TORTS
IN A NUTSHELL
FOURTH EDITION

By

EDWARD J. KIONKA
Professor of Law Emeritus
Southern Illinois University School of Law

THOMSON

™

WEST

Mat #40234504

Nutshell Series, In a Nutshell, the Nutshell Logo and West Group are trademarks registered in the U.S. Patent and Trademark Office.

COPYRIGHT © 1977, 1992 WEST PUBLISHING CO.
© West, a Thomson business, 1999
© 2005 Thomson/West
      610 Opperman Drive
      P.O. Box 64526
      St. Paul, MN 55164–0526
      1–800–328–9352

Printed in the United States of America

ISBN 0–314–15219–9

PREFACE

This book, like all others in the Nutshell series, is intended for anyone seeking a concise exposition or review of the basic principles of American law. Its main value, however, will probably be to first-year law students taking the course in torts, who are struggling to get a glimpse of the elusive "big picture" of which my former dean and colleague John Cribbet of Illinois so often spoke. (Every law student and lawyer should know his famous "big picture" story. See John E. Cribbet & Corwin W. Johnson, PRINCIPLES OF THE LAW OF PROPERTY xi (3d ed. 1989).)

This Nutshell, again like all others, must be used with caution and with a clear understanding of its limitations. Overall, I believe that it presents an accurate "big picture" of the subjects discussed. But many of the rules are subject to minor exceptions and qualifications which space does not permit to be mentioned. Some rules and subrules, not essential to an understanding of the basic principles, have been omitted altogether. Some hard problems are only alluded to. In addition, the tort law of every jurisdiction is a little bit different from that of every other, and each contains its own idiosyncrasies, judicial and sometimes statutory. This text must not be taken as the law of any particular jurisdiction, but rather as a composite view.

The law student would be well-advised to base his or her study of tort law primarily on other sources. There is no substitute for a careful analysis of casebook materials for a more thorough treatment and for a necessary perspective of tort law in action. And it would be wise to flesh out one's knowledge of the various areas by study of a more complete text, such as Dan B. Dobbs excellent Hornbook, THE LAW OF TORTS (2000), and also of the Restatement (Second) of Torts and, as it emerges, the Restatement (Third). Reference to other sources available in the law library is sometimes necessary in areas where enlightenment seems slow to come. Nevertheless, it is my firm belief that law students (as all of us are) must have a clear view of the forest before we can truly understand and appreciate the various trees. I hope that this book will help to provide that overview, a solid structural framework of concepts to which the elaborations and refinements of ever more specific rules can be attached. May it serve as an entree into the proverbial seamless web.

No single Nutshell could do justice to all of tort law. This one's focus is the basic principles of liability, defenses, and damages. The volatile area of products liability, discussed briefly here, is the subject of a separate Nutshell (Jerry J. Phillips, PRODUCTS LIABILITY IN A NUTSHELL (6th ed. 2003)). And the law governing the liability of those who provide medical services has been undergoing rapid growth and change, and there are important statutory developments in this area. See Marcia Boumil, Clifford E. Elias, & Diane Bissonnette Moes, THE LAW OF MEDICAL LIABILITY IN A NUTSHELL (2d ed. 2003).

On the other hand, I have covered some subjects not normally included in basic torts texts and courses (see, e.g., Chapter 1 and §§ 8–14, 8–15, 8–21, and 8–22) because I believe that they are important to an accurate overview.

I am deeply grateful to all those—students, lawyers, and legal scholars—who have helped me learn about tort law and its processes. Deepest thanks also to my colleagues, friends, and family who have long supported me in this project—especially Terri, my life partner, soulmate, and spouse, whose support and understanding never wanes. Many thanks also to Southern Illinois University School of Law, which, as always, has provided excellent support and encouragement to faculty scholarship. And thanks, Pete, for your invaluable help editing the first edition.

Portions of the Restatement of the Law, Second, Torts (copyright 1965, 1971, 1972, 1976, 1977, 1979 by the American Law Institute) are reprinted herein with the permission of the American Law Institute.

EDWARD J. KIONKA

Carbondale, Illinois
January, 2005

*

EXPLANATORY NOTES

The following notes may be helpful in using this book.

Cases. For obvious reasons, cases have been cited sparingly. In general, the cases cited are either (1) leading authorities on a particular point, (2) landmark cases, or (3) illustrative cases.

Only the name, court of decision, and date are cited in the text. The full citation may be found in the Table of Cases. If only the name of the state is given, it is the highest court of that state.

Restatement of Torts. The Restatement of Torts (First and Second) has been particularly well regarded by the courts, and it is highly authoritative in most jurisdictions. Frequent references to it are given, but I have not cited every relevant section. Ordinarily it is cited where the provision or its comments provide further illumination of the point under discussion. Citations are to the Restatement (Second) unless otherwise noted. For simplicity and to save space, I use the form "R. § ___." The Restatement (Third) of Torts is now being developed, and eventually it will supplant the Restatement (Second). As of this writing, two parts have been finally adopted: the Restatement (Third) of Torts: Products Liability (1998), and the Restatement (Third) of Torts: Apportionment of Liability

(2000).[1] I have cited certain relevant provisions, but it is too early to tell whether the Restatement (Third) will be accorded the same authority as its predecessors.

Texts. Texts and articles are cited only occasionally. In its day, the most authoritative and useful text was the Hornbook originally authored by the late Dean William L. Prosser, PROSSER & KEETON, THE LAW OF TORTS (5th ed. 1984), fifth edition by W. Page Keeton, Dan B. Dobbs, Robert E. Keeton, and David G. Owens. For convenience, it is cited as "Prosser." Although it remains a valuable reference, the Prosser Hornbook has not been updated since a 1988 supplement was released. The current Torts Hornbook is Dan B. Dobbs, THE LAW OF TORTS (2000), which is an excellent successor to Prosser.

There is also a useful six-volume treatise, FOWLER V. HARPER, FLEMING JAMES, JR. & OSCAR S. GRAY, THE LAW OF TORTS (2d ed. 1986), which is gradually being replaced by a third edition, of which one volume has been published. Texts on individual subtopics are also available.

References to Parties. For convenience and consistency, the terms "plaintiff" and "defendant" are used throughout to include not only persons who

[1] For the record, it should be noted that there is also a Restatement (Third): Unfair Competition (1995), that contains some topics that fall under the torts umbrella. However, those topics are beyond the scope of the first-year law school torts course.

technically have that status (i.e., those who have brought suit or been sued) but also persons who *potentially* occupy one status or the other—one who has been harmed, or one who is arguably a tortfeasor. Also, plaintiffs and defendants are personalized by use of the pronouns that refer to natural persons (e.g., "he"), which should be read to include, where appropriate, legal entities such as corporations. And male and female nouns and pronouns are used throughout in a generic sense to include both men and women.

Where appropriate, the term "plaintiff" should be read to include one who was *fatally* injured. Technically, in such a case the proper term would be "plaintiff's decedent," since the plaintiff would be a living person or entity suing on behalf of the decedent's estate or beneficiaries. To conserve space, I use the term "plaintiff" generically to mean the immediate victim of the tortious conduct.

The terms "injury" or "harm" include fatal injuries unless the context requires otherwise.

*

OUTLINE

PART IV. IMMUNITIES

PART V. SURVIVAL AND WRONGFUL DEATH

PART VI. INJURIES TO OTHER INTERESTS

OUTLINE

TABLE OF CASES

References are to Pages

A

B

E

F

G

H

L

M

N

P

R

T

U

V

W

Y

*

TORTS
IN A NUTSHELL
FOURTH EDITION

*

PART I

INTRODUCTION

CHAPTER 1

PROLOGUE: ORIGINS, OBJECTIVES, AND OVERVIEWS OF TORT LIABILITY

§ 1–1. The Definitional Dilemma

"Tort" is an elusive concept. The word is not used in common speech. Although it describes one of the major pigeon-holes of the law, the concept has defied a number of attempts to formulate a useful definition. The dilemma is that any definition that is sufficiently comprehensive to encompass all torts is so general as to be almost meaningless.

Closely related to the definitional dilemma is the classic question, is there a general principle of tort liability? Or are there only the laws of the individual "torts," a miscellaneous and more or less unconnected collection of nominate civil actions grouped together merely for convenience of reference? Legal scholars have debated this issue for more than a century, without resolving it satisfactorily.

If there is any such general principle, it has yet to be adopted by Anglo–American courts and legislatures. The common law developed as a system of individual named torts—trespass, deceit, slander, and later assault and battery, conversion, and so on—each with its own more or less unique rules. In fact, until 1859 there was no legal treatise bearing the name "torts." As yet, except for the tort called "negligence," there has been little synthesis of the nominate torts into larger categories.

The one common element of all torts is that someone has sustained a loss or harm as the result of some act or failure to act by another. Beyond this, accurate generalization becomes impossible. Virtually all of the infinitely diverse forms of human activity—driving a vehicle, engaging in business, speaking, writing, owning and using real or personal property, making love—may be a source of harm and therefore of tort liability. This diversity of conduct resists broad generalizations, and so does the tort liability on which it is based.

Tort law is perhaps the last bastion of the common law. Even in this age of legislation, with its proliferation of codes and uniform acts, tort law remains uncodified and in large part unaffected by statute. This may tell us something about its fundamental nature. In any event, in view of the fact that it evolved a posteriori, inductively, from particular cases, and not a priori, it is not surprising that a number of diverse and independent torts emerged. And perhaps this very diversity results, overall, in a closer approximation of justice than could be achieved by the application of more general rules.

Sometimes it is suggested that a common element of tort liability is *fault,* that tortious conduct is that which falls below accepted community standards of behavior. Some sort of fault is common to many torts, although it might more accurately be described as conduct that creates an unreasonable or unacceptable risk of harm. But even in this sense, fault cannot be said to be a universal principle of liability. Various kinds of blameworthy conduct resulting in damage do not give rise to tort liability. Conversely, the law sometimes imposes tort liability simply because a particular activity can and should bear the cost of damage associated with it, regardless of the fact that the conduct of the "tortfeasor" was morally blameless.

The common law system of nominate torts does not seem to have impeded the creation of new causes of action. For example, the action for invasion of privacy, now well established, had its genesis in a law review article published in 1890. Nor has this system stifled change. Within the confines of the nominate torts, the law has persistently evolved toward expanded liability by modifying existing rules. In less than a century, the law of product-caused injuries moved from rules highly favoring the manufacturer (caveat emptor) to a form of strict liability.

One may well ask whether there is need for a general principle of tort liability. The boundaries of the spheres of the nominate torts intersect, often overlap. If one's damage is not actionable, it is almost certainly not for lack of a name or a general principle, but rather because the existing law deliberately refuses to shift the loss.

One might also ask whether our law would be appreciably different even if such a general principle were announced. The codes of the European and other civil law countries usually contain a provision such as § 1382 of the French Civil Code:

> Every act whatsoever of an individual which causes injury to another obliges the one by whose fault [*faute*] it has occurred to make reparation for it.

Yet the tort law of these countries is remarkably similar to ours. The California Civil Code includes some general tort liability provisions (e.g. §§ 1708, 1709, 1714), but the structure and rules of California tort law are indistinguishable in form from those of other states.

If a definition of "tort" is necessary, it will have to be something in the nature of this:

> A civil wrong, wherein one person's conduct causes a compensable injury to the person, property, or recognized interest of another, in violation of a duty imposed by law.

Obviously, this does not tell us very much. To say that the breach of a law-imposed duty creates tort liability begs the question. Moreover, not *all* violations of legal duties are torts. This does not even distinguish tort from breach of contract, since in the final analysis the binding effect of contractual duties is limited to that imposed by law. Some have defined "tort" by excluding "mere" breaches of contract, but this glosses over the fact that the breach of a contractual duty under certain circumstances can be the basis for tort liability.

Even the simple term "cause" has no external reference. Many times courts have denied liability because of the absence of legal cause, even though the conduct in question was rather clearly a substantial cause in fact of the harm.

Tort law is a complex machine for shifting human losses. Like other complicated machinery, for most practical purposes it is best understood as the sum of its individual component parts. Efforts to change these parts to make them more similar may only impair their individual performance.

§ 1–2.　The Jurisprudence of Tort Law

In general, "jurisprudence" is philosophy as applied to law. It is the study of the first principles or fundamental premises that underlie a legal system. When we speak of the jurisprudence of tort law, we refer to those ideas that provide the foundation upon which tort law rules are built.

There are various ways to think about the aims, functions, goals, and justifications that drive tort law. First, we can look behind the rules to try to see what motivated them. Particular rules might reflect (1) morality or corrective justice, (2) social utility or policy, (3) process or procedural considerations, (4) purely formal reasoning, or (5) some combination of these. Sometimes a court will state a justification for a tort law rule that falls into one or more of these categories. Often, the court will not, and we are left to guess.

Morality or corrective justice attempts to hold defendants liable only when it seems fair or "right" to do so. For example, if we judge a particular defendant's conduct to be blameworthy, then we think it just to hold that defendant liable for injuries caused by that conduct. One criterion of justice is current community standards of fairness.

Social utility or policy considerations can also play a role in the choice of a rule. For example, if we impose liability on a defendant for certain unsafe conduct that we wish to discourage, then that defendant and others will be deterred from engaging in that conduct. The deterrent effect of tort law serves the social policy of making our society safer. Economic policy is a particular social policy that is sometimes used to help derive tort law rules, when economic efficiency points toward a particular rule.

Process considerations motivate us to create rules that can be fairly and effectively administered. Tort law rules are enforced through litigation. A rule that is too cumbersome or difficult for judges or juries to understand or apply or which cannot be administered fairly and consistently from one case to another may be rejected because of such process considerations. In addition, rules must be such that litigants, reviewing courts, and the public can verify the correctness of their application and believe that the tort system is operating fairly and efficiently.

Formal reasoning is the mechanical application of preexisting rules of law without regard to justice, policy, or process considerations. Lower courts often have little or no discretion to make or modify rules, and in such cases their task is merely to discover and apply the appropriate rule by application of formal reasoning.

Tort law has three main functions or goals: (1) compensating persons sustaining a loss or harm as a result of another's conduct; (2) placing the cost of that compensation on those who, in justice, ought to bear it, but only on such persons, in accordance with one or more of the jurisprudential considerations mentioned above; and (3) preventing future losses and harms.

Compensation. The victim of a tort has sustained certain harm(s) or loss(es) that we will call "costs." Tort law is predicated on the idea that all these costs—tangible and intangible—can be measured in money. The basic (and usually exclusive) tort remedy is to require the tortfeasor to pay the victim the sum of these costs as "compensatory damages."

Note that in most tort cases—the automobile "accident" is a typical example—the loss to the victim is also a net loss to the economic system. The loss-producing event ordinarily does not result in a corresponding economic gain to the tortfeasor that could be returned to the victim. The main jurisprudential issue in tort law is, under what circumstances can we justify compelling another to compensate the victim for these costs?

If compensation—relieving the victim of the sudden and substantial burden of these costs—were our only goal, there are more efficient ways than tort litigation. The law permits (and could require, as it occasionally does) first party insurance—life, health and accident, disability, fire, theft, etc. Or government could impose a tax-financed compensation system, similar to social security. A portion of the tangible costs of physical harm to persons and property are already reimbursed by insurance, employment benefits, and governmental benefits. By expanding the coverage and limits, such compensation could be made to serve as a substitute for tort damages in the vast majority of cases now processed through the tort system. Why use the more cumbersome, inefficient and expensive method?

The answer is found in our notions of justice and social policy, described above, and to some extent other considerations.

Justice.

Fairness. Fundamentally, justice is the result of the application of current community standards of fairness. If a loss-producing event is a matter of pure chance, then the fairest way to relieve the victim of the burden of its costs is insurance or governmental compensation. In this way, all of us share the risk and its costs. If the risk differs for different groups but is more or less random within each group, premium classifications can equitably adjust these differences.

But where (1) we can identify a particular person as responsible for the creation of the risk (the "tortfeasor"), (2) the risk is not inconsequential nor of a type that the community customarily accepts, and (3) the tortfeasor is at least theoretically capable of reducing or eliminating the risk or its consequences, the balance of fairness shifts. At some point on the continuum of these factors, it becomes more just to impose the loss on the tortfeasor than to permit it to remain on the victim or to be shared by the community. Ideally, at precisely this point tort liability attaches.

Cause In Fact. Causation is, for obvious reasons, the sine qua non. Tort liability is only just if the actor's conduct was a substantial factor in bringing about the victim's loss or harm.

Fault. Fault is usually a necessary element of the liability equation. It is not enough that one has caused harm to another; ethically, we find it difficult to justify liability unless the actor's conduct was somehow culpable. One is not required—in most cases—to insure others against the risks inherent in socially accepted conduct. But the requisite "fault" need not be narrowly defined, nor need the actor be subjectively aware that his conduct carries an unacceptable risk of harm. Clearly, if one intentionally harms another, or knows (or is presumed to know) that his conduct creates a substantial certainty of harm, liability naturally follows.

Motive (actual or inferred) can thus be an element of fault. However, "fault" also includes conduct where no harm was intended or even foreseen, where an ordinary person *should have foreseen* that such conduct created an *unreasonable* risk of harm to others. According to Judge Learned Hand's classic formula, conduct is wrongful if the burden of alternative conduct that would have prevented the harm is less than the foreseeable probability and gravity of the harm. In measuring this burden we may consider the necessity and utility of the harm-producing conduct as compared to its alternatives. Thus, fault may lie in merely creating an unnecessary or unreasonable risk, however unknowingly. In this sense, one can find a fault element even in some forms of so-called strict liability.

Fault Substitutes. Sometimes other factors may partly or entirely substitute for the fault requirement. These include:

(1) Economic efficiency. Principles of economics suggest that, in general, the costs of an activity should be internalized. Where an activity causes harm, the cost of that harm ought to be reflected in the overall cost-price structure of that activity. Workers' compensation statutes and products liability rules to some extent reflect this idea. It is also suggested that the law may consider the relative capacity of the parties to absorb or spread the costs. Thus, as between (a) one who carries on an insurable activity or an activity with respect to which income is received and (b) an injured person with

limited resources, the former is deemed better able to absorb and distribute the costs of harm resulting from the activity, thereby reducing what Guido Calabresi calls the "secondary costs" of the injury.

A corollary principle is that it is often more efficient to require an *activity* to be insured against the non-intentional harms it causes than to require an *individual* to insure generally against such harms and others.

(2) Vicarious liability. Tort liability is sometimes imposed on one in the absence of any fault on his part for a tort committed by another who is acting on his behalf or with his express or implied permission—most commonly employees, and sometimes independent contractors and others. In addition to the economic efficiency reasons, and the justification that such liability promotes care in the selection, training and supervision of one's agents (which is doubtful), the principal basis for vicarious liability is the simple idea that one, in justice, ought to be liable for the torts of those who act in his stead—in effect, their acts are his when committed in that capacity.

(3) Economic benefit. Earlier it was noted that in most tort cases, the harm results in a net economic loss. But this is not always so. In many situations, the creation of the risk is of benefit to the creator. Speeding saves time, which we are fond of saying is the equivalent of money. Cornercutting of all kinds often reduces the costs of the activity. This benefit to the actor is not often articulated as a justification

for liability, but there is some evidence that courts and legislators will more readily impose liability where this element is present.

There are other cases where defendant's wrongful conduct causes a direct pecuniary loss to plaintiff and a corresponding direct pecuniary gain to defendant—for example, misrepresentation in a sales transaction or conversion of a chattel. In such cases compensation may also be termed reimbursement or restitution, and here, too, it is more readily awarded.

Fault Without Liability. There are cases where the actor's conduct is a cause in fact of another's harm, and all of the usual fault requirements are met, but for reasons of social policy no tort liability exists. The concepts *duty, proximate cause, privilege,* and *immunity* are the means by which the courts (and legislatures) balance the burden of liability against other social values.

Plaintiff's Fault or Consent. The victim's tort recovery may be reduced or denied when he has consented to encounter the risk or when his own fault contributed to his injury. Where there has been a true consent or a knowing and voluntary assumption of the risk, denial of all recovery may be just. However, until the last quarter of the twentieth century, most jurisdictions denied recovery entirely in cases where defendant's conduct was negligent or even "reckless" (a twilight zone between negligent and intentional) if the victim's conduct of the same kind contributed, however slightly, to the unfortunate result. Under prevailing notions of justice, this is unsound. The victim's fault is by definition only a portion of the total loss-producing fault; it does not negate or supersede the fault of others. The more logical approach is to compare the fault of all parties to the loss-producing event and reduce the damages of each in proportion to his own contributory fault. This is now accomplished by statute or court decision in almost all of the states, and even before was frequently accomplished by juries ad hoc.

Prevention of Future Costs. The third primary function or goal of tort law is to prevent future torts by regulating human behavior. In this respect, the law serves an educational function, and operates prospectively. Theoretically, a tortfeasor held liable for damages will be more careful in the future, and the general threat of tort liability is an incentive to all to regulate their conduct in accordance with the established standards. To this extent tort law supplements and extends the criminal law; indeed, tort sanctions can often be more potent. Punitive damages, allowable in most tort actions involving intentional or reckless misconduct, are intended to reinforce this function.

Although this function is frequently asserted to be a justification for tort liability, we do not yet know enough about whether it works. Does tort liability—actual or prospective—in fact affect human behavior, and if so, to what extent? Perhaps future empirical research will provide some answers; so far, that research has only just begun.

Other Justifications. These are not the only functions, goals or justifications of rules of tort law, but merely the primary ones. There are others. For example, in some cases the provision of a remedy in tort will serve to vindicate the plaintiff, quite apart from any compensation he may receive. And it is widely assumed that it deters individual retaliation and resort to violent or otherwise improper self-help remedies for a perceived wrong.

The Real World. All of the foregoing justifications for the existing rules of tort liability are to some extent based on an idealization of the operation of the tort system. The underlying assumptions need to be tested to determine whether they have any basis in fact. We need to know more about external influences—for example, the widespread availability and use of insurance. And we need better information about the results of the system in actual operation in the real world. Litigation is an expensive, time-consuming and uncertain means of compensation that can be justified only if it adequately achieves defined goals. Many proponents of "no-fault" compensation systems assert that tort law has failed this test. Some also suggest that in certain kinds of cases—notably auto crashes—our basic assumptions about fault and its determinability are erroneous. The fundamental question that must continually be asked is, does the tort system achieve its stated goals—compensation, justice, deterrence—sufficiently well to justify its costs?

§ 1–3. The Evolution of Tort Concepts and Remedies

Evolution of Tort Remedies. English law in its earliest stages did not differentiate between tort and crime; indeed, such terms were unknown. When one person harmed another, the available remedies included a private war or "feud" in retaliation, the object being to cause an equivalent harm to the wrongdoer. As the law began to intervene in these private disputes, it first merely provided incentives for the parties to settle by an agreed compensation. Soon it began to require resort to a primitive form of trial (by ordeal or oaths) in lieu of the feud. If plaintiff won, defendant had to pay some fixed sum to the plaintiff (called "bot") and to the king ("wite"), computed on the basis of plaintiff's value ("wer") and the nature of the injury, or on the value of the property. If the defendant could not pay (which was probably the usual case), he was punished.

The Anglo–Saxon courts were local and applied local laws. After the Norman Conquest (1066), the royal courts were created and gradually took jurisdiction over a specified list of wrongs, such as felonies where there was a breach of the "king's peace" (the domain under the king's protection) and disputes involving land. Minor wrongs (what we now call misdemeanors) continued to be handled in the local courts as before. It is well to remember that even as late as the thirteenth century, there was little "common law"—that is, law that was uniform throughout the country—except with respect to land. Both local laws and the royal law were primarily customary law, and in most matters local customs varied. In addition to the local county courts, there were ecclesiastical courts, baronial courts, manorial courts, and borough courts, all applying local or specialized law. But by the end of the thirteenth century, the royal courts had come to dominate the legal system.

At first, all prosecutions for "wrongs" in the king's courts were brought by the individual harmed (or his representative). Plaintiff accused defendant of a wrong in open court and offered the appropriate form of trial—combat, ordeal or oaths, depending on the type of wrong and other factors. This procedure was known as the "appeal of felony." If the plaintiff won, the defendant was punished, but no compensation was awarded to the plaintiff in this action, except that in an appeal of larceny, the goods (if available) were returned to the plaintiff. In 1166, the presentment (grand) jury was instituted, and a century later lesser crimes could be prosecuted by public officials upon an information, but the appeal of felony remained optional for many years.

Much of the king's business was accomplished by royal writ, and this included the administration of justice. Such writs became the grant of jurisdiction to a royal court to adjudicate a case. Gradually, a formal system of named writs evolved, and it became necessary for the plaintiff to purchase an appropriate writ from the king's chancellor in order to commence his action. As the result of various political and judicial pressures, the writs became crystallized into certain forms and contents, corresponding to the available actions, and if the plaintiff could not fit his case into one of the prescribed writs, he had no action in the royal courts. By the fifteenth century it had become possible, and common, to commence an action by bill (complaint) instead of a royal writ. But the plaintiff's declaration still had to state a cause of action in the recognized form, corresponding to the writs that could have been selected.

The most important personal civil action was trespass, called by Maitland "that fertile mother of actions." Its origins are obscure, but shortly after 1250 it seems to have been in common use and to have been one of the writs of course. For some time, its limits were not clearly defined, and it was used in a variety of cases where one person had harmed another. Its great significance lay in the fact that plaintiff recovered his actual damages, if any, rather than damages according to a fixed scheme of compensation. For many years it also retained a quasi-criminal character in that a vanquished defendant was usually imprisoned or fined. In a short time it became immensely popular and largely supplanted the "appeal" in felony cases accept, curiously, for homicide. No civil action was permitted in the king's courts for wrongful death until the passage of Lord Campbell's Act in 1846. In addition, it provided a remedy in the royal courts for a number of lesser harms that theretofore could be redressed only in the less effective local courts.

Three common forms of the writ soon developed: (1) trespass *vi et armis* (with force and arms) for assault, battery, and false imprisonment; (2) trespass *de bonis asportatis* (taking of goods) for trespass to chattels; and (3) trespass *quare clausum fregit* (breach of the "close") for trespass to land. In time the criminal penalties were dropped, but the plaintiff could still recover in trespass even though he could not prove actual damage.

Concurrent with the growth of trespass there developed a practice of issuing and honoring writs for wrongs that did not fit within the confines of the designated trespass actions. Such writs eventually became classified as an action of trespass on the case or, more correctly, "action on the case." Unlike the trespass writs that had been developed into inflexible forms, the "case" writs set forth the facts of plaintiff's particular case in considerable detail. By the sixteenth century, case had become a distinct and generic form of action.

As time went on, certain of the recurring case actions crystallized and were separated into named actions having rules and writs of their own. Trespass, together with case and its progeny, account for virtually all the actions to which we now refer collectively as the law of torts.

Assumpsit, which eventually became the primary remedy for breach of contract, began life as a special form of case. In the fourteenth century (some believe even earlier), case provided a remedy where one undertook to provide a service and expressly agreed to exercise care and skill but instead damaged the plaintiff or his property. (Where a "common calling" was involved, the law implied the undertaking.) The breach of this promise or assumpsit was a wrong. Gradually assumpsit became a means for enforcing other contracts not under seal. It then became an independent contract action, while case remained an alternative remedy in tort for breach of certain kinds of contractual undertakings, primarily involving misfeasance (as opposed to a total failure to perform).

Case also came to provide a remedy for deceit. There was an original writ called deceit, but it concerned abuse of legal procedure, construed as a fraud on the courts. But as the idea of assumpsit developed in case, a related case action for deceit developed for breach of an express warranty. During the nineteenth century implied sales warranties developed, and the law of warranty became classified as a part of the law of sales, but some of its tort origins remain visible. In the meantime, the tort action for deceit continued to develop under the aegis of case.

Trover began to emerge as an action separate from case during the sixteenth century. It developed as a remedy for conversion and certain kinds of damage to chattels in situations where replevin, detinue, or trespass *de bonis asportatis* did not apply or where these remedies were inadequate. Eventually, it became concurrent with all of them.

Case was the general form of action under which most other torts evolved. Nuisance, defamation, interference with economic relations, and malicious prosecution were case actions. So were certain kinds of strict liability, such as that of certain classes of bailees or for the spread of fire. And so was the most important of the tort causes of action, negligence, when it finally emerged as an independent basis of liability.

Evolution of Theories of Liability. In the final stages of their evolution, there were at least two (perhaps three) basic differences between trespass and case so far as tort remedies were concerned.

(1) Trespass was applicable when the injury was *direct* and *immediate;* case was the remedy for *indirect* or *consequential* harm. The best known articulation of this principle is the oft-cited *Scott v. Shepherd* (K.B. 1772), but the principle clearly predates that case.

(2) Case actions required proof of *actual damage,* whereas trespass actions did not.

(3) According to some legal historians, proof of defendant's *fault* was required in case, but not in trespass.

Trespass. As previously noted, the English court system in its early stages consisted of not one but many courts—royal, feudal, and communal—each with a jealously guarded jurisdiction of its own. The royal courts first entertained the action of trespass on the theory that it involved a breach of the "king's peace," which was for a time a necessary allegation. These courts' jurisdiction was thus limited to the more serious and inflammatory civil wrongs, and to actions to try title to property, for which trespass was often used. Eventually it became established that the essence of trespass was that defendant had committed some *affirmative* act that caused a *direct* and *immediate* injury to the plaintiff. Assault and battery "with force and arms," a forcible entry onto plaintiff's land, or the forcible taking of his chattels were the types of cases for which the action was most clearly designed. But it was not so limited. The requirement that the plaintiff prove a *forceful* trespass was eventually dropped, although for a time it was still formally alleged.

Thereafter, the plaintiff could recover for any direct and immediate trespass to his person or property, however slight the contact or harm, and if he could not prove actual damages nominal damages were awarded.

At one time, it was generally thought that trespass liability was strict, or nearly so. It was said that plaintiff did not have to prove defendant's fault. More recent analyses, however (see, e.g.,

S.F.C. Milsom, Historical Foundations of the Common Law (2d ed. 1981)), suggest that the situation may have been more complicated, and to some extent may be beyond our knowledge because of our incomplete knowledge of the applicable rules of procedure and the limited reports available. As we have seen, the plaintiff pleaded his case using formal writs that, at least to some extent, masked the true facts. If, as often happened, the defendant pleaded the *general issue—in nullo est inde culpabilis,* "in no way is he to blame"—the claim was sent out for a jury trial, and the results of that trial were not reviewable and were not reported. Milsom suggests that under the general issue, defendant could probably show that he was not at fault. But it is clear that fault was not part of the plaintiff's case; absence of fault was, at best, a defense, and it was not an absolute one because the jury might decide for the plaintiff anyway.

The reported cases arose when the defendant did not plead the general issue, but instead made a *special* plea in *justification.* It is from the reports of rulings on demurrers to these pleas that we see glimpses of other defenses, such as self-defense and the use of force to repel a trespass or to effect a lawful arrest. However, we also see occasional dictum that "inevitable accident" would excuse a trespass (e.g. *Weaver v. Ward*, K.B. 1616), but apparently this defense was never successfully invoked *as a special plea* prior to the nineteenth century, so long as the act of the defendant was voluntary.

Case. The action on the case was the remedy for indirect injury. The classic illustration of the distinction between trespass and case is that of the log thrown onto a highway. One struck by the log as it fell could maintain trespass against the thrower; but one hurt by stumbling over it as it lay in the road was required to sue in case. In addition, case required allegation and proof of a breach of a duty, ordinarily by proof of defendant's fault—that is, that his conduct was illegal, intentionally wrongful, or unreasonably dangerous. And being wholly a civil action, actual damages were essential.

Negligence. Unlike trespass, the action on the case in most instances required allegation and proof of fault to establish a breach of duty to plaintiff. (It has been suggested that case was thought proper when a bare statement of defendant's conduct was not sufficient to show its wrongfulness.) This fault could be the performance of a lawful act in a dangerous manner. Thus negligence (often under a different name) was, until recently, merely one basis of liability in a number of different civil actions for which case was the appropriate writ.

There is no clear path by which we can trace the development of the negligence concept from the emergence of case in the thirteenth century to the latter part of the eighteenth century when negligence came to be recognized as a special form of the action. From the beginning the common law had no difficulty in imposing liability for a wrongful act even though the harm it caused was indirect or delayed in time. Not so, however, if the wrong was instead a *failure* to act. Liability for nonfeasance was first imposed on those who undertook to perform some service and breached an express promise to exercise care or skill. This was extended to those engaged in "common callings"—common carriers, innkeepers, public warehousemen, and other public servants (and for a time surgeons, smiths, carpenters, tailors, and barbers). As to them, in the absence of an express promise a promise to exercise care and skill was implied. Gradually the idea was extended to the neglect of other duties, and with it came the tendency to allege that defendant had acted "negligently and recklessly" or similar words. During the eighteenth century liability for nonfeasance was considerably expanded, and the term "negligence" changed from a mere descriptive term to the standard characterization of the wrongful conduct, whether action or inaction.

By 1800, "case for negligence" was a common expression, and soon thereafter writers began to classify a large number of previously unclassified tort actions under that heading. As the vitality of the forms of action declined, intentional harms, direct and indirect, came to be grouped as a separate field of liability, and a general concept of negligence took hold. Thus, negligence came to be regarded as itself an independent tort. It is important to remember, however, that the term continues to be used in both senses. It is the name of a tort cause of action, and it also describes the actor's conduct in this and other torts.

United States. In this country, all of the states (except Louisiana) received the common law of England including its forms of action. But during the formative period of U.S. law, significant changes occurred. One was the abolition, to a greater or lesser extent, of the forms of action, which were replaced either by a single civil action at law or by a limited number of actions such as trespass (for all torts) and assumpsit (for contracts). Another was the restriction of tort liability.

Fault was established as a necessary element of plaintiff's case in a trespass action, both in this country and in England. The leading case was *Brown v. Kendall* (Mass. 1850). Defendant raised a stick to separate two fighting dogs, and in doing so accidentally struck the eye of plaintiff who was standing behind him. Plaintiff sued in trespass for assault and battery. Although the court held that trespass was the proper form of action, it found for defendant, holding that liability in trespass required either intentional or negligent misconduct. The *Brown* case was widely cited and followed. Eventually most states applied the same rule in cases of trespass to land and chattels.

Liability was limited in other ways as well. Charities and units of government were given total immunity for the torts of their employees. Employers generally were protected from liability to their injured employees by the strict application of the doctrines of contributory negligence, assumption of the risk of known hazards in the work situation, and the fellow-servant rule. Courts in the nineteenth century largely rejected the English doctrine of strict liability for harm caused by abnormally dangerous activities (§ 3–3). A consumer injured by all but the most dangerous products had a cause of action, if any, only against his immediate vendor. The fault ethic was so strong that the New York Court of Appeals in 1911 held the state's first workers' compensation statute unconstitutional because it imposed liability without fault.

Beginning in its second decade, the twentieth century has seen a dramatic reversal of this attitude. Workers' compensation statutes have been passed and sustained in every state. Charitable and governmental immunities have crumbled. Strict liability for abnormally dangerous activities is now the general rule. Manufacturers as well as retailers are strictly liable for defective products in most states. Comparative negligence (in lieu of the total bar of contributory negligence) has become the rule in all but four states. New causes of action, such as for invasion of privacy and negligent infliction of psychic trauma, have been created. Procedural reform, such as the abolition of the forms of action in almost all states and improved discovery procedures, has removed many of the barriers to the successful prosecution of meritorious claims. Vestiges of its ancestry are still discernible, but the tort law of today, like society itself, is far different from that which our ancestors knew.

§ 1–4. The Roles of Judges and Juries

In the United States, the vast majority of tort (and especially accident) cases are settled prior to filing suit or prior to trial, but they are settled largely on the basis of counsel's judgments as to what a jury verdict in the case is likely to be. In those tort cases that reach the litigation stage, trial by jury is usually demanded. The remainder of this book will briefly sketch the rules of tort law, but it is well to remember that for the most part, these rules do not decide actual cases. The preeminent power in resolving tort cases lies with the "trier of fact," most often a jury.

It is commonly said that questions of *law* are for the court and questions of *fact* are for the jury. This is not entirely true, and can be a little misleading, since judges possess the ultimate power to decide which is which, and legal issues frequently have a fact component. But through well-established rules and customs, and by use of the general verdict, juries are given wide latitude to decide these controversies without court interference.

Jury questions are of three kinds. R. § 328C. First, the jury must determine what in fact occurred—was the light red or green when defendant drove through it, did defendant utter certain words, did plaintiff look before he stepped, and the like. Then, in most cases, the jury is required to make one or more decisions as to the *legal consequences* of these facts—was plaintiff or defendant negligent, were the words defamatory, was plaintiff a trespasser, licensee, or invitee, etc.—usually on the basis of some general legal definition given by the court. Finally, the jury must determine whether plaintiff was damaged by defendant's tortious act and the dollar value of plaintiff's compensable damages.

Questions of law for the court are also of three kinds. R. § 328B. First, certain issues are invariably issues of law such as (1) whether defendant owed plaintiff any recognized legal duty, or, conversely, whether plaintiff has a legally protected right; (2) the elements of proof necessary to establish liability (or nonliability) and the measure of damages; and (3) whether, on the facts, some particular rule of law imposes or excuses liability as matter of law— for example, the rule that violation of a certain safety statute is negligence per se, or that false statements of intent are not actionable misrepresentations. The latter are sometimes stated in terms of duty or "scope of liability" rules, but they are more particularized standards of conduct than the broad general rules usually associated with the term "duty," such as the duty to exercise reasonable care in operating a motor vehicle. It will be seen that by embodying particular standards of conduct in rules of law, courts take from the jury the power to determine the legal consequences of certain facts, and thereby transform questions of fact into questions of law and enable the court to decide the case instead of the jury.

Second, all issues that are ordinarily questions of fact for the jury become questions of law for the court if the judge decides that the evidence on that issue so overwhelmingly favors one conclusion that reasonable persons could not reach the opposite conclusion.

Third, judges alone apply rules of procedure, which may have an important effect upon the outcome of the case, especially rules concerning the admission and exclusion of evidence, burden of proof, presumptions, and the applicability of res ipsa loquitur.

However, in spite of the ultimate powers of decision retained by the courts, the fact is that courts do permit juries to render the ultimate judgment in a substantial proportion of tort cases, particularly where the controlling issues involve disputes as to what occurred or mixed questions of law and fact such as breach of duty, status, damages, causation, and the like.

Thus, it is important to understand that tort law is not merely a system of rules of actionable or nonactionable conduct, but also of rules that determine when the law will *not* decide cases and instead will leave the decision whether to impose liability to the more or less unfettered discretion of the jury. In fact, one leading torts scholar suggested that "nearly all legal theory in negligence cases is designed to serve the ends of allocating the power of judgment respectively to judge and jury." (Leon Green, JUDGE & JURY 261 (1930)). In many—perhaps even most—tort cases, rules of law take one only so far, and the lawyer or judge cannot determine the ultimate liability question. In such cases, it is necessary and entirely appropriate to say that beyond a certain point, the remaining issues are jury questions, and therefore whether or not the particular defendant is liable to the particular plaintiff is merely an educated guess.

See generally R. §§ 285, 328B, 328C; Harper, James & Gray ch. 15; Dobbs, ch. 2.

CHAPTER 2

CAUSE IN FACT

§ 2–1. Cause in Fact

The most basic element of any tort cause of action is some causal connection between the act or omission of the tortfeasor and plaintiff's injury. Yet the application of this simple concept has proved one of the most troublesome tasks in all of tort law. No other topic has occasioned so much controversy and confusion among both courts and legal scholars.

One source of confusion has been the common tendency of judges to discuss all causation problems under the term "proximate cause." It is preferable to divide causation problems into two distinct categories: (1) cause in fact and (2) "legal" cause, or scope of liability. "Legal cause" is primarily a device for limiting the scope of liability to those consequences of defendant's conduct that bear some reasonable relationship to the risk he created. Problems of legal cause or scope of liability arise most often in cases of nonintentional physical harm, and therefore will be discussed in § 4–4, infra.

In its simplest form, cause in fact is established by evidence that tends to show that defendant's act or omission was a necessary antecedent to plaintiff's injury. Courts sometimes express this in the

31

form of a rule commonly known as the "but for" or "sine qua non" rule: defendant's conduct is not a cause of the event, if the event would have occurred without it.

Proof. A large number of cause in fact problems are merely problems of proof. Plaintiff's decedent is found at the bottom of defendant's stairway, obviously killed by a fall. The stairway is littered with debris and poorly lit, or otherwise defective. Was the decedent's death a result of the negligent maintenance of the stairway? The usual rules of circumstantial evidence apply, and if the jury can draw a reasonable inference of causation, its determination is final. Compare *Wolf v. Kaufmann* (N.Y.App.Div. 1929) and *McInturff v. Chicago Title & Tr. Co.* (Ill.App. 1968) (cause not proved) with *Wright v. Stech* (Ill.App. 1972) and *Ingersoll v. Liberty Bank* (N.Y. 1938) (jury question). If resolution of the cause issue requires special knowledge beyond that possessed by the average juror, plaintiff must produce satisfactory expert testimony. E.g., *Stubbs v. City of Rochester* (N.Y. 1919) (cause of typhoid fever).

Courts will occasionally relax the usual proof requirements for policy reasons, for example, where the defendant's negligent conduct was partly responsible for the proof problem. See, e.g., *Haft v. Lone Palm Hotel* (Cal. 1970) (burden shifted to defendant to prove that negligent failure to provide lifeguard in motel pool was not a cause in fact of drownings).

Multiple Causes. In real life, of course, every occurrence has many causative antecedents. Recognizing this, the test for tort liability is whether the cause for which defendant was responsible was a *material element* and a *substantial factor* in bringing about the event. It need not be the sole cause, nor (contrary to the implication of the term "proximate") the last or nearest cause, and thus there may be two or more causes that were material and substantial. Such multiple causation cases often present special problems, and the "but for" or "sine qua non" rule usually breaks down.

A defendant is not relieved of liability merely because others are also responsible for the same harm. Where the negligence of two drivers concurs to produce a collision that injures a bystander, both may be held jointly and severally liable, even though there was no concert of action and despite the fact that the negligence of neither driver alone would have resulted in injury.

Going one step further, there may be two culpable acts or omissions that concur to cause plaintiff's harm, either one of which alone would have been sufficient to produce the same result. For example, two fires, each negligently set, combine to destroy plaintiff's property; either one alone would have done the same thing. In such cases, the "sine qua non" rule is inapplicable, and both defendants may be held jointly and severally liable for the whole loss.

Suppose, however, there are two sufficient causes and one is blameless—in the last example, one of the fires was set by lightning. The better rule holds the negligent defendant liable, since the fortuitous intervention of a natural event ought not to exonerate him when he would have been liable without it, and he would have been jointly and severally liable if the other cause were the culpable act or omission of another.

In general, if there are two or more causative agents and each is responsible only for a divisible part of plaintiff's harm, the law will hold each culpable defendant liable only for his respective portion of the damages, unless the defendants were acting in concert or engaged in a joint enterprise. For example, if several riparian owners pollute a stream, each is liable only for that portion of the damage caused by his contribution. See Restatement (Third) of Torts: Apportionment of Liability § 26.

One exception to this principle is where A's act injures plaintiff and also foreseeably exposes him to an increased risk of further injury by B. Driver A runs down plaintiff and renders him helpless in the roadway where he is struck again by B, who was also negligent; A is liable for plaintiff's entire damage, but B only for that portion he caused. Another relatively common example is where A negligently injures plaintiff and B, a doctor, aggravates the injury by negligent treatment. A is again liable for all of plaintiff's damages, including those caused by

B's malpractice, for which B is also jointly and severally liable.

Subject to this exception, the traditional rule has been that plaintiff's damages must be apportioned if they are even theoretically divisible. In other words, in any case where a given defendant was *in fact* responsible for less than all of plaintiff's damages, plaintiff may have judgment against that defendant for no more than his share, and the burden is on the plaintiff to prove his contribution or fail to recover against him at all. As a practical matter, in many cases adequate proof is impossible, with the result that plaintiff may have been seriously damaged by several defendants and be unable to recover anything from any of them. However, courts have often come to plaintiff's rescue with the aid of various devices, such as finding concerted action, or an indivisible injury for which all are jointly liable, by relaxing standards of proof, or, sensibly, by shifting the burden of apportionment to the defendants. See R. § 433B(2).

Alternative Liability. A special variation of this case is where there is clearly established double fault and alternative liability. Suppose two defendants negligently and simultaneously fire shotguns in the direction of plaintiff, and he is struck by the shot from only one, but cannot prove which. Rather than find a dubious concert of action (as a few courts have done), the California Supreme Court in such a case shifted the burden of proof on the issue of causation to the defendants, and imposed liability on both unless and until one or the other could prove that he was *not* the cause of plaintiff's injury. *Summers v. Tice* (Cal. 1948). See R. § 433B(3).

Enterprise and Market Share Liability. In product liability cases involving an injury caused by a product from an unidentifiable manufacturer, some courts have been willing to create new rules of causation when the plaintiff can prove that similar products were marketed during the relevant time by a group of manufacturers. These cases necessarily involve an injury caused by a common design feature of the similar products.

In one variation, known as enterprise liability, (1) the injury-causing product was manufactured by one of a small number of defendants in an industry, (2) the defendants had joint knowledge of the risks inherent in the product and possessed a joint capacity to reduce those risks, and (3) each of them failed to take steps to reduce the risk, delegating this responsibility to a trade association. Most, if not all, the manufacturers must be joined as defendants, and those joined are jointly and severally liable to the plaintiff. *Hall v. E.I. DuPont De Nemours & Co.* (E.D.N.Y. 1972) (blasting caps).

Another type is known as "market share" liability. The plaintiff must join defendants representing a substantial share of the relevant market at the relevant time. Depending on which variation has been adopted, the defendants will each be liable to the plaintiff for some fractional share of plaintiff's total damages calculated in reference to that defendant's market share. Jurisdictions differ as to whether to recognize this form of liability (compare *Sindell v. Abbott Laboratories*, Cal. 1980 (yes), with *Mulcahy v. Eli Lilly & Co.*, Iowa 1986, and *Smith v. Eli Lilly & Co.*, Ill. 1990 (no)) and, among those that have adopted it, they differ in the operative details (compare *Brown v. Superior Court*, Cal. 1988, *Collins v. Eli Lilly Co.*, Wis. 1984, *Martin v. Abbott Laboratories*, Wash. 1984, and *Hymowitz v. Eli Lilly & Co.*, N.Y. 1989) (all DES cases).

Liability for Reduced Chance. Suppose that defendant's tortious conduct does not "cause" plaintiff's harm in a "but for" sense, but merely reduces plaintiff's chances of a favorable outcome. For example, suppose that plaintiff's decedent, having contracted a form of cancer, had a 40% chance of cure if he had received proper treatment. As a result of defendant's negligence in failing to make a prompt diagnosis, his chance of cure was reduced to 25%, and he died. *Herskovits v. Group Health Co–Op.* (Wash. 1983). Is defendant liable, and if so, for how much? The courts are divided. Some strictly apply traditional cause-in-fact requirements, denying all recovery unless the victim's chances were initially over 50%. Some (e.g. *Herskovits*) allow damages if the jury determines that the defendant's negligence was a "substantial factor" in hastening or precipitating the adverse result, without requiring the plaintiff to prove that the initial chance was over 50%; this is referred to as the "relaxed causation" rule. And some allow damages based on the percentage difference (in this case, 15%) attributable to the defendant's negligence times the plaintiff's total damages. In effect, this creates a cause of action for the value of the lost chance itself. See Joseph H. King, Jr., *Causation, Valuation and Chance in Personal Injury Torts Involving Pre-existing Conditions and Future Consequences*, 90 Yale L.J. 1353 (1981), generally regarded as the genesis of this idea, and *"Reduction of Likelihood" Reformulation and Other Retrofitting of the Loss-of-a-Chance Doctrine*, 28 Mem. St. U.L. Rev. 492 (1998).

PART II
PHYSICAL HARM
CHAPTER 3
STRICT LIABILITY

§ 3–1. Basis of Strict Liability

Modern tort law classifies the cases involving physical harm to persons and property according to the degree of fault inherent in the tortious conduct: intentional, negligent (including reckless or "wilful and wanton" misconduct), and a third category called "strict liability," "absolute liability," or "liability without fault."

As previously noted (§ 1–3), some believe that strict liability was the prevailing rule of the early common law. Whether it was or not, fault is now the norm. The negligence concept carries with it the requirement that defendant's conduct be blameworthy in the sense of creating an unreasonable risk of harm. The intentional torts require fault in the form of intent. But there remain a few situations where the historically-rooted strict liability has been preserved.

Writers have disagreed as to whether there is any liability without an element of fault. The issue is largely definitional. Legal fault is not the same as moral blame; it is merely a deviation from some standard of conduct required by society for the protection of its members. If the departure is innocent, or if defendant cannot help it, he may be *morally* blameless but he is nonetheless *legally* at fault.

The activities that give rise to strict liability—e.g., blasting, storing dangerous substances, keeping dangerous animals—are not so unreasonable as to be prohibited altogether; indeed, they may be socially useful or necessary. But they are sufficiently dangerous or create sufficiently *unusual* risks that the law requires them to be carried on at the actor's peril. Thus, it has been suggested that the fault is *conditional,* arising only if and when harm results, or that there is an element of fault in carrying on the activity at all but that the activity is privileged so long as it does not cause harm. Such analyses are, of course, somewhat tautological; they equate fault and legal liability. It may be just as valid to ignore "fault" and to say that certain activities, for reasons of social policy, may be conducted only if the person conducting them is willing to insure others against the harm that results from the risks they create.

There are a number of instances in the law of liability without fault, besides those (discussed in this chapter) which traditionally are collected under the heading "strict" or "absolute" liability. Certain statutes (e.g. workers' compensation) create it. It is found in an employer's liability for the torts of her employees, in common law liability for defamation, and in some forms of liability for selling defective products. The common thread that runs through all forms of strict liability is that, irrespective of the care with which it is conducted, a particular activity ought to carry with it the costs of the risks it creates. If it helps one to stretch the concept "fault" to include the creation of these risks, perhaps no harm is done, but it would seem preferable to view strict liability as special instances of mandatory insurance against particular designated risks imposed as a matter of policy irrespective of fault.

§ 3–2. Animals, Statutory Strict Liability

Animals. Strict liability for damage caused by animals has survived (with modifications) the general shift to the fault requirement, probably because of the special risks they create. Since animals have no conscience with which to restrain themselves, and possess great capacity to do mischief if not restrained, those who keep them have a duty to restrain them or pay.

Trespassing Animals. In most jurisdictions, the general rule is that keepers of all animals, including domesticated ones, are strictly liable for damage resulting from the trespass of their animals on the property of another.

There are three principal exceptions:

(1) Owners of dogs and cats are not liable, absent negligence, for their trespasses, except

where strict liability is imposed by statute or ordinance.

(2) There is no liability without negligence for damage caused by the trespass on property adjoining a road by livestock straying from the road.

(3) In some parts of the western United States, certain farm animals (especially cattle) by custom or statute are permitted to graze at large on the range, and their owners are not strictly liable for their trespasses. In some states there are "fencing out" statutes that require landowners who wish to exclude such animals to construct a certain type of fence; having done so, the animals' owner is strictly liable for subsequent trespasses. In other states, "fencing in" statutes relieve the animal's owner of strict liability if he has constructed a certain fence to keep his animals on his own property.

The basis of liability for animal trespass is possession and control. Hence, if the owner surrenders possession to another, the bailee becomes liable. Except perhaps as to wild animals or animals known to be dangerous, the bailment relieves the owner's liability.

Liability Apart From Trespass. For purposes of liability for harm other than trespass, the law distinguishes between animals domestic and wild. In the case of animals that are customarily domesticated and kept in that region (e.g., in the U.S., dogs, cats, cattle, sheep, horses, etc.) the keeper is strictly liable for the harm they cause only if she had actual knowledge (or had knowledge of facts which ought to have given her notice) that the animal had the particular trait or propensity that caused the harm. The trait must be a potentially harmful one, such as viciousness or destructive tendencies (as opposed to, e.g., excessive playfulness), and the harm must correspond to the knowledge; notice that a dog will attack other dogs is not, of itself, notice that he will attack humans. Thus, it is often said that "every dog is entitled to one bite," but this is not necessarily true since the keeper may be on notice by reason of other known facts. In some jurisdictions, statutes impose absolute liability for certain types of damage (e.g., dog bites) without requiring scienter.

Keepers of species that are normally considered "wild" in that region (e.g., in the U.S., bears, lions, elephants, monkeys, etc.) are strictly liable for the harm they cause if they escape, whether or not the animal in question is known to be dangerous. And because such animals are known to revert to their natural tendencies, they are considered to be wild no matter how well trained or domesticated. However, where the injury occurs on the owner's premises while the animal is confined or restrained, the cases tend to deny strict liability, commonly on a theory of assumed risk.

Statutory Liability. Occasionally, a statute may impose strict liability for harm caused by a particular activity. See, e.g., N.Y. Envtl. Conserv. Law § 23–1717 (release of LP gas).

§ 3–3. Abnormally Dangerous Activities

Strict liability for harm resulting from abnormally dangerous conditions did not develop in the United States until well into the twentieth century, but its roots are found in earlier forms of liability without fault. The doctrine originated in a leading English case, *Rylands v. Fletcher* (Exch.Ch. 1866, aff'd, H.L. 1868). Defendants, mill owners in Lancashire, constructed a reservoir on their land to provide water for their mill. The water broke through the filled-in shaft of an abandoned coal mine and flooded along connecting passageways into plaintiff's active coal mine nearby, flooding their mine. The trier of fact found that defendants were ignorant of the abandoned mine shaft and free of negligence. The lower court held for defendants.

On appeal, the Exchequer Chamber decided to impose strict liability, but the case did not fit into the existing tort pigeonholes. There was no trespass, perhaps because the flooding was not direct or immediate (the premises of plaintiff and defendants did not adjoin) or because defendant acted through an agent. Nor was there any nuisance (as the term was then understood) since there was nothing offensive to the senses and the damage was not continuous or recurring. Using analogies to strict liability for trespassing cattle, dangerous animals, and "absolute" nuisance, Justice Blackburn concluded:

> We think that the true rule of law is, that the person who for his own purposes brings on his

lands and collects and keeps there anything likely to do mischief if it escapes, must keep it in at his peril, and, if he does not do so, is prima facie answerable for all the damage which is the natural consequence of its escape.

Defendants appealed to the House of Lords, which affirmed, but the rule of the case was more narrowly stated by Lord Cairns:

The Defendants ... might lawfully have used [their] close for any purpose for which it might in the ordinary course of the enjoyment of land be used; and if, in what I may term the natural user of that land, there had been any accumulation of water, either on the surface or underground, and if, by the operation of the laws of nature, that accumulation of water had passed off into the close occupied by the Plaintiff, the Plaintiff could not have complained. . . .

On the other hand, if the Defendants, not stopping at the natural use of their close, had desired to use it for any purpose which I may term a non-natural use, for the purpose of introducing into the close that which in its natural condition was not in or upon it, for the purpose of introducing water either above or below ground in quantities and in a manner not the result of any work or operation on or under the land,—and if in consequence of their doing so, or in consequence of any imperfection in the mode of their doing so, the water came to escape and to pass off into the close of the Plaintiff, then it appears to me that

that which the Defendants were doing they were doing at their own peril....

Thus, the emphasis in the House of Lords was upon the activity's nonnatural character, as well as its escape from the premises.

Rylands v. Fletcher must be viewed in its historical context. The judges may have been operating from a tradition of strict liability, or at least from a context in which fault was not an element of the plaintiff's claim. In addition, the common law rules governing the tort liability of owners and occupiers of land refused to impose liability when harm to persons outside the premises resulted from a "natural" (as opposed to an "artificial" or man-made) condition. Thus, the decision may simply have been an application of the then-current principle that a landowner was liable for an artificial (i.e., nonnatural) condition on his land that caused injury to his neighbor's land. And one author has persuasively shown that the decision may have been motivated in large part by the courts' concerns about a serious contemporary problem, unsafe reservoirs. Simpson, *Legal Liability for Bursting Reservoirs: The Historical Context of Rylands v. Fletcher*, 13 J. Legal Stud. 209 (1984).

Whatever may have been its original meaning, subsequent cases—English and U.S.—have interpreted *Rylands* to impose strict liability if the harm results from the miscarriage of an activity that, though lawful, is unusual, extraordinary, exceptional, or inappropriate, in light of the place and manner in which the activity is conducted. Thus, water collected in household pipes or a stock watering tank or a cistern is a natural use; but water collected in large tanks in dangerous proximity to plaintiff's land is not. Gas or electricity in household pipes or wires is a normal use, but not so gas stored in large quantity or high-voltage electricity under the street. Although the automobile is manifestly dangerous, the risks of harm it creates, absent negligence, are common and accepted; but those created by a ten-ton traction engine or a steam roller are not. The storage in quantity of explosives or flammable liquids, blasting, accumulation of sewage, emission of creosote fumes, and pile driving all have been held to be sufficiently unusual and excessive under the circumstances to justify strict liability.

The same activity may be appropriate or normal in one location but not in another. This suggests that the primary basis of liability is the creation of an extraordinary risk, either in kind or degree. A water reservoir might be an inappropriate use of land in a coal mining area, but not in West Texas (*Turner v. Big Lake Oil Co.*, Tex. 1936). The storage of explosives in quantity, or blasting, create unusual and unacceptable risks in the midst of a large city, but not in remote rural areas. An oil well in the oil fields of Pennsylvania is a natural use of the land and there is no strict liability for resulting harm; but the opposite is true of an oil well drilled in a thickly settled residential area of Los Angeles. If the activity is appropriate to the area, there is strict liability only if it is conducted in an unusual or abnormal way (e.g., crop dusting).

Until 1947, the English cases had applied the doctrine broadly. While the rule was originally framed in terms of an "escape" of that which caused the harm, subsequent cases imposed no such requirement. And the rule was extended to cover personal injuries as well as property damage. But in *Read v. J. Lyons & Co., Ltd.* (1947), the House of Lords refused to impose strict liability in favor of a government inspector injured in an explosion at defendant's munitions plant on the ground that there had been no escape of a dangerous substance from defendant's land. In addition two of the judges thought that the rule did not apply to personal injuries. And in *Cambridge Water Co. v. Eastern Counties Leather Plc.* (H.L. 1994), the English version of the rule was further narrowed, being seen as merely an extension of nuisance liability to an isolated escape from the defendant's premises, and requiring that the harm be of a type that is reasonably foreseeable.

At first, the doctrine was widely rejected by U.S. courts. (Interestingly, a number of cases spurning the "rule" rejected it in the broad form stated by Justice Blackburn, ignoring or overlooking the fact that the final formulation by Lord Cairns was somewhat narrower.) Much of the earlier hostility to the rule was probably due to the strength of the fault ethic and to a desire to protect emerging industries. More recently, the policy pendulum has swung to the view that hazardous enterprises, however use-ful, must pay their own way. At present, virtually all U.S. jurisdictions accept the rule, in name or in fact, but some tend to apply it very narrowly. No U.S. case has yet applied the doctrine to electricity in any form or place (although they uniformly re-quire a high degree of care commensurate with the danger). But see *Ferguson v. Northern States Power Co.* (Minn. 1976) (rule cited with approval).

Even where *Rylands v. Fletcher* is expressly re-jected or narrowly applied, the same result may be reached by other means. The principal alternate theory is "absolute nuisance," under which negli-gence or intent to do harm need not be proven. Trespass is another. In cases involving damage caused by blasting (an activity often cited to typify a *Rylands v. Fletcher* situation) some courts (e.g., New York) imposed strict common law trespass liability for harm caused by debris thrown off defen-dant's premises, in lieu of adopting *Rylands*. The catch was that under this theory, there was no strict liability for damage caused solely by vibration or concussion, since there was no trespass. Most of the jurisdictions that once made this distinction have now repudiated it and impose strict liability for all blasting-caused damage, direct and indirect, with or without accepting *Rylands*.

Aviation has been a source of controversy. So far as passengers and cargo are concerned, the usual rules of negligence law have always been applied. But as to ground damage caused by falling aircraft or objects or forced landings, various rules have been applied or suggested. Some early cases imposed strict liability on a trespass theory. The Uniform Aeronautics Act, promulgated in 1922, provided for strict liability, and it was adopted (sometimes with modifications) in several states. So did the Restatement (First) of Torts § 520, comment b (1939). However, as the industry has passed from its infancy and become a common and safe means of transportation, there has been something of a retreat toward negligence.

The Uniform Act was withdrawn in 1943. Several state statutes have been modified or repealed. Some strict liability decisions have been overruled (e.g., see *Wood v. United Air Lines, Inc.*, N.Y. 1962).

Even though it now is generally agreed that aviation no longer creates abnormal or unusual risks, it has also been recognized that there remain good reasons to justify strict liability for ground damage. The probability of harm is small, but the potential gravity is great and there is simply no way for those on the ground to avoid the risk. Thus, the Restatement (Second) of Torts § 520A provides strict liability for ground damage caused by "the ascent, descent or flight of any aircraft, or by the dropping or falling of any object therefrom." It must be remembered, however, that statutes in almost half the states supersede the common law to a greater or lesser extent.

The advance of technology will likely provide new illustrations of this rule. Two cases have imposed strict liability for damage caused by rocket testing. And it seems certain that the same result will be reached if the case ever arises involving nuclear energy.

In this area, the Restatement of Torts has been of questionable value, and has not accurately mirrored the case law. The first Restatement limited strict liability to "ultrahazardous" activities which the actor "should recognize as likely" to cause harm "by the unpreventable miscarriage of the activity" (§ 519). An activity was said to be ultrahazardous if it "(a) necessarily involves a risk of serious harm ... which cannot be eliminated by the exercise of the utmost care, and (b) is not a matter of common usage" (§ 520). Generally speaking, the case law did not require that the harm be unpreventable, that the risk necessarily be a "serious" one, nor that the plaintiff prove the foreseeable *probability* of the harm. In addition, the formulation was thought to be misleading, since there is probably *no* activity that is not perfectly safe if the *utmost* care is used in conducting it (including the choice of location). The Restatement (Second) §§ 519, 520, approved in 1964, simply provides strict liability for activities which are "abnormally dangerous," to be determined by considering six factors:

(a) whether the activity involves a high degree of risk of some harm to the person, land or chattels of others;

(b) whether the gravity of the harm which may result from it is likely to be great;

(c) whether the risk cannot be eliminated by the exercise of reasonable care;

(d) whether the activity is not a matter of common usage;

(e) whether the activity is inappropriate to the place where it is carried on; and

(f) the value of the activity to the community.

Not all courts will consider all factors, and some factors are or ought to be of greater significance than others. Whether strict liability is appropriate requires a complex balancing of policy considerations that can only be done on a case-by-case basis.

§ 3–4. Scope of Strict Liability

All forms of strict liability have similar limits and defenses.

Scienter. Unless otherwise provided by statute, defendant must *knowingly* engage in (or authorize) the activity. Fairness dictates that if liability is strict, at least the risk must be consciously assumed.

Proximate Cause. For similar reasons, courts tend to invoke a narrower rule of proximate cause than in negligence cases (see § 4–4, infra). Thus, liability is confined to those consequences, the risk of which made the activity abnormally dangerous in the first place (R. § 519(2)), and to those persons foreseeably within the zone of danger, the courts applying a slightly more restrictive view of what is foreseeable.

In negligence cases, defendant is ordinarily not excused by the fact that the harm was brought about by an unforeseeable intervening cause (such as an "act of God") so long as the result is within the scope of the risk he created. However, in strict liability cases unforeseeable intervening cause is a defense. See, e.g., *Madsen v. East Jordan Irrigation Co.* (Utah 1942) (blasting caused frightened mother mink to kill her kittens); *Kaufman v. Boston Dye House* (Mass. 1932) (flammable liquid discharged into stream ignited by sparks from passing truck). The Restatement (First) and (Second) § 552 are contra, but so far the courts have refused to follow this section, apparently on the theory that one who is held to the liability of an insurer at least ought to be able to predict the limits of his risk with reasonable certainty.

Contributory Negligence, Assumption of Risk. The traditional rule was that contributory negligence is not a defense in a strict liability case. R. § 484(1). At first glance, this may seem incongruous; plaintiff's fault will negate or reduce defendant's liability when he is also at fault but not when he is innocent. But recall that strict liability is based on the *willful* creation of an abnormal risk by unusual conduct; inherent in the creation of such a risk is the possibility that others may fail to anticipate or guard against it. However, under the Restatement (Second) of Torts, the plaintiff's conduct in voluntarily and unreasonably subjecting himself to the risk—one form of assumption of the risk—is a defense. R. § 484(2). Thus, if this rule is applied,

one who brings himself within the reach of, or
provokes, a dangerous animal cannot recover if he
knew of the danger or if it was obvious. And,
according to the Restatement, while strict liability
ordinarily extends to invitees, licensees, and even
known trespassers on defendant's premises (R.
§ 512), such persons cannot recover if they knew of
the danger and proceeded to bring themselves within its zone.

Note, however, that the encountering of the risk
must be both voluntary and *unreasonable*. Defendant, by creating a patently dangerous condition,
may not unreasonably limit plaintiff's freedom of
action or unreasonably restrict the use of neighbor-
ing land. And in many situations (e.g., a circus) the
plaintiff may reasonably assume that defendant will
protect him against the obvious risks.

In contrast, the Restatement (Third), Apportionment of Liability, § 8, provides that in all cases
involving physical injury, the factfinder should as-
sign shares of responsibility to each party, regardless of the legal theory of liability. This means that
shares of fault can be assigned to a negligent plaintiff even if the defendant's liability is strict. Nevertheless, while it is true that in most cases, plaintiff's
foolishness in encountering a known risk is properly
characterized as mere negligence, certain cases may
remain where the plaintiff's conduct may evidence
his implied consent to subject himself to the risk
and thereby relieve the defendant of liability entirely.

Legislative and Public Duty Privileges.
When legislation expressly authorizes or imposes a
duty to carry on an activity, strict liability is usually
not imposed. R. §§ 517, 521. E.g., *Pumphrey v. J. A.
Jones Constr. Co.* (Iowa 1959) (blasting under state
contract); *Guzzi v. New York Zoological Soc'y* (N.Y.
1922) (custodian of public zoo); *Pope v. Edward M.
Rude Carrier Corp.* (W.Va. 1953) (common carrier
required to accept dangerous cargo). Contra: *Smith
v. Lockheed Propulsion Co.* (Cal.App. 1967) (rocket
testing under government contract); *National Steel
Service Center, Inc. v. Gibbons* (Iowa 1982) (railroad
tank car explosion).

Federal Tort Claims. The Federal Tort Claims
Act waives the sovereign immunity of the United
States for harm caused by the "negligent or wrongful act or omission of any employee of the Government," but this language has been construed to
exclude claims based on strict or absolute liability.
Laird v. Nelms (U.S. 1972).

CHAPTER 4

LIABILITY FOR NEGLIGENT CONDUCT

§ 4–1. Standards of Conduct: Of Risks and Reasonable Persons

The term "negligence" is used in two senses. First, it is the name of a tort cause of action, notable for its breadth. It is the closest thing there is to a general principle of tort liability. As a general rule, all persons are under a duty to conduct themselves in all of their diverse activities so as not to create unreasonable risks of physical harm to others. In certain cases, as will be noted later, this duty is limited or denied, but unless such a special exception exists one may be held liable for the consequences of his negligent conduct, at least if it causes physical harm.

Second, "negligence" describes that form of wrongful conduct itself which is an element of various tort causes of action (or defenses), including the action of that name. Thus, the components of the cause of action for negligence are:

(1) A *duty* owed by the defendant to plaintiff (or, more accurately, the absence of any rule limiting the general duty of ordinary care) (§ 4–5);

(2) A breach of that duty by the defendant's failure to conform to the required standard of conduct (i.e., *"negligence"* or negligent conduct);

(3) A sufficient *causal connection* between the negligent conduct and the resulting harm (§§ 2–1, 4–4); and

(4) Actual *loss* or *damage* of a recognized kind.

Plaintiff's *contributory negligence* (or certain other kinds of fault) will reduce her damages or, in some cases, defeat her claim entirely. Contributory negligence is an affirmative defense.

In analyzing the negligence cause of action, we will first consider the nature of negligence itself. What criteria do we use to determine whether defendant's act or omission may be deemed to be negligent?

General Characteristics of Negligence. According to the accepted definition, "negligence is conduct that falls below the standard established by law for the protection of others against unreasonable risk of harm." R. § 282. Always bear in mind that negligence is conduct.

To nonlawyers, "negligence" imports the absence of carefulness as a state of mind. The root word "neglect" implies forgetfulness or inattentiveness, determined subjectively and individually. In this sense, negligence and moral fault coincide.

But this is not the accepted legal concept. As the definition indicates, legal negligence is *conduct*. If one's conduct creates an unreasonable risk of harm, he may be held negligent even though his actual state of mind was one of anxious concern for the safety of others. In such cases, legal fault and moral blame diverge.

This is not to suggest, however, that the actor's state of mind is irrelevant. Whether or not his conduct in question was reasonable may depend, in part, on what he actually knew. For example, whether one who operates an automobile with defective steering is negligent may depend upon whether he knows of the defect. The distinction, so far as negligence liability is concerned, is between (1) knowledge and perception and (2) motive and intent. In judging whether conduct is negligent, the actor is charged with what he actually knew and actually perceived, as well as what he ought to have known and perceived. However, we do not permit the actor to defend his conduct by proof that his subjective intent or motive was to act nonnegligently. The ultimate issue is the reasonableness of his conduct, not the reasonableness of his belief that he was acting with appropriate care. Conversely, if defendant's *conduct* did not subject plaintiff to an *unreasonable* risk of harm defendant was not negligent, even though his state of mind was that of total obliviousness to the safety of others.

The Reasonable Person. In general, in judging whether conduct is negligent the law applies objective standards of reasonableness. It does not make special allowance for the particular weaknesses of the actor. The clumsy, rash, timid, forgetful, the chronically careless person, the fool, the ignorant, the slow reactor, the person with low intelligence— all are held to the general standard of reasonable care, whether or not they are capable of meeting it. Conduct that creates an unreasonable risk of harm is no less dangerous simply because the actor lacked the capacity to conform to an acceptable level of performance. While it may be somewhat unfair to such persons to hold them to a standard that they cannot always meet, it would be more unjust to require the innocent victims of their substandard conduct to assume such risks.

The standard is usually stated as "ordinary care" or "due care" or "reasonable care," measured against the hypothetical conduct of a hypothetical person—the "reasonable person of ordinary prudence." The question is, what would the "reasonable person" (sometimes the "ordinarily prudent person") have done under the same circumstances as those in which defendant found himself? R. § 283.

The reasonable person is, of course, a creature of the law's imagination. He or she is not the average or typical person, but rather an idealized image of such a person—a composite of the community's judgment as to how the typical community member *ought* to behave in each of the infinite variety of circumstances and activities in which there is a potential or actual risk of harm to the actor or others. The test is not what the typical respectable citizen in fact does, nor what the majority of the community does, since the behavior (e.g., jaywalking) may fall below the community's standards of safety.

On the other hand, the reasonable person is not perfect or infallible. She is permitted errors of judgment, mistakes in perception; she may even be momentarily distracted. She is human. But such errors must have been reasonable or excusable under the circumstances; they must have been consistent with the exercise of ordinary care.

Attributes of the Reasonable Person.

Knowledge, Experience and Perception. Tort liability for physical harm is founded upon defendant's knowledge (actual or constructive) of the risk and of some degree of probability that it will be realized (harm to the plaintiff). In negligence (as distinguished from intentional torts), the actor does not desire the injurious consequences of his conduct; he does not know that they are substantially certain to occur, nor believe that they will. There is merely a risk of such consequences sufficiently great that the ordinarily prudent person will anticipate them and guard against them. Thus, the normal actor (plaintiff or defendant) is charged with his *actual* knowledge and perceptions, and also with certain basic knowledge common to the community and with the ability to observe and understand his environment.

Obviously, conduct must be judged in light of what the actor *actually* knows and observes, since the reasonable person always takes this into account. If by chance she discovers that a product has a latent dangerous defect, if she sees another vehicle approaching without lights at night, she must act accordingly, even though she would not have been negligent in failing to discover or observe these things. R. § 289.

In addition, most persons are deemed to have the knowledge and experience, and the ability to perceive, understand and remember, of the hypothetical reasonable person. Thus, in the absence of overriding extenuating circumstances, one must see the clearly visible and hear the clearly audible. A driver approaching a railroad crossing where the view is unobstructed will not be heard to say that he did not see the approaching train or hear its whistle. And one cannot deny personal knowledge of those things that are commonly known in the community: basic principles of physics (e.g., materials that are combustible, the danger of electricity, principles of leverage), the limits of the body's physical capacity, the natural propensities of children and animals, the dangers of common sports, the effects of intoxicating beverages, and the like. R. § 290. Moreover, one must take notice of what one does *not* know (such as when walking in a strange dark hallway, or using an unfamiliar product or substance) and exercise caution commensurate to one's ignorance.

One who undertakes an activity ordinarily is charged with the knowledge common to those who regularly engage in it. A product manufacturer must know the characteristics and dangers of its product, at least to the extent that they are generally known in the industry or reasonably knowable. A motorist must know the rules of the road. And knowledge must keep reasonably current.

Special Skills. If the actor has chosen to engage in an activity requiring special skills, education, training or experience, then the standard by which her conduct is measured is that of the reasonably skilled, competent and experienced person who is a qualified member of the group authorized to engage in that activity. R. §§ 299, 299A. Typically (though not necessarily) these are activities that are licensed—physicians and surgeons, lawyers, architects, barbers, pilots, motorists, and the like—in general, the professions and skilled trades. The public properly relies upon the special expertise of those who engage in such activities, so that persons who undertake (even gratuitously) to perform them are judged by the standards of conduct of those properly qualified to do so, whether or not the actor is in fact a recognized member of the group in question. For example, a druggist who undertakes to diagnose and prescribe medication for an illness described to her by a customer will be judged by the standards applicable to a physician.

With respect to medical doctors (and sometimes dentists and others), the standard of care has been limited by the so-called "locality rule." See § 8–18, infra.

If the profession recognizes specialists—as do medicine and dentistry, for example—a certified specialist is held to the higher standard of the specialist subgroup. And, like all reasonably prudent persons, the actor who possesses more than the minimum level of knowledge, skill, training or experience for that activity is required to apply it, especially where he holds himself out to the public as possessing such special competence.

As to all specialized activities, the law generally has refused to create a subgroup for novices. The learner, the beginner, the trainee—pilot, automobile driver, employee, professional—is held to the standard of conduct of persons who are reasonably skilled, learned and experienced in the activity. The law does not require the general public to assume the risk of the neophyte's lack of competence. True, these activities typically are socially useful and, of necessity, all those who would engage in them must be more or less unskillful and incompetent at first. The beginner is thus held to a standard that he sometimes cannot meet. But at least the beginner can take his lack of skill and experience into account and act accordingly, whereas the public is usually defenseless against these risks. Of course, in a given case the victim may be found to have knowingly and voluntarily assumed this risk (e.g., a flight instructor), but this does not affect the general standard of care to which the novice is held.

Physical Characteristics. The "reasonable person" standard is subjective to the extent that the actor's actual *physical* characteristics are taken into account. The test is, what is reasonable conduct for an ordinarily prudent person with the actor's physical characteristics? Or, what would the reasonably prudent person do under the circumstances, his physical handicap constituting one of those circumstances? R. § 283C. The blind, the deaf, the crippled, and all others physically impaired are no less entitled to live as fully as they can, and it would be an unfair burden to require them to conform to a standard of conduct physically impossible for them to meet. At the same time, the physically handicapped person must act prudently in light of his infirmity, and he may be negligent in taking a risk that is unreasonable in view of his known physical limitations.

Mental Capacity. In judging the actor's conduct, no allowance is made for subjective deficiencies in the actor's mental capacity to conform to the standard of the reasonably prudent person. The fact that one is mentally deficient (in intelligence, judgment, memory, emotional stability, etc.), voluntarily intoxicated, or even insane, ordinarily does not excuse his failure to act as a reasonably prudent sane, sober and normal person would have acted under the same circumstances. R. §§ 283B, 895J. Although this imposes a standard of behavior that such persons often cannot possibly meet, their mental incapacity itself poses a threat to the general security and increases the risk of unreasonably dangerous conduct. As between such persons and their innocent victims, it is deemed preferable that the former (or those responsible for them) should bear this risk.

However, as to contributory negligence the reason for the rule does not apply with equal force, and some courts have applied a subjective standard and permitted the jury to excuse a plaintiff who lacked the mental capacity to appreciate the risk or avoid it (other than by intoxication). In particular, the elderly whose mental faculties are impaired by senility or other diseases associated with aging may qualify for subjective treatment.

Evidence of intoxication is frequently admitted on the issue of negligence, but the better view is that drunkenness is not negligence per se but does not excuse conduct otherwise negligent. Its true function in such cases is probably, to aggravate the wrong. It is usually negligent (or even reckless) to undertake certain activities at all (e.g., driving) while intoxicated.

Minors. As a general rule, children, like other incompetents, are liable for their torts. R. § 895I. But children as a class are expected to be more or less incapable of meeting adult standards of behavior, and are judged by a lesser standard. Thus, where the plaintiff or defendant is a minor, the test is, what is reasonable conduct for a child of the actor's *age, intelligence,* and *experience.* R. § 283A. Aside from society's general tolerance for the unintended misdeeds of its youth, there are several justifications for applying a subjective standard. For the most part, children do not engage in the high-risk activities of adults. Due to their smaller size and subjection to adult supervision and control, their negligence overall does not create the same magnitude of risk as that of adults. Also, children as a group are readily identifiable on sight, and thus others can frequently adjust their conduct to make allowance for them and their "childish" behavior.

A number of courts have gone so far as to establish arbitrary age ranges within which children are "presumed"—rebuttably or conclusively—to be incapable of negligence. In many states, children below a certain age (usually seven) are legally ("conclusively presumed") incapable of negligence. In the next higher range (usually seven to fourteen) they are rebuttably presumed incapable; above that, no presumption operates, which means that they are capable of negligence as a matter of law. Sometimes these presumptions apply only to the minor's contributory negligence. These multiples of seven were borrowed from rules of criminal responsibility, which in turn were derived from ancient mythology, and there is little justification for their use. It would seem preferable to leave the question of capacity to the jury in each case.

Tort law applies the statutory age of majority (18) for purposes of these rules and all those this age or above will be held to adult standards of conduct.

There is one major exception to the standard for minors. If the child is engaging in what is deemed to be an "adult" activity—such as operating an automobile or flying an airplane—he will be held to an adult standard of care. It is doubtful that the courts really intend to use the appellation "adult" in any literal sense, since minors are freely permitted to engage in them and regularly do so. Rather, this is merely an application of the rule, previously discussed, that *whoever* engages in a potentially hazardous activity that requires special skill, experience, training, or education will be judged objectively by standards of reasonable competence for that activity, for the protection of the public, regardless of age.

Emergencies. The law recognizes that even the reasonably prudent person is susceptible to errors of judgment in emergency situations. Thus, in such cases the test is, was the actor's conduct in the emergency a reasonable response under the circumstances, even though in retrospect another course of action might have avoided the injury. R. § 296.

It must be remembered, however, that failure to anticipate an emergency may itself constitute negligence. The owner of a theater must consider the possibility of fire; the proprietor of a swimming pool or beach cannot ignore the likelihood of emergencies that threaten drowning; a certain level of "defensive" auto driving is required.

Moreover, the actor may have been negligent in creating the emergency in the first place, in which case he may be held liable for that negligence, even though his conduct in the emergency was acceptable.

Conduct of Others. The reasonable person will regulate his conduct in light of his expectations of the conduct of others. This is merely an application of the principle requiring him to know his environment.

This duty includes anticipating not only the reasonably prudent conduct of others, but in some cases their negligence or even unlawful conduct, at least where such conduct is reasonably foreseeable. It is sometimes said that an actor may assume that others will act lawfully and carefully. This may be true in specific situations, but it is equally clear that if she has reason to anticipate the contrary she must act accordingly. Thus, it may be negligence to leave one's car unlocked with the keys in the ignition due to the foreseeable risk of theft, or to fail to slow down in the vicinity of a school yard where children may negligently dart into the street. R. §§ 302A, 302B.

When Is a Risk "Unreasonable"? In general, and in the absence of some more specific rule of conduct, negligence is the doing of an act (or omitting to do an act that some duty requires), without wrongful intent, under circumstances where our hypothetical reasonably prudent person would foresee that he is thereby exposing another (or himself) to an *unreasonable* risk of harm. R. § 284. (Of course, the harm must be to a legally protected interest. This is a matter of duty, which will be discussed in § 4–5, infra, and throughout this book.)

When is the risk unreasonable? The classic formulation is that of Judge Learned Hand—when the foreseeable *probability* and *gravity* of the harm outweigh the *burden* to the actor of alternative conduct that would have prevented the harm. *Conway v. O'Brien* (2d Cir. 1940); *United States v. Carroll Towing Co.* (2d Cir. 1947). Compare Terry, *Negligence*, 29 Harv.L.Rev. 40 (1915); R. §§ 291–292.

The *probability* or likelihood that harm will result together with the *gravity* or seriousness of the potential harm, in combination, determine the magnitude of the risk (sometimes called the "hazard" or "danger"). R. § 293. Thus, it may be negligence to dash across a little-traveled highway without looking for traffic, even though the statistical probability that you and a fast-moving car will reach the same point at the same time is very low; the potential harm is very great. Conversely, the failure to repair a hole in a rarely-used sidewalk might not be negligence, whereas it would be if the sidewalk is heavily traveled. The gravity of the harm includes both the extent of the damage and the relative societal value of the protected interest; for example, one such value is that people are more valuable than property. R. § 293(a).

Note particularly that the actor's conduct is judged by the *foreseeable* risk, viewed at the time and place of the conduct.

The *burden* of reducing or eliminating the risk by alternative conduct is placed on the other side of the scale. A number of considerations may be relevant: (1) the importance or social value of the activity or goal of which the actor's conduct is a part (for example, rescuers are often held not negligent in situations where similar conduct would clearly have been negligent for any other purpose); (2) the utility of the conduct as a means of conducting the activity or reaching the goal; (3) the feasibility of alternative, safer conduct; (4) the relative cost (in money, time or effort) of safer conduct; (5) the relative utility of safer conduct as a means of achieving the same end; (6) the relative safety of alternative conduct; and perhaps others as well. For example, suppose the question is whether it was negligence to give a transfusion of whole blood that (unknown to the hospital) contained hepatitis virus. So far as the *burden* aspect is concerned it would be relevant to consider: (a) the purpose of the transfusion; (b) its anticipated medical value; (c) whether other blood was available; (d) whether a substitute (e.g. plasma) would have worked as well; (e) whether it was possible to detect the virus, and at what cost; (f) whether better screening of donors would have significantly reduced the risk; and the like. Thus, all of these factors are proper subjects of proof.

Reducing the risk does not always require that the conduct or condition creating it be modified. In certain cases, this can be accomplished by an adequate warning of the danger. And where a warning would be appropriate and effective, the burden of providing one is ordinarily very slight, and in such cases negligence may thus be found if there is any significant risk of harm at all.

Judge and Jury. Whether conduct was negligent is preeminently a question of fact, which means it is ordinarily for the jury (see § 1–4). Fundamentally, the attributes of the reasonable person are matters of common sense and community values, and so are the factors that determine whether a risk was unreasonable. Thus, it is common practice to give the jury merely a short general definition of negligence and the reasonable person test, leaving it to the jury to apply its common experience to the evidence. R. § 285. The jury is left ignorant of the elaborations of these concepts that fill the pages of lawbooks.

However, in certain cases, the decision is one for the court. The judge may decide, based on her own experience and her legal knowledge of the underlying principles, that there is no question for the jury because the conduct in question so clearly was or was not negligent that no reasonable person could reach any other conclusion. The elaboration of the attributes of the reasonable person and of the balancing test for determining reasonableness of the risk derive mainly from appellate decisions in cases where the trial court decided the question, or one of the parties contends that it should have.

There are situations, however, in which the jury receives further guidance. The jury will be told if some special variation of the reasonable person test applies, such as in the case of physicians, minors, etc. Further, courts will sometimes go so far as to declare that certain kinds of conduct in certain situations are (or are not) negligence as a matter of law, or presumptively negligent, or evidence of negligence, and the jury will be so instructed. Sources of these specific standards of conduct will be discussed in the section that follows.

§ 4–2. Sources of Standards of Conduct

Rules of Law. As we have seen, the standard of conduct required of the plaintiff or defendant in the circumstances of the particular case is ordinarily fixed by the trier of fact (the jury), and is derived from its own knowledge and experience. Thus, each jury is usually free to make its own independent ad hoc determination of what the reasonable person would or would not have done, subject only to the court's power to decide the case when it feels strongly one way or the other (by directing a verdict).

However, in reviewing trial court rulings appellate courts are frequently required to state whether or not, as a matter of law, certain conduct was negligent or nonnegligent in particular circumstances. Under principles of stare decisis, these decisions become precedents in future cases. As similar fact situations recur, there is an inevitable tendency to generalize, with the result that some types of conduct become fixed as standards by rules of law.

Within proper limits, this is necessary and desirable. Jury trials of clear cases are a waste of time and resources, and occasionally (due to prejudice, sympathy, error, etc.) the jury will reach an improper result, at least as judged on a purely rational basis. A certain amount of judicial control lends stability, certainty and meaning to the negligence concept.

Occasionally, however, courts and scholars have gone too far and attempted to establish rules of conduct of universal application to which no exceptions are permitted. Invariably, the rule eventually breaks down in the face of the obvious necessity of basing the standard on the particular circumstances of the case, the apparent risk, and the actor's opportunity to deal with it. No fixed rule can be justly applied in every case, nor ignore the changing conditions and expectations of society.

The classic example is the so-called Pennsylvania rule concerning the standard of care of motorists approaching railroad crossings. In *Baltimore & Ohio Ry. v. Goodman* (U.S. 1927), Mr. Justice Holmes (a leading advocate of setting standards by rules of law) attempted to "lay down a standard once for all" requiring a driver to stop, look and listen and, if necessary, to leave his vehicle and walk out onto the tracks to ascertain whether a train is coming. It soon became apparent that such a rule was too harsh and unjust in many cases, and made it virtually impossible to recover for a crossing accident. Moreover, the standard was clearly unworkable, since compliance would often unreasonably delay vehicular traffic, might itself be dangerous, and in some situations would not even accomplish the desired result. Finally, in *Pokora v. Wabash Ry.* (U.S. 1934), *Goodman* was overruled.

"Illustrations such as these," said Mr. Justice Cardozo, "bear witness to the need for caution in framing standards of behavior that amount to rules of law.... Extraordinary situations may not wisely or fairly be subjected to tests or regulations that are fitting for the commonplace or normal."

Similar rules—such as that it is *always* negligent to drive at such a speed that it is impossible to stop within the range of vision, that a motorist must always sound his horn when a pedestrian is in or about to enter his path, and the like—have met a similar fate.

This is not to say, of course, that courts may not take the case from the jury where there would be general agreement that on the particular facts the conduct in question clearly was negligent (or was not). But given the infinite variety of fact situations in which injuries occur, virtually all rules of conduct must be sufficiently flexible to admit of exceptions and excuses.

Legislation. Legislation—federal and state statutes, municipal ordinances, even administrative regulations—will often prescribe standards of conduct for the protection of others from harm. For purposes of tort law, such legislation may be classified in two categories: (1) statutes that expressly or by necessary implication themselves create a civil cause of action for damages; and (2) those that do not, ordinarily providing criminal penalties for their violation.

If the statute itself provides for a civil remedy, it creates in essence a statutory tort cause of action, and the only questions are whether the statute is valid and whether the facts of the case are within its terms. Examples include the Federal Employers Liability Act, the Jones Act, and state employee safety and dram shop acts. In a proper case, a civil remedy may be found to have been given by necessary implication, even though not expressly provided. See, e.g., Mowe, *Federal Statutes and Implied Private Actions*, 55 Ore. L.Rev. 3 (1976); R. § 874A.

In the second category, where no civil remedy is expressly or impliedly provided, courts will nevertheless permit the statute to be introduced into evidence to establish the standard of conduct. Some courts have constructed the doubtful fiction that this is what the legislature intended. Others have suggested that the reasonable person obeys the criminal law; while this is no doubt often true, this rationale does not account for all the cases. Perhaps the most satisfactory justification is that the statute embodies a legislative judgment that certain conduct either is required or is unreasonable (depending on the type of statute) which the courts will apply in civil cases where logic dictates that the issue is directly analogous. Negligence is the breach of a duty imposed by law, and in most cases it matters not whether the law is of judicial or legislative origin.

When is the statute a relevant standard? The fundamental limitation is legislative purpose. The court must first find that the statute was intended, at least in part, to protect a class of persons that includes the plaintiff (or defendant, as the case may be) against the particular hazard and kind of harm that resulted. R. §§ 286, 288. If the legislature's standard is to be adopted, then the court must also adopt the limits of the purpose for which the statute was intended, for those are presumably the limits of its validity. Thus, a statute prohibiting certain activities on Sunday is intended to protect the public peace and morals, and therefore is irrelevant on the issue whether the activity was conducted negligently. Violation of a speed limit enacted solely to conserve gasoline is irrelevant in determining whether the excessive speed was unreasonably dangerous. An act requiring certain safety features in factories may be held to be for the protection of employees, not casual visitors or trespassers. A statute, intended to prevent the spread of disease, requiring separate pens for animals transported by ship was not admissible in an action for loss of plaintiff's sheep that were washed overboard during a storm at sea, even though as chance would have it the required pens would have prevented the loss.

On the other hand the class of those protected may be construed very broadly, especially where the danger is great. Thus, statutes regulating the sale of firearms, gasoline, explosives, intoxicants and poisons have been held to protect all those likely to be injured by the violation, including those injured as a result of subsequent criminal acts.

Legislative purpose is, of course, whatever the courts say it is, and their predilections vary. Thus, different courts have held that similar statutes requiring that upon leaving an auto the driver must remove the key and lock it were, and were not, intended for the protection of persons struck by a thief operating the car. In general, however, courts have taken a reasonably broad view of safety statutes. For example, a statute requiring open elevator shafts to be fenced, obviously intended primarily to prevent workmen accidentally falling into them, was held to encompass protection against a radiator placed near the opening being accidentally knocked into the opening and killing a workman below. *De Haen v. Rockwood Sprinkler Co.* (N.Y. 1932). Moreover, statutes by their terms not applicable to the case at bar may be invoked by analogy, more or less as a statutory custom, as where a statute setting safety standards for a private power company was admitted as tending to establish a standard for one municipally owned.

Licensing statutes—such as for doctors, lawyers, auto drivers, etc.—present a special problem. Most courts have held that defendant's failure to comply with a licensing statute is not admissible, since it does not tend to prove that he was negligent on the occasion in question. This is consistent with the evidentiary rule that one's reputation for a particular character trait (e.g., as a careless driver) is not admissible to prove that he was careless at the time and place in question. This has troubled some courts and dissenters, since such a rule seems to authorize violations and exposes the public to the very risk—lack of skill and competence—against which the licensing statute was intended to protect. A better rule might be to permit the violation of a licensing statute to create a presumption of negligence, which would shift to the defendant the burden of establishing that he exercised the requisite care and skill.

Where a statute is used to establish the standard of care in a negligence case, what weight should it be given and how is it to be invoked? Preliminarily, the court must determine whether the statute is applicable. If it is, most jurisdictions hold that violation of the statute is *prima facie* negligence or negligence *per se*. R. § 288B. Thus, in the absence of evidence excusing the violation, negligence is conclusively established and the jury is so instructed. However, in a considerable minority of jurisdictions the violation is merely *evidence* of negligence, which the jury may consider together with all other evidence in the case in determining the standard of care and whether it was breached. In such cases the statute is not binding on the jury even in the absence of evidence by defendant excusing the violation.

Even in those states that follow the "negligence per se" rule, most statutes have the effect of establishing negligence but no more. Plaintiff must still establish causation—for example, that the violation of a speed statute was a cause of the collision. And in most cases, contributory negligence and assumption of the risk (if otherwise available) are defenses. There are, however, statutes such as child labor laws, factory safety laws, and laws regarding the operation of school buses that are intended to protect a particular class of persons against their own inability to protect themselves, where the courts refuse to permit such defenses. And courts will sometimes apply expanded versions of the proximate cause rule, particularly where the statute creates a civil remedy for its violation.

When may a violation of the statute be excused?

A few statutes are held to impose an absolute duty of compliance, where to hold otherwise would be inconsistent with a strong legislative safety purpose. In such cases, any violation, however innocent or well-intentioned, is negligence, and to this extent the liability is strict. These include some types of statutes for the protection of workers (the Federal Safety Appliance Act, child labor laws, some factory and construction safety acts), pure food acts, building regulations, and some motor vehicle equipment and maintenance laws.

However, as to most statutes courts hold that in proper circumstances a violation may be excusable, in recognition of the fact that the civil standard of *reasonable* care will not invariably require obedience to the letter of the criminal law. In those jurisdictions where violation of a statute is merely *evidence* of negligence, any countervailing evidence that tends to excuse or justify the violation is, of course, admissible. Moreover, even in those states in which the violation is negligence *per se,* certain types of excuses are recognized. These include physical circumstances beyond the actor's control, innocent ignorance of facts that make the statute applicable, sudden emergencies not of the actor's making, and even situations where it would be more dangerous to comply with the statute than to violate it. See R. § 288A. Sometimes courts merely require the exercise of reasonable care to attempt to comply. And although there is authority to the contrary, the better rule would refuse to recognize obsolete, unenforced or clearly unreasonable legislation that remains on the books solely because of legislative inaction.

The converse issue is, may a defendant show *compliance* with a statute as proof that he exercised reasonable care? Yes, but (except for statutory torts) such proof is ordinarily not conclusive and is merely some evidence for the trier of fact to weigh, since the statute prescribes only minimum standards of conduct that may or may not have been sufficient under the circumstances. R. § 288C.

§ 4–3. Proof of Negligence

Burden of Proof and Presumptions. In order to win a negligence case, the plaintiff must produce sufficient evidence to tip the scales of probability in his favor with respect to each "element" of his cause of action—duty, negligence, causation, and damages. R. § 328A. The ordinary rules of evidence apply and these are beyond the scope of this discussion. However, a few rules of proof that regularly arise in negligence cases are worthy of special note.

Negligence law has its own set of legal presumptions. Most presumptions are merely formalized rules of circumstantial evidence. Upon proof of a certain fact or facts (A), called the "basic" facts, the law presumes the existence of fact B, the "presumed fact." In other words, fact B is established by proof of A, unless and until rebutted by other evidence. For example, the fact that a person properly addressed, stamped and mailed a letter (A) gives rise to a presumption that the letter was received by the addressee (B). Some presumptions merely codify common knowledge, for lack of better evidence, such as the presumption that the instinct for self-preservation has induced the plaintiff (normally a careful person) to exercise due care for his own safety. And some presumptions are mainly designed to shift the burden of producing evidence where the fact to be presumed is statistically probable and the true facts are within defendant's control (sometimes called "smoking out" presumptions). Examples of the latter include the presumption of a carrier's negligence when a passenger is injured by a cause within the carrier's control, the presumption that the discharge of a firearm that occurred while the firearm was in defendant's possession and control was intentional or negligent, and the presumption that a vehicle normally used in the owner's business was being driven by the owner's employee within the course and scope of his employment.

The procedural effect of a presumption in the face of contrary evidence varies, depending on the type of presumption and the rules of that jurisdiction. Consult an evidence law treatise for further elaboration of these rules.

Experts and Opinion Evidence. Expert witnesses are frequently necessary or desirable in tort litigation. Their chief functions at trial are: (1) to provide the jury with data beyond the common knowledge of jurors, such as scientific data, computations, tests, experiments, and the like; (2) to assist the jury by applying their expertise to the facts of the case and rendering opinions; and (3) in professional negligence cases, to establish the standard of care.

As a general rule of evidence, witnesses must testify only to *facts,* not opinions or conclusions, since it is the jury's task to determine the inferences to be drawn from the evidence. At one time, this rule was particularly strong against opinions on so-called "ultimate issues," such as whether defendant was negligent. However, the prohibition was never absolute; and at least as to intermediate issues, such as whether plaintiff's injuries were caused by the occurrence in question, whether defendant was intoxicated, and the like, the value of testimony in the form of an opinion outweighs any possible prejudicial effect and hence it is admissible. Recognizing that the jury is never bound by the witness's conclusions anyway, the rule today is that where the underlying facts are such that the witness is better able (by reason of her expertise or experience) to evaluate them than the jury, the witness may assist the jury by giving her opinion, even on the ultimate issue. Thus, experts have been permitted to testify that a railroad crossing was "extrahazardous," that a product was unreasonably dangerous, and even that a doctor in a malpractice case was negligent.

Res Ipsa Loquitur and Circumstantial Evidence. Like the rules of presumptions, res ipsa loquitur is basically a rule of circumstantial evidence, and the doctrine can only be understood as such. It does not shift the burden of proof or change the standard of care. It is merely a method of proving negligence by circumstantial evidence, except that the inference has been formalized into a rule of law.

Virtually any fact can be proved circumstantially, and it is probably the rare lawsuit in which one or more facts are not so proved. Speed can be inferred from skid marks; age from appearance; the point of collision from the position of the vehicles afterward. The classic illustration is that of the careless cross-examiner who asked one question too many. After eliciting from the witness testimony that he did not actually see defendant bite off plaintiff's nose, he asked: "Well, then, how do you know he did?" The witness replied, "I saw him spit it out." In that case, the fact that defendant bit off the plaintiff's nose was proved circumstantially. If other facts or conditions are used to establish the happening of some event in lieu of direct, eyewitness testimony of the event itself, then such event is being proved by circumstantial evidence.

Res ipsa loquitur ("the thing speaks for itself") is merely a special application of this rule to proof of defendant's conduct—perhaps more accurately, it sanctions circumstantial evidence that defendant must have performed some act (or omitted to perform some act) under circumstances where such conduct may be deemed negligence. See R. § 328D.

The basic requirements for invoking the doctrine are merely codifications of common sense principles of circumstantial evidence.

(1) *Control by Defendant.* It must be shown that plaintiff's injury or damage was caused by an instrumentality or condition that was under defendant's management or control at the relevant time(s). At one time, some courts applied this requirement restrictively, ruling that such control or management must have existed at the time of the injury. However, the better and logical rule requires only that the jury be able to find that the negligence, if any, occurred while the instrumentality was within defendant's control. In cases where the injury occurred after the instrumentality had left defendant's control, this requirement is usually met by evidence that tends to exclude other possible causes subsequent to defendant's possession. For example, res ipsa is often invoked in exploding bottle cases upon a showing of careful handling

between the time the bottle left the possession of defendant bottler and the time of the explosion.

This requirement ordinarily precludes use of res ipsa against multiple defendants, except in cases of vicarious liability or shared responsibility for the same instrumentality or condition such that either all or none were similarly negligent. A striking exception is *Ybarra v. Spangard* (Cal. 1944) where the plaintiff, unconscious during an appendicitis operation, sustained a traumatic injury to his shoulder, and res ipsa loquitur was applied against all of the doctors and hospital employees connected with the operation although clearly not all of them were negligent. Given the special relationship between medical personnel and patients and the notorious reluctance of the former to testify against one another, the court decided to shift the burden of explanation under such circumstances to those with sole knowledge of the true facts. Accord: *Anderson v. Somberg* (N.J. 1975) (burden of proof shifts to defendants).

(2) *Inference of Negligence.* The circumstances must be such that, in the ordinary course of events, the plaintiff's harm would not have occurred if defendant had used ordinary care while the instrumentality was within his management or control. In other words, it must be inferable that some negligence on the part of defendant was the cause of the damage. Note that other possible causes need not be excluded to a certainty; plaintiff need only show that defendant's negligence is the most probable

explanation. There are many possible reasons for the explosion of a bottle; but upon proof that it was properly and carefully handled after leaving the bottler's possession, we are left with the inference that the bottler must have been negligent somewhere in the bottling process. Note also that the inference need not be of any *particular* negligence; it is sufficient if the jury can find that of the several possible causes that might have occurred while the instrumentality was under defendant's control, the possibilities for negligence outweigh the nonnegligent possibilities. A bottler may have failed to detect a defect in one of its bottles, or it may have overcharged a sound bottle; if negligence in one process or the other is more probable than the sum of the remaining (nonnegligent) possibilities, this requirement is satisfied. For this reason, the doctrine is sometimes called "general negligence" because the jury is told that it can find for the plaintiff without determining exactly what the defendant did wrong.

If the inference of negligence depends on facts beyond the common knowledge of jurors, such facts may be supplied by testimony, and in appropriate cases (e.g., professional negligence) an expert witness may testify directly to the inference itself—for example, that plaintiff's injury would not have occurred if the doctor had not been negligent.

(3) *Plaintiff's Conduct.* At one time, the courts generally imposed a third requirement, that the event was not due to any cause for which plaintiff

was responsible. Originally, this required the absence of any "voluntary act" (or significant contribution) by the plaintiff, but this evolved into a requirement that she not have been contributorily negligent. Most jurisdictions have now dropped this third element on the theory that it is inconsistent with the modern rule that plaintiff's contributory fault is not necessarily a total bar to his recovery, but rather a damage-reducing factor. This overlooks the original purpose of this element, which was to help negate inferences that anything other than defendant's negligence was responsible for the harm. In the final analysis, however, the second element adequately covers the same ground, so the omission of the third is of little significance.

Courts sometimes say (almost always in dictum) that res ipsa applies only where evidence of the true facts of the occurrence is more accessible to the defendant than to the plaintiff. However, this is more properly a *policy justification* for the rule than a requirement, and very few courts have elevated it to the latter.

Whether a particular case is appropriate for the application of res ipsa loquitur is decided in the first instance by the court, but the credibility and weight of the inference is for the jury. In other words, once the plaintiff introduces sufficient evidence to raise a jury issue on each requirement, the court instructs the jury on res ipsa loquitur and the decision whether it has been sufficiently proved and what inferences should be drawn is for the jury, the same as in any other circumstantial evidence case. Most courts require res ipsa to be specifically pleaded in the complaint, but will permit alternative pleading and proof and will permit the case to go to the jury on both theories, proof of specific acts of negligence and res ipsa, so long as they are consistent—that is, so long as plaintiff's proof of specific negligence does not itself negate the res ipsa inferences or requirements.

Once a res ipsa case is established prima facie, what is the procedural effect? While courts occasionally have held that it creates a presumption or otherwise permits a directed verdict for plaintiff in the absence of sufficient explanatory evidence by defendant to overcome it, most courts hold that the weight and credibility of the inference are for the jury and the jury is free to decide for the defendant even in the absence of an explanation by the defendant, unless the inference is so strong that reasonable jurors could reach no other conclusion.

Suppose the defendant introduces explanatory evidence. In most cases, unless defendant's evidence destroys the inference of negligence so completely that a directed verdict for defendant is proper, both the res ipsa inference and defendant's explanation must be weighed by the jury. In other words, the res ipsa inference ordinarily survives the introduction of contrary evidence by defendant and the jury must decide which is stronger.

There is an analogous circumstantial evidence rule applied in strict product liability cases which holds that plaintiff need not prove the exact defect in the product that caused the occurrence in question, so long as the evidence tends to show that the product malfunctioned in such a way that the existence of a defect may be inferred and also tends to exclude possible causes other than a product defect.

Custom, Habit, and Character. Evidence of the usual and customary conduct or practice of others under similar circumstances is normally admissible as tending to establish the proper standard of reasonable conduct. R. § 295A. Such evidence is frequently used in cases of alleged negligence in some business activity, where the nature and operation of the business or industry are beyond the common knowledge of jurors. For example, evidence that all other manufacturers of punch presses incorporate a certain safety switch in their machines would tend to show that its absence from defendant's press was unreasonable and therefore negligent. And conversely, evidence that the defendant (or plaintiff) conformed to the usual and customary practice is some evidence that his conduct was reasonable and therefore not negligent. However, in neither case is evidence of conformity or nonconformity conclusive, since the jury is the final arbiter of whether the reasonably prudent person would have done more or less than was customary.

Evidence of a person's habit—that he consistently responds to a particular environmental stimulus in a certain way (e.g., always activates his turn signal before making a turn)—is admissible as circumstantial evidence that he did that act on the occasion in question.

On the other hand, evidence of a pertinent character trait is normally inadmissible to show that the person acted accordingly on the occasion in question. Its slight probative value is outweighed by its prejudicial effect. By the same token, evidence of prior specific acts is inadmissible to prove the person's propensity to act in that manner. However, such evidence may occasionally be admissible on a narrow issue, where relevant, such as to show notice or knowledge of a condition, custom, or some other fact in issue.

Trade Rules and Standards. Rules and standards for the conduct of an activity are frequently available. Sources include accrediting agencies, trade associations, safety organizations (e.g., the National Safety Council, Underwriters' Laboratories), federal and state agencies, and even the rules and bylaws of the defendant itself. Like evidence of custom, these are normally admissible (if sufficiently authoritative) as some evidence of the proper standard of conduct, but are not conclusive.

§ 4–4. Scope of Liability: Proximate or "Legal" Cause

"Proximate cause" is one of the more elusive concepts in tort law. As previously noted (§ 2–1), the term is loosely (and confusingly) used to encompass both (1) questions of cause in fact and (2) issues that might better be called "legal cause" or "responsible cause." More properly (and as used herein) it refers to the latter only—those more or less undefined policy considerations that limit a defendant's liability to persons and consequences that bear some reasonable relationship to the tortious act or omission. Thus, it is really a scope of liability issue.

Ironically, "proximate cause" issues have little to do with either proximity (in time or space) or causation. They are not questions of fact; they arise only after cause in fact is established. The term "proximate cause" is descriptive only in the sense that it refers to those rules that require that there be a *legal* proximity, a proximity in the sense of justice or fairness, between the cause of the harm (the tortious conduct) and its consequences. Suppose that defendant negligently drives his car so as to strike another auto, causing it to leave the roadway and knock down an electric utility pole. The wires break, and electricity is shut off to a certain area. Clearly, defendant's negligence is the cause in fact of any harm that results from the electrical failure. But rules of proximate cause will be applied to excuse defendant from liability for at least some of those consequences, simply because fundamental notions of fairness tell us that they are too far removed from the risks of negligent driving. The principal cause in fact of the Great Chicago Fire may have been Mrs. O'Leary's negligent placement of her lantern, but obviously no court would impose tort liability upon her for the full consequences of that negligence.

Thus, at bottom, proximate or legal cause is essentially a question of *duty*—was the defendant under a duty to protect this particular plaintiff against the particular event that injured him or the consequences of that event? The trouble is, courts often do not see it or articulate it as such. They will sometimes say that the defendant's conduct was not the proximate cause of plaintiff's harm when they really mean that the defendant was not negligent at all, or that the plaintiff's own negligence or assumption of the risk or misuse of the product was a superseding cause of the harm. As a leading torts scholar put it: " 'Proximate cause' . . . has been an extraordinarily changeable concept. 'Having no integrated meaning of its own, its chameleon quality permits it to be substituted for any one of the elements of a negligence case when decision on that element becomes difficult. . . . No other formula . . . so nearly does the work of Aladdin's lamp.' " (Prosser, § 42 at 276.)

Dean Leon Green logically proposed (with little success) that *all* limitations on liability other than those imposed by the cause in fact requirement be administered as a part of some issue other than cause.

Even when properly characterized as a policy question, the concept has defied attempts to articulate workable general rules or formulae to use in deciding cases. For example:

Nearest cause. It has long been recognized that proximity in time or space has little bearing; causes remote in that sense may be legally proximate because they are directly and foreseeably related to the result.

Last Human Wrongdoer. The last human wrongdoer may or may not be liable depending upon intervening causes and the scope of the risk he created; and an earlier tortfeasor may not be relieved of liability by the conduct of a later one if the former was under a duty to protect the plaintiff against the risk of the latter.

Cause vs. Condition. Some courts have sought to distinguish active "causes" from passive "conditions" upon which they operate, and hold that a defendant who merely creates the latter is not liable. Besides the fact that such a characterization is purely arbitrary in many cases, this test overlooks the fact that a failure to act when there is a duty to do so may be just as culpable as active wrongful conduct.

Substantial Factor Test. The substantial factor test is useful on the issue of cause in fact, but it has little value on the question of proximate cause, which is not factual or quantitative.

Clearly, all such "tests" are inadequate and even misleading. Proximate or legal cause cannot be reduced to absolute rules. The best statement concerning the problem is that of Street in FOUNDATIONS OF LEGAL LIABILITY 110 (1906):

It is always to be determined on the facts of each case upon mixed considerations of logic, common sense, justice, policy, and precedent.... The best use that can be made of the authorities on proximate cause is merely to furnish illustrations of situations which judicious men upon careful consideration have adjudged to be on one side of the line or the other.

Thus, it is better to view proximate or legal cause as several distinct scope of liability problems, more or less unrelated. The principal ones are (1) unforeseeable consequences, and (2) intervening causes.

(1) Unforeseen Consequences. Perhaps the most troublesome and controversial proximate cause or scope of liability problem is that of liability for the unforeseen and unforeseeable consequences of admittedly wrongful conduct. Conduct is said to be negligent (or reckless or intentional) because it involves a *foreseeable* and unreasonable risk (or certainty) that it will cause harm. Suppose that certain conduct is negligent, but the resulting harm is different in kind or degree from that which was or should have been foreseen. Defendant negligently operates his auto and thereby collides with a truck. He did not know (and had no reason to suspect) that the truck was carrying dynamite. The ensuing explosion injures the plaintiff, two blocks away. Obviously, the contemplated risk of negligent driving, to the reasonable person, would not include any injury to the plaintiff. Is defendant liable for plaintiff's harm?

There are two competing schools of thought. The prevailing view limits a defendant's liability (1) to those consequences, the foreseeability of which made defendant's conduct negligent in the first place, and (2) to persons within that foreseeable zone of danger. In other words, the test for whether a given result is proximately caused by defendant's negligence is essentially the same, so far as foreseeability limitations are concerned, as for determining whether defendant's conduct was negligent at all. This is commonly known as the *risk principle*.

The opposing view—held by fewer courts and writers—is that a consequence is proximate to a cause if it occurs as a *direct* result of the tortious act (regardless of whether it was foreseeable). The result is direct if it follows in an unbroken natural sequence from the effect of defendant's act upon conditions existing and forces already in operation at the time, without the intervention of any external forces that were not then in active operation. And direct consequences are *always* proximate.

The classic case on proximate cause is *Palsgraf v. Long Island R.R.* (N.Y. 1928). Two of defendant's employees helped a passenger board a train as it pulled away from the station. In doing so, one of them negligently dislodged a package, wrapped in newspaper, which the passenger was carrying. The package contained fireworks, which exploded when it fell. The explosion caused some scales located on the platform some distance away to tip over on Mrs. Palsgraf and injure her.

Clearly, while the defendant's employees could have foreseen some harm (e.g., to the contents of the package or to the passenger) as a result of their negligence, they had no reason to foresee any harm to Mrs. Palsgraf. Should defendant be liable to her?

A judgment for the plaintiff was reversed, 4–3. Writing for the majority, Judge Cardozo saw the problem as one of duty, not causation (although as previously noted proximate cause is basically a duty question). Negligence toward *someone* is not enough; there must be a breach of a duty (negligence) toward the *plaintiff,* and there is none unless harm to the plaintiff was *foreseeable.* Plaintiff must "sue in her own right for a wrong personal to her, and not as the vicarious beneficiary of a breach of duty to another." See R. § 281.

Judge Andrews, writing the dissent, took a broader view. The duty to exercise care is owed to all. If defendant's conduct unreasonably creates a risk of harm to others, it is negligent. And within broad limits (set by rules of proximate cause), one is liable for the consequences of that negligence, foreseeable or not. Proximate cause establishes the point beyond which the law declines to trace a series of events, and is determined by considerations of "convenience, of public policy, of a rough sense of justice." Foreseeability may enter in, but only as one factor; it is never determinative. Thus, Andrews' idea of proximate cause closely approximates the "direct causation" test noted above. And he would permit the jury to set the limits.

The *Palsgraf* case has been extensively discussed and debated. Although essentially a problem of the "unforeseeable plaintiff," it has been cited in connection with almost every conceivable proximate cause problem because it so effectively contrasts the ideas of limitations based on scope of the risk and foreseeability of harm on the one hand, and the directness of the consequences on the other.

A series of English cases illuminate the problem in terms of foreseeability of consequences. In *In re Polemis and Furness, Withy & Co.* (K.B. 1921), the negligence of the defendant's stevedores caused a wooden plank to fall into the hold of the plaintiff's ship, striking a spark that ignited petrol vapor in the hold. The ensuing fire destroyed the ship. Although the arbitrators specifically found that the spark was not foreseeable, recovery was allowed because the damage was a direct consequence of the negligence. *Polemis* was overruled in 1961 by a case commonly known as *Wagon Mound No. 1* (the ship involved), where the court refused to impose liability for the destruction by fire of plaintiff's dock caused by the ignition of an oil spill because the trier of fact found that it was not foreseeable that the oil would catch fire and burn. However, in a later action for damage to some ships caused by the same fire (*Wagon Mound No. 2*) there was evidence that defendants should have been aware of some *slight* risk of fire, and in view of the total lack of utility of defendant's conduct, it was not justified in ignoring even this slight risk and was therefore liable.

Even though liability be limited to foreseeable consequences within the risk and to foreseeable plaintiffs, there is still much room for flexibility and for the application of special rules.

(a) *Definition of "foreseeable."* Obviously, courts have ample maneuverability even within the foreseeable consequences rule, depending upon how broadly or narrowly the foreseeable event is defined and how probable it has to be. Thus, it is usually held that it is not necessary that the exact manner in which the harm occurs be foreseeable, but only that harm of the same general type as that sustained by plaintiff be foreseeable. R. § 435. For example, if one of the foreseeable risks of negligent driving is broadly defined as *injury* to pedestrians, then a negligent driver may be held liable where he strikes a utility pole and knocks it on a pedestrian, or perhaps even where he incapacitates a traffic control device and thereby contributes to a separate car-pedestrian collision. On the other hand, if the risk is narrowly defined as *colliding* with pedestrians, the latter would not be included. Further, few consequences of a negligent act are *entirely* unforeseeable, especially in retrospect. As illustrated by *Wagon Mound No. 2*, a willing court can attach liability to consequences that are mathematically rather improbable. This is sometimes facilitated by characterizing the result as "not unforeseeable" rather than marginally foreseeable.

(b) *Definition of "hazard."* Liability may be expanded or contracted depending upon how one defines the hazard or risk that makes the conduct wrongful. Thus, it is usually held that a tortious act that threatens only property damage will nevertheless support liability for personal injury, even though unforeseeable. (However, liability based on violation of a statute is generally limited to consequences against which the statute was intended to protect.) And it is often held that where some harm is foreseeable, defendant will not be excused from liability because the harm is greater in degree than was foreseeably within the risk. Some writers have sought to explain the *Polemis* case on this basis, since some damage to the ship or its cargo might have been expected from knocking the plank into the hold; therefore, defendant is in no position to complain that the damage was merely greater in amount than foreseen.

(c) *Rescuers.* It is generally held that rescuers, as a class, are always foreseeable when defendant's negligence endangers anyone, including himself. *Wagner v. International Ry.* (N.Y. 1921) (Cardozo, C.J.). This appears to be more a matter of policy than foreseeability, as even rescuers of rescuers are protected.

(d) *Physical consequences.* It is uniformly held that defendant takes the plaintiff as he finds him, and is liable for all the physical consequences of his injuries, however unusual or unforeseeable (sometimes referred to as the "thin-skulled" or "eggshell" plaintiff rule). R. §§ 435(1), 458, 461. Thus, if plaintiff has hemophilia or some other special susceptibility to harm, and dies from what would be a minor injury to almost everyone else, defendant is nevertheless liable for his death. A corollary principle is that defendant is liable for damages based on the plaintiff's actual income (where this is one element of damages) even though defendant has no reason to foresee that his income was very large.

(e) *Intentional torts; strict liability.* Courts tend to expand proximate cause limits where the tort is intentional. R. § 435A. For example, defendant shoots at A, misses him and hits plaintiff whom he had no reason to expect to be in the line of fire. Under the doctrine of transferred intent, plaintiff has a cause of action for battery. Conversely, where liability is strict, courts tend to restrict liability to foreseeable consequences and persons.

(2) Intervening Cause. Intervening cause describes the second important category of scope of liability problems. See R. §§ 440–453. In these cases, there are two (or more) causes in fact of plaintiff's harm; one is defendant's tortious conduct, and another is a subsequent act or event that *intervenes* between defendant's conduct and the injury. The intervening cause may be human conduct (tortious or not) or a natural force or event. The question is, under what circumstances does the intervening cause *supersede* defendant's tortious conduct and excuse his liability. If it does, the term "superseding cause" is applicable.

A cause is intervening, by definition, only if it comes into active operation as a cause *subsequent* in time to the tortious conduct of the defendant. If it was operating at the time of defendant's conduct, then it is a concurrent cause, and as we saw in § 2–1, will not excuse defendant's liability.

The essence of an intervening cause is that it changes the fact situation that existed when defendant acted. Therefore, if defendant is to remain liable, it must be because he ought to have *foreseen* the intervening cause and taken it into account in his conduct. Thus, the test is again one of foreseeability (seen, as always, in hindsight). Was the intervention of the later cause so significant a part of the risk involved in defendant's conduct, or so closely connected to it, that defendant's responsibility for his own conduct ought not to be terminated by it?

Obviously, defendant remains liable if the risk of the intervening cause was the very thing that made his conduct negligent. Thus, one is negligent in spilling a large quantity of gasoline because of the risk that it will be ignited, and he is not relieved of liability merely because the ignition occurs by the independent act of another. And he also remains liable if his negligence was the sufficient cause in fact of the harm, in spite of the fact that a foreseeable act or omission of another (or a natural force) intervened, altering the effect of the harm or failing to prevent it. The risk of negligently starting a fire will ordinarily include the risk of delays by others in notifying the fire department, or of foreseeable changes of wind direction or velocity.

Foreseeability of subsequent events—like foreseeability of consequences, previously discussed—is often improved by hindsight. Courts will sometimes say that an intervening cause was foreseeable because it was not unforeseeable or abnormal, even though it seems clear that no ordinary person would actually have had such an event within his contemplation. A driver who negligently strikes a pedestrian does not usually consider in advance the fact that he may be left unconscious in the roadway and run over by another car, or negligently treated by a physician, but these events are not so bizarre or improbable as to constitute superseding causes. R. §§ 457, 460.

Foreseeable events include forces of nature (such as wind, rain, lightning, freezing temperatures, etc.) so long as not abnormal, as well as human conduct. In appropriate cases, negligence and even criminal conduct by others is deemed foreseeable. Thus, one who spills gasoline must anticipate that another will negligently ignite it. And one who leaves an automobile on a city street, unlocked with the keys in the ignition, creates a foreseeable risk that it will be stolen. Rescuers—even negligent ones—are to be expected. And a defendant who negligently creates an emergency must anticipate negligent (but not foolhardy or unreasonable) defensive acts by those in peril. Even suicide has been held not to be a superseding cause of the victim's death when it results from an insanity, cause by defendant's tort, which prevents the victim from realizing the nature of his act or controlling his conduct. R. § 455.

Conversely, superseding causes are those that are unforeseeable and produce unforeseeable results.

The abnormal, the unpredictable, the highly improbable—whether forces of nature or acts of people—will relieve defendant of liability, so long as the results they produce are also unforeseeable. A defendant who negligently requires plaintiff to make a detour is not liable for his death caused by an airplane falling upon him, or by an unexpected flood, or by a robber (so long as defendant had no reason to know he was subjecting plaintiff to an increased risk of such an attack). An owner who negligently facilitates the stealing of his car is generally held not liable to a victim of the thief's negligent driving unless he should have foreseen a greater than normal risk of such harm (e.g., he leaves his auto in a neighborhood populated by derelicts and drunks).

Suppose that the *result* is foreseeably within the risk created by defendant's negligence, but is actually brought about by an unforeseeable intervening cause. For example, defendant negligently maintains its rotten telephone pole so as to create an unreasonable risk that it will fall over of its own accord and injure a pedestrian; instead, however, a negligent driver strikes the pole and knocks it upon the plaintiff. Or explosive gas is negligently permitted to accumulate in an oil barge, but it is unforeseeably ignited by lightning. In such cases, defendant is held liable, even though the intervening cause was unforeseeable, because the result was within the foreseeable risk for which defendant is responsible.

There are two exceptions, if they may be called that, to the foregoing rule. First, if the intervening cause is the intentional or criminal conduct of a third person, defendant is excused, provided the risk of that conduct is not what made the defendant's act tortious in the first place. Thus, if in the preceding examples someone intentionally ignited the gas, or intentionally pushed the pole over on the plaintiff, considerations of justice may require that the third person and not the defendant be held responsible. Second is the situation where a third person discovers the danger that defendant has created, under circumstances where the third person has some duty to act. There are two groups of such cases. Defendant permits some dangerous chattel (e.g., dynamite caps) to get into the hands of a child. The parent discovers the danger, takes the chattel away from the child, but fails to prevent him from obtaining possession of it again and the child is then injured. Similarly, a third person discovers the danger that defendant has created, and *deliberately* ignores it and thereby exposes others to its risks. For example, a retailer discovers that certain bottles of defendant's product marked "kerosene" actually contain dangerous amounts of gasoline, but he continues to sell them without any warning. In all of these cases, the intervening cause is deemed sufficiently strong and independent to shift liability from defendant to the intervening third person, and defendant is exonerated.

In the second situation, however, it can be argued that both the first and second actors should be liable, rather than the first actor excused. Courts developed the old rules before the advent of comparative fault and contribution, and it would seem preferable to apply these doctrines rather than to exonerate an actor whose tortious conduct plainly contributed to the plaintiff's harm.

§ 4–5. The Concept of Duty

The duty concept is not limited to negligence law. In fact, all rules of law that define the boundaries of one's legal liability to another may be phrased in terms of some duty, whatever the conduct or activity. One has a duty not to utter defamatory falsehoods; to refrain from unexcused breaches of valid contracts; to support one's minor children. The difference is that in areas other than negligence law the liability rules are sufficiently specific that there is ordinarily no occasion to create rules that further limit the scope of these already narrowly defined duties. This is not to say that there are not exceptions and limitations to such liability rules, but merely that courts do not find it necessary to use a "duty" analysis.

In contrast, negligence is a broad and pervasive principle of liability. The general rule is that one is under a duty to all persons at all times to exercise reasonable care for their physical safety (and that of their property). At the same time, justice and policy considerations require that particular classes of persons and particular activities be subject to greater or lesser standards of liability. For example, in most jurisdictions a product manufacturer is strictly liable for the physical harm caused by certain product defects, even though the manufacturer was not negligent. On the other hand, there is no general liability for negligent conduct that causes only mental suffering, or that causes harm to a trespasser. Those rules that create exceptions to the general principle of negligence liability by narrowing its scope can best be analyzed as duty limitations.

It is sometimes stated that in order for negligence to be actionable, it must constitute a violation of some *legally recognized duty* to another. This is true, but it misplaces the emphasis. It is preferable to view duty in negligence law in terms of a broad *general duty* of reasonable care with *exceptions,* rather than as a series of specific duties that vary according to the facts of the case.

Confusion often results from the loose use of the term "duty" as a substitute for a proper analysis of some other element of the negligence equation. For example, court may hold that a bottler has a "duty" to inspect its bottles for defects; strictly speaking, its failure to do so is merely a specific illustration of negligent conduct.

The scope of one's legal duty is a *question of law* to be decided by the *court* and never by the jury. Thus, perhaps it is only natural for courts to speak in terms of duty when they are promulgating fixed rules of conduct as rules of negligence, causation, or contributory negligence of general application. In fact, if the court really intends to establish a fixed rule of liability or nonliability with respect to certain specific conduct, it probably does no harm to characterize these rules as duties. But there is danger in using the term when no such arbitrary rule is intended, for judicial approval of the finding of a jury may thereby become transformed unwittingly into a static rule of general application in future cases. While some legal scholars (e.g., Dean Leon Green and Justice Holmes) have favored the proliferation of such specific standards of conduct and the consequent narrowing of the role of the jury, experience has shown that many such arbitrary rules are too rigid and inflexible. See § 4–2, supra. Thus, they must be developed cautiously and deliberately, and clarity is facilitated if the term "duty" is used only with respect to general liability limitations imposed by law.

Numerous duty-limiting rules are sprinkled throughout the negligence cases; some are statutory. Some are broad and general, others quite narrow and specific. Each jurisdiction has a few peculiar to itself. The principal common ones include the following.

Relationship Between Plaintiff and Defendant. The principal development of negligence as a separate tort cause of action occurred during the nineteenth century when the fault ethic was particularly strong and liability rules tended to favor defendants. This may explain the fact that early in this development both English and U.S. courts developed the rule that no action could be founded on the breach of a legal duty owed to some person other than the plaintiff. In other words, there must be some *relationship* between defendant and his victim sufficient for the court to find that defendant's duty to exercise reasonable care ought to run in favor of that particular person. "Negligence in the air, so to speak, will not do." The catch is that there is no standard except the judge's conscience for determining when the relationship is sufficient to raise a duty. The basic question remains a philosophical one: whether plaintiff's interests are entitled to protection against defendant's conduct. It would be hard to conceive of a case where the court could not find such a relationship if it chose to do so. In cases where the connection between defendant's negligence and plaintiff's harm is tenuous, the scope-of-liability ("proximate cause") rules previously discussed (see § 4–4) are adequate protection.

In fact, recall that in the *Palsgraf* case discussed in § 4–4, Judge Cardozo saw the issue as whether the negligence of defendant's employees was a breach of a duty to Mrs. Palsgraf, and concluded that it was not; Andrews on the other hand saw the issue as one of proximate cause. Proximate cause rules themselves may be seen as duty limitations; one may well ask why two separate sets of liability limiting rules are necessary. Perhaps it is because some courts confuse legal cause and cause in fact and send questions of proximate cause to the jury. Nevertheless, both sets exist, and on similar facts some courts will analyze the issues in terms of duty while others will use proximate cause. The desired result can be reached with either concept.

Nature and Scope of the Risk. Suppose defendant's conduct threatens harm to a particular interest or of a particular kind, but results in harm to a different interest or of a different kind. For example, an act may be negligent only because it threatens property damage, but it results in some unforeseen personal injury (e.g., *Palsgraf*). Or it may be negligent to entrust a child with a pistol because of the danger of accidental discharge, but instead he drops it on the plaintiff's foot—a risk as to which (let us assume) the entrustment was not unreasonable. In such cases, many courts will say that there was no duty to protect plaintiff against the harm that actually resulted, or to protect the interest that was actually invaded. As we have seen, other courts will reach the same result by applying principles of proximate cause. Again, either way, the result is the same.

Of course, not all courts would deny liability in these situations. As we saw in our discussion of proximate cause, the nature and scope of the risk may be broadly defined so as to encompass the harm that occurred. Duty is no less elastic than proximate cause.

Interest Invaded. Certain types of interests for various reasons have been afforded relatively little protection against negligent invasion. Interests of a solely pecuniary nature such as the right to have a contract performed, the expectation of financial advantage, damage caused by negligent misrepresentation, and other kinds of pecuniary harm present special problems that are discussed elsewhere.

There are interests that traditionally have been given less than full protection even though the harm is physical, although the scope of these limitations appears to be narrowing. For example, prior to the mid-twentieth century, recovery was denied for injuries to an unborn child. Some courts said that a fetus was not a "person" to whom a duty of care was owed, but the more likely reason was that courts were skeptical of the medical proof of cause and effect. This duty limitation no longer exists, provided the child is born alive, and the child may recover for his personal injuries or his survivors for his subsequent death. The courts are still split, however, on whether a wrongful death action may be maintained if the child is killed while still in the womb, but the trend has been in favor of permitting suit. See § 8–20, infra.

U.S. courts have also been slow to allow recovery for illnesses resulting entirely from negligently-caused psychic trauma. This subject is discussed in § 8–19, infra.

Misfeasance vs. Nonfeasance. The law of negligence, from its inception, has distinguished between liability for the consequences of affirmative acts—"misfeasance"—and liability for merely doing nothing—"nonfeasance." The early law of wrongs was concerned only with the more important forms of misconduct, and was less concerned with punishing inaction. Courts have hesitated to force people to act affirmatively to prevent physical harm to others, however strong the *moral* duty may be. Affirmative negligent acts create a new risk of harm, but nonfeasance at least does not make matters worse and perhaps merely fails to benefit another by interfering in his affairs.

The problem is that almost any inaction can be characterized as "misfeasance" if the court is so disposed, and often inaction is substantially the equivalent of active misconduct. The failure to blow a horn may be seen as active negligence in the operation of a train or auto. A failure to repair may be deemed active mismanagement on the part of one responsible for that which is broken. Thus, as in other duty issues, the fundamental question is whether there is a sufficient relationship between the one who failed to act and the one injured thereby that the court deems it just to impose liability. In an oft-quoted case, Judge Cardozo characterized the problem as whether the defendant has gone so far in what he has actually done, and has got himself into such a relation with the plaintiff, that he has begun to affect the interests of the plaintiff adversely, as distinguished from merely failing to confer a benefit upon him. *H. R. Moch Co. v. Rensselaer Water Co.* (N.Y. 1928).

A common example of this limitation is the absence of a duty to go to the aid of one in peril, in the absence of some pre-existing status or relationship that would require it. R. § 314. Thus, an expert

swimmer with a boat and rope at hand is not
required—so far as U.S. tort law is concerned—to
attempt to rescue one who is drowning, unless the
swimmer happens to be a life guard hired for that
purpose. A physician who by chance happens upon
the scene of an accident is under no duty to render
emergency medical care, unless the victim also happens to be the doctor's patient. This rule has troubled many courts and writers, at least in cases
where aid could be offered or a rescue attempted
with little or no risk to the actor, especially since
such a duty is imposed by legal systems of other
countries. Thus, U.S. courts will tend to find that
this duty exists if there is any sort of preexisting
relationship between the parties such that the victim might reasonably expect aid, such as carrier-
passenger, innkeeper-guest, employer-employee,
jailer-prisoner, school-pupil, parent-child, husband-
wife, and even store-customer and host-guest. R.
§§ 314A, 314B. The requisite relationship is found
where defendant's conduct is responsible for plaintiff's peril, whether or not defendant's conduct was
negligent. R. § 322.

Moreover, duties of affirmative action that would
not otherwise exist may be voluntarily assumed. It
is commonly held that one who gratuitously undertakes to render aid to another assumes a duty to act
with reasonable care, a duty that, once assumed,
may not be abandoned at will. R. § 324. While
consistent with the principles of negligence law, this
rule is said to have the negative effect of stifling
charitable impulses and deterring would-be res-

cuers, and has resulted in the enactment of "Good Samaritan" acts in many states that relieve physicians (and certain others) who render emergency medical aid from all liability for negligence.

While early cases held that there was no tort liability for failure to perform a gratuitous promise, more recent cases have permitted recovery where there was reasonable detrimental reliance. And once defendant has commenced performance, it is clear that he has assumed a duty to perform with reasonable care. R. §§ 323, 324A.

The principle of voluntary duty assumption has been broadly applied, and is by no means confined to rescue situations. It has been extended to landlords who make repairs on leased premises, railroads that provide extra protection at crossings, and even to workers' compensation liability insurers who undertake safety inspections of the insured's premises. Liability is usually justifiable on the ground that defendant has increased the danger, or misled the plaintiff into a false sense of security, or deprived plaintiff of the possibility of help from other sources. However, liability need not depend upon the existence of these factors; the better approach is simply to impose liability on the basis of the general duty of reasonable care.

Relationships of the kind referred to above (carrier-passenger, innkeeper-guest, employer-employee, etc.) may give rise to other duties of affirmative action, such as to protect the subordinate or dependent party against harm that may be foreseeably caused by third persons (other passengers, guests, employees, etc., or others outside the relationship) or to protect those outside the relationship from harm caused by those under defendant's control (e.g., the parent's duty to control his child, the duty of the owner-passenger of an auto to exercise control over the driver). See R. §§ 315–320.

Special Duty Rules. Tort law has created special duty rules for certain kinds of defendants or activities. These include owners and occupiers of land, manufacturers and suppliers of products, automobile owners and operators, and others. The trend is toward abolishing these special duty rules, insofar as they arbitrarily restrict the duty of ordinary care. These rules will be discussed in Chapter 8.

In addition, there are certain status immunities, such as sovereign immunity and intra-family immunities. Strictly speaking, these are not duty limitations but limitations on the availability of a remedy. However, as a practical matter, they have the same effect. These will be discussed in Chapter 11.

§ 4–6. Degrees of Negligence

Regrettably, negligence law has been the victim of attempts to refine the negligence concept by subdividing negligent conduct into narrower categories. There are two closely-related but distinguishable approaches—degrees of care, and degrees of negligence.

High Degrees of Care. Common carriers (operators of airplanes, ships, buses, railroads, taxicabs, and even elevators, escalators, and amusement devices) are said to owe their passengers "the highest degree of care consistent with the mode of conveyance used and the practical operation of its business." Similarly, those responsible for certain dangerous instrumentalities (e.g., explosives, high-voltage electricity) must, say the courts, exercise a "high degree of care," commensurate with the danger, to protect others from harm.

While these and other similar statements might be interpreted as creating a higher duty of care, in most cases this is not what is intended. Negligence is the failure to exercise reasonable care. The amount of care—that is, the conduct—that is *reasonable* for a given situation depends on various factors, including the relationship between the parties and the nature and extent of the risk inherent in that situation. Brain surgery requires greater care in the wielding of the knife than does carving a turkey. Transporting dynamite or paying passengers on a public conveyance requires different conduct than does hauling potatoes. But even though a high risk or a heavy responsibility may be involved, there is no logical reason to depart from the usual standard of *reasonable care under the circumstances,* and there is no such departure so long as the jury is instructed in the usual way.

However, most jurisdictions have authorized jury instructions phrased in terms of the "highest degree of care" standard in suits by passengers against common carriers, and occasionally "high degree of care" instructions are permitted in other cases. Such instructions are theoretically objectionable as giving undue weight to the obligations of these defendants, since the law only requires, for example, a carrier to behave as would a reasonably prudent carrier under the same or similar circumstances. Instructions like these may well result in a heavier burden of liability by encouraging the jury to find liability for conduct that would not otherwise constitute a breach of the duty of reasonable care.

Degrees of Negligence. The idea that negligence may be classified as slight, ordinary, or gross apparently found its way into the English law of bailments from the Roman law, and thence into our law, where it has persisted. For an injury to the goods bailed, a bailment for the benefit of the bailee (such as in the case of a bailee for hire) results in liability for slight negligence. A bailment for the mutual benefit of both parties requires ordinary care. And a gratuitous bailment for the benefit of the bailor makes the bailee liable only for gross negligence.

Except for bailments, however, U.S. courts have almost entirely rejected as unworkable the notion of degrees of negligence. For a time during the nineteenth century, Illinois and Kansas tried a form of judicially-created comparative negligence in which these concepts were used, but the system had to be abandoned when the decisions as to which was which became hopelessly confused. Legal writers have almost uniformly condemned the idea of degrees of negligence.

Apparently, however, the state legislatures did not get the word, and there are statutes in many jurisdictions in which the term "negligence" is preceded by some adjective such as "gross" or "willful." In most cases, the statute applies only to a particular situation, activity, or type of defendant; but the general comparative negligence statute of South Dakota uses "slight negligence," and until 1992 Nebraska used "slight" and "gross" negligence.

"Slight" negligence is the failure to exercise *great* care; it is *not* a slight departure from ordinary care (except in the comparative negligence context).

Some jurisdictions, rather than (or in addition to) making common carriers liable for failure to exercise the "highest degree of care," hold them liable for slight negligence. Is there a distinction? Technically, yes; practically, no. Technically, slight negligence is the failure to exercise *greater* care than the circumstances would ordinarily demand; whereas the "highest degree of care" is itself, by definition, the standard that the circumstances require, and therefore one who does not conform to that standard is, strictly speaking, guilty of ordinary (not slight) negligence. However, as a practical matter, while the form of the instructions to the jury may be different depending upon which approach is used, the net effect is the same in either case, since the ultimate question is whether defendant failed to exercise a high degree of care.

"Gross" negligence is an even more troublesome concept. Any definition, such as "the failure to exercise even slight care," is virtually indistinguishable from willful and wanton misconduct (see § 4–7, infra). Some courts have therefore treated these concepts as identical, but most have struggled to preserve some distinction between them. The best that can be done is to say that gross negligence is something more than ordinary negligence but only in degree; and it is something less than recklessness, which is conduct evincing a conscious disregard of the safety of others. The distinction is important, since contributory negligence sometimes does not reduce or negate liability for willful and wanton misconduct, and a finding of willful and wanton misconduct will usually support an award of punitive damages whereas gross negligence will not.

§ 4–7. Willful and Wanton Misconduct

Lying on the fault continuum between mere negligence and the intent required for liability for one of the intentional torts (see § 6–1) is a gray area known by various names, such as "willful and wanton" or "reckless" conduct. "Willful and wanton" is the term most commonly used by the courts and lawyers in practice; the Restatement uses the term "reckless." See R. §§ 500–503. The term "willful" in this context can be misleading, since no intent to cause injury is required, and the cases do evidence some confusion of terminology. Bear in mind that "willful and wanton" cannot be taken literally; it is an idiom for that conduct that can best be described as characterized by a reckless disregard of the safety of others.

Definitions of reckless or willful and wanton conduct vary among the jurisdictions, and sometimes within the same jurisdiction depending upon the type of case. The most common general definition is unreasonable conduct committed under circumstances in which the actor knew or had reason to know (that is, had knowledge of facts from which he ought to have been aware) that (1) his conduct created an unreasonable risk of physical harm, and (2) that risk was relatively high, either in degree or in the probability that harm would occur. Compare R. § 500. It is sometimes said that it is conduct that evidences a conscious disregard or indifference to the safety of others. The actor is aware of the danger but he is indifferent to it, or he recklessly disregards the fact that his conduct has created a substantial risk of harm.

Thus, such conduct differs from negligence in degree as well as in kind. It differs in degree in the sense that the risk of harm is greater; and it differs in kind because of the different mental state of the actor. He is (or is presumed to be) *conscious* of the risk, and yet chooses to proceed (or to fail to act) in spite of his awareness. In contrast, mere negligence ordinarily consists of inadvertence, inattention, thoughtlessness, or incompetence; there is no awareness of an imminent and considerable danger. Recklessness also differs from intentional tortious conduct (see § 6–1), in that the latter requires an awareness that the injury is certain or substantially certain to occur so that we may infer that the actor intended to bring about that result. In contrast, the reckless actor did not intend to injure anyone, but he knew or had reason to know that the *risk* of harm was quite substantial.

Reckless conduct is a hybrid, with attributes of both negligence and the intentional torts. It will often support a claim for punitive damages (see § 9–3). Traditionally, contributory negligence was not a defense to reckless conduct (contributory reckless conduct was). Almost all jurisdictions have adopted comparative negligence, and some now hold that plaintiff's contributory negligence will reduce his recovery even against defendant's reckless conduct. See § 5–4.

As in the case of negligence, an action based upon willful and wanton misconduct requires that plaintiff establish that defendant owed him a duty of care, and the same duty limitations apply. See § 4–5 and Chapter 8. Proximate cause rules, in a form slightly more favorable to the plaintiff than in negligence cases, are applicable (see § 4–4). And actual damages must be shown.

In certain situations, a finding that defendant's conduct was reckless is a prerequisite to liability. For example, the general rule (subject to various exceptions) is that a possessor of land is liable to a trespasser injured on the premises only for willful and wanton misconduct. And there are numerous statutes that exempt certain defendants from liability for ordinary negligence, thereby requiring at least recklessness—e.g., certain governmental immunity acts and "Good Samaritan" laws.

To avoid the arbitrary and sometimes harsh results that often flowed from a strict application of automobile guest statutes, premises liability rules, and the doctrine of contributory negligence, some courts bent and stretched their definitions of willful and wanton misconduct to the point that they were very close to ordinary negligence. For example, in Illinois willful and wanton misconduct used to be defined as the failure to exercise ordinary care after actual or constructive knowledge of an existing danger. Such liberal definitions probably did little harm in most cases, except that in jurisdictions that allow punitive damages in any case of reckless conduct, they may have had the effect of authorizing punitive damages for conduct that amounted to little more than mere negligence. Now that the harsh effects of the contributory negligence rule have been greatly ameliorated and the guest statutes have been abolished, the courts are evolving a stricter definition of reckless conduct.

CHAPTER 5

DEFENSES TO NEGLIGENCE LIABILITY

§ 5–1. Contributory Negligence

Until the late twentieth century, the general common law rule in the United States was that a negligent tortfeasor was entirely excused from liability to a plaintiff whose failure to exercise reasonable care for his own safety was a contributing cause of plaintiff's injury. R. § 467.

The justifications advanced for this rule do not withstand close scrutiny, at least by modern standards. For example, it has been suggested that plaintiff is being punished for his own wrongdoing; but why should he bear the entire punishment when defendant was also at fault? Some argued that courts will not aid those who do not come with clean hands. This is perhaps a variation of the old rule that courts will not apportion damages among joint tortfeasors. The weakness of this argument is that in other contexts, courts often grant relief to plaintiffs who were to some extent at fault; moreover, in most cases the refusal to apportion was simply arbitrary and unjust.

It has also been suggested that the rule deters negligent conduct. But common sense teaches that few will exercise greater care for their own safety than that which is motivated by the fear of personal injury; no additional incentive is added by the contemplation of the uncertain outcome of some future lawsuit. And since the negligence of many defendants (corporations, manufacturers, landowners, etc.) creates no corresponding risk of personal injury to them, any rule (such as contributory negligence as a total bar) which reduces a defendant's liability exposure operates to reduce the sum total of the incentives toward safety which negligence law creates.

One of the most common justifications for the "all-or-nothing" rule of contributory negligence was that plaintiff's own negligence had become the direct, immediate and superseding cause of his own injury. The case traditionally cited as originating the rule, *Butterfield v. Forrester* (K.B. 1809), appears to be based on this idea, which perhaps reflects the early common law notion that there is but a single proximate cause of every injury. This often led to a search for the "last human wrongdoer" on whom the blame was fixed. In some (but not all) cases, this was the plaintiff, where his negligence occurred after that of the defendant. Of course, this "single cause" notion is simply not true. We now recognize that the negligence of several persons may combine to produce a single indivisible injury for which all are jointly and severally liable.

In light of the rule's shaky foundations, it is not surprising that it was often ignored. It was well known that juries frequently violated the court's instructions and awarded the plaintiff some damages despite his contributory negligence, although less than he would have received if he were free from fault. In other words, juries commonly fashioned and applied their own rule of comparative negligence.

The weakness of the rationale for the "total bar" rule led the courts and legislatures to find ways around it—for example, the doctrine of "last clear chance" and the rule that the bar could not be invoked by a defendant whose conduct was "willful and wanton." But until late in the twentieth century, most U.S. courts persistently refused to abandon the rule. Perhaps this was because comparative negligence is complex to implement and administer, and the "all or nothing" rule was so firmly established. However, as we shall see (§ 5–2, infra), the pressure to abandon the old rule finally became irresistible, and comparative fault is now the norm in all but a few states.

Note, however, that except for changing from a total bar to a damage-reducing factor, virtually all of the characteristics of contributory negligence are the same today as before. In other words, the *concept* of contributory negligence survives; only its effect on plaintiff's recovery has changed. Moreover, in most jurisdictions plaintiff's contributory negligence can still be a total bar to his recovery if his share of the fault is sufficiently large. Therefore, the characteristics of contributory negligence continue to be important.

Contributory negligence is an affirmative defense that must be pleaded and proved by the defendant. R. § 477.

In general, the same standards apply for determining whether conduct is contributorily negligent as are used to determine whether conduct is negligent. R. §§ 463, 464, 466, 470. Plaintiff must act as a reasonably prudent person. However, the results of applying this standard are not necessarily the same for plaintiffs as for defendants. Reasonable care for one's *own* safety is not always the same as reasonable care for the safety of others. Generally speaking, courts and juries have tended to be more lenient with plaintiffs, so that the same conduct that would have made a defendant negligent may be found to be reasonable (or less culpable) as to a plaintiff. And courts more often have found that questions of contributory negligence are for the jury. The Restatement (Third) of Torts: Apportionment of Liability § 3, abolishes all special ameliorative doctrines for defining the plaintiff's contributory negligence.

As to causation, the same "substantial factor" test applies as in the case of defendant's negligence. R. § 465. In addition, the defense is usually strictly limited to the risk that made the conduct negligent. R. § 468. For example, a plaintiff who is negligent for standing on an unsafe platform is not contributorily negligent with respect to injuries sustained when an adjacent wall collapses upon her.

The defense is often not available when plaintiff's action is based on some other theory of liability. For example, it is not a defense to an intentional tort. Nor, if contributory negligence operates as a total bar, does it bar a cause of action based on willful and wanton misconduct. R. §§ 481, 482. And it is not a defense to liability for breach of warranty, strict liability for abnormally dangerous activities, or, in some jurisdictions, strict product liability. As a defense to strict liability, a few jurisdictions have used a form of contributory negligence which consists of plaintiff's voluntary exposure to a known danger, but this is more often classified as assumption of risk.

Nor is contributory negligence a defense to the tort liability created by certain types of statutes which are intended to protect certain classes of persons from dangers against which they are incapable of protecting themselves—for example, child labor laws, statutes prohibiting the sale of certain articles to minors, and certain factory acts and other statutes for the protection of workmen. R. § 483.

At one time, a doctrine called "last clear chance" negated the bar of contributory negligence under certain circumstances in which the negligence of the defendant was subsequent in time to that of the plaintiff, and the defendant had the last opportunity to avoid the accident by the exercise of ordinary care. See R. §§ 479, 480. Where comparative fault is the rule, the doctrine is no longer necessary, and it has been abandoned in almost all jurisdictions. It is still available, however, in those few jurisdictions that have not adopted comparative fault.

§ 5–2. Comparative Negligence

From the middle of the twentieth century on, dissatisfaction with the "all or nothing" contributory negligence rule greatly increased. As late as 1968, only seven states (and Puerto Rico) had comparative negligence rules of general application. But during the last third of the century, a strong trend, following the lead of the other common law nations, resulted in almost all states embracing the civil law and maritime doctrine of comparative negligence.

At first, courts were reluctant to adopt comparative fault by judicial decision. Contributory negligence as a total bar was a time-honored fixture in tort law, and courts were hesitant to make such a drastic change, preferring to defer to the legislative branch. Nevertheless, judicial dissatisfaction became increasingly apparent in decisions, and many courts openly warned that they would reconsider the rule if the legislature failed to do so. Finally, judicial impatience resulted in a wave of court decisions adopting the "pure" form of comparative negligence. In some cases, these decisions were followed by legislation codifying the doctrine, often in a somewhat different form. As of this writing, all but five U.S. jurisdictions (Alabama, Maryland, North

Carolina, Virginia, and D.C.) have some form of comparative fault.

Under comparative fault, plaintiff's negligence is not a complete bar to his recovery. Instead, his damages are calculated and then reduced by the proportion which his fault bears to the total causative fault of his harm. For example, assume the trier of fact decides that defendant's negligence contributed 75% and plaintiff's negligence 25% to plaintiff's injury, and that plaintiff sustained $10,000 damages. Plaintiff will be awarded a judgment for $7,500.

There are two basic versions. About a dozen jurisdictions have adopted the "pure" form in which plaintiff may recover no matter how great his fault in comparison to that of defendant. Thus, if plaintiff is 80% at fault and defendant 20%, plaintiff still recovers 20% of his damages. However, most comparative negligence jurisdictions have adopted the "modified" form, of which there are two versions—"49%" and "50%"—under which plaintiff recovers nothing if his negligence was "as great as" (50%) or "greater than" (51%) that of defendant. The modified form of comparative fault, representing a partial retention of contributory negligence, is not logically defensible, but probably reflects a compromise view that a plaintiff who is equally or largely responsible for his own injury is unworthy of compensation. (South Dakota has a different standard, allowing recovery when plaintiff's negligence is "slight.") The Restatement (Third) of Torts: Apportionment of Liability § 7 advocates the pure form of comparative fault.

The shift to comparative fault has created a number of problems of adjustment. In most cases, the solutions depend in part on the wording of the particular statute, and thus vary from state to state. Some of the principal problems include:

Multiple Parties. Suppose plaintiff's harm is caused in part by several joint tortfeasors, all of whom may or may not have been sued. In most jurisdictions, plaintiff's fault is compared to that of all tortfeasors collectively, including those who are not defendants. However, there is a minority view that plaintiff's fault is compared only to that of those who are parties to the lawsuit; this rule unfairly distorts the calculation of plaintiff's share.

A minority of states continue to recognize the doctrine of joint and several liability in its original form. But in most states, the advent of comparative fault—which means that a negligent plaintiff can still recover damages—has been seen as a policy change sufficient to justify a different rule. Some states have adopted a rule of "several" liability, so that each defendant is liable to the plaintiff only to the extent of that defendant's proportional share of the fault. Most states have a hybrid system, having aspects of both joint and several liability and several liability.

Counterclaims. If one or more defendants are also injured, they can counterclaim against the plaintiff and each other. Such counterclaims are each treated as separate lawsuits. Note, however, that if more than one claimant is successful, the better rule is that the damages are *not* offset.

Assumption of Risk. Is it still a complete bar to plaintiff's recovery? Only if and to the extent that it is not merely another form of contributory negligence. See § 5–4, infra.

Willful and Wanton Misconduct. Even if defendant's conduct may be characterized as willful and wanton misconduct, which would defeat the defense of contributory negligence (§ 4–7), in some jurisdictions comparative negligence is nevertheless applicable to reduce plaintiff's damages.

Punitive Damages. Where defendant's reckless misconduct is sufficient to justify punitive damages, such damages are not reduced under the comparative negligence rule.

Strict Liability. Where defendant is held strictly liable (see Chapter 3, supra, and § 8–9, infra), does the comparative negligence rule or statute apply? Much will depend on the statutory language, but it would seem that it should unless some statute requires otherwise.

Violation of Safety Statute. Where defendant's liability is based upon the violation of certain statutes intended to protect persons more or less unable to protect themselves against certain risks, some courts have held contributory negligence no defense. Does this rule apply to prohibit reduction of plaintiff's damages under comparative negligence? The prevailing view is that it does not, unless the statute requires otherwise.

Role of Court and Jury. The trier of fact allocates the parties' fault in percentages, and assesses plaintiff's total damages. Who then does the arithmetic and determines whether and how much plaintiff will recover? The statutory provisions, if any, control, and they vary. Where the question is open, it would seem preferable (and would reduce confusion and error) to use a special verdict procedure, asking the jury to decide only the fault percentages and total damages and permitting the court to make the computations.

§ 5–3. Imputed Contributory Negligence

Tort law includes the principle of vicarious liability, by which *A* is held liable for the wrongful act of *B* solely because of the existence of some prior relationship between *A* and *B*. The most common examples of such relationships are employer-employee, partnership, joint venture or enterprise, and in some instances employer-independent contractor. Thus, if the requisite relationship exists, a third person *(C)* may sue *A* for injuries caused by the wrongful conduct of *B*, even though *A* was innocent of personal fault so far as *C's* injuries are concerned. See §§ 8–16–8–18, infra. This vicarious liability may be thought of as a form of imputed negligence.

Given this principle, the question naturally arises, should imputed negligence work both ways, that is, when *A* is suing as well as when he is defending? In other words, if both *B* and *C* were concurrently negligent, resulting in injury to *A* or his property, should *B*'s negligence be imputed to *A* so as to reduce or bar his recovery from *C* under the contributory negligence rule?

The answer ought to be no. The policy considerations that justify vicarious liability simply do not apply in reverse. Nevertheless, despite this and the general hostility to contributory negligence, where the relationship is one of those which will support vicarious liability (such as employer-employee and joint venture or enterprise) most courts have applied a rule of imputed contributory negligence to bar plaintiff's recovery from a third person where plaintiff's agent was also negligent. This is still the majority view, and that of the Restatement. R. § 486; Restatement (Third) of Torts: Apportionment of Liability § 5.

Incredibly, at one time some courts went further and imputed contributory negligence on the basis of other relationships that do not even support vicarious liability. Thus, the negligence of the driver of a vehicle was imputed to his injured passenger, apparently on the theory that the passenger should have had better sense than to ride with one who might be negligent. The negligence of one spouse was imputed to the other. The negligence of a parent was imputed to the child, despite the fact that the child was innocent and incapable of negligence, thereby burdening the child with the parent's sins. The negligence of a bailee of a chattel was imputed to the bailor to bar the bailor's recovery from a third person for damage to the property. Happily, these decisions are now almost entirely overruled or obsolete. R. §§ 487, 488, 490, 494A.

A special case is created by the financial responsibility statutes enacted in about a dozen states (§ 8–16, infra) that make the owner of a motor vehicle liable for the negligence of its driver. A few courts have held that these statutes apply both ways and bar the owner's recovery from a negligent third person where the driver was also negligent. However, the better view refuses to interpret these statutes to impute contributory negligence, as they obviously were not intended to do so. *Mills v. Gabriel* (N.Y. 1940).

Imputed contributory negligence, if applicable at all, does not apply to suits between those within the relationship (e.g. by an employer against his employee), except that a member of a joint enterprise cannot recover from another *non-negligent* member (on a vicarious liability theory) for injuries caused by the negligence of a third member of the enterprise. R. § 491.

All of the foregoing assumes that plaintiff was not himself guilty of any *personal* contributory negligence. There are a number of cases in which the courts seem to talk in terms of imputed or vicarious contributory negligence, but in fact the negligence was that of the plaintiff himself, such as in failing to exercise care in the selection or control of his agent.

§ 5–4. Assumption of Risk

Assumption of risk is another of those elusive concepts that has meant different things to different judges and legal writers. Much of the confusion arises from attempts to relate it to the duty concept. Thus, it is said that plaintiff's assumption of the risk of defendant's negligence operates to relieve defendant of his duty to exercise care for plaintiff's safety. Conversely, others maintain that the term really describes those areas where there is no duty in the first place, and that therefore plaintiff is required by law to accept those risks when he chooses to encounter them.

Such analyses, while perhaps technically accurate under some definitions of "duty," are of doubtful value and can be quite misleading. For almost all purposes, it is preferable to keep the two concepts separate. All persons are under a duty to exercise reasonable care for the safety of others, except as limited by the law's specific duty limitations (§ 4–5) and scope of liability rules (§ 4–4). Assumption of risk, when available, is an affirmative defense, to be pleaded and proved by defendant, which will operate to defeat or reduce defendant's tort liability despite the fact that she owed plaintiff a duty of care and that she was negligent. Duty is a question of law for the court; assumption of risk is a question of fact for the jury. Analyses which commingle the two concepts—and there are many examples in the law books—can only lead to error.

Another fertile source of confusion is the failure to distinguish and eliminate from consideration those cases where defendant was not negligent at all. Absent negligence, we do not even reach the question of assumption of risk. Yet there are cases (and writers) that talk in terms of assumption of the risk of dangers that were not created by negligence in the first place. Bear in mind throughout this discussion that we are here concerned only with risks that were created by some negligent conduct on the part of the defendant.

Finally, much confusion is generated by the fact that implied assumption of risk overlaps contributory negligence. In fact, some say that assumption of risk is simply a form of contributory fault and therefore should be abolished as a separate concept.

Theoretically, assumption of risk is plaintiff's voluntary *consent* to encounter a known danger created by defendant's negligence. Contributory negligence is *unreasonable conduct*. Thus, the distinction is between *consent* and *conduct*. The same facts may give rise to one or both defenses. For example, assume that defendant offers plaintiff a seat in defendant's chair, which has a defective leg. Plaintiff accepts, the chair collapses and plaintiff is injured. If plaintiff knew that the leg was broken, he may be said to have assumed the risk of that defect. In addition, his conduct may also have been negligent because the reasonably prudent person would not have used the chair. But if plaintiff did not actually know of the defect, then he did not consent to assume that risk, even though his conduct may or may not have been negligent depending on whether a reasonably prudent person would have noticed the defect or inspected the chair before using it.

Assumption of risk may be *express* or *implied*.

Express Assumption of Risk. In general, persons entering into a relationship may voluntarily agree that one will consent in advance to assume the risk of the other's negligence. R. § 496B. Ordinarily principles of contract law apply. These agreements sometimes take the form of releases or disclaimers.

However, courts have often refused to enforce such agreements where one party is at such an obvious disadvantage in bargaining power that he is placed at the mercy of the other's negligence, or where some other strong overriding public policy is operative. Thus, they may not be enforced in favor of employers, public utilities or others engaged in public callings, public bailees, carriers, and in some cases landlords and others where there is some strong public interest disfavoring immunity.

The agreement must be knowingly and voluntarily made. And such contracts will not be enforced as to risks of willful and wanton misconduct or intentional torts.

Implied Assumption of Risk. According to the traditional view, consent to relieve another from liability for negligence may also be inferred from plaintiff's conduct. R. § 496C. It is here that the principal difficulties have arisen. For purposes of this analysis, the cases will be divided into three general groups.

Primary assumption of risk. In the first group are the cases where plaintiff voluntarily enters into some relationship with defendant with knowledge that there are certain inherent but commonly accepted risks against which defendant will not protect him. This would include spectators and participants in sporting events, those who accept hazardous employment, and the like. It is these cases which are most often analytically unsound. What risks are assumed? In general, one assumes the ordinary foreseeable hazards of the activity; but as to these, there is *no negligence* on the part of defendant, and therefore no assumption of the risk of *negligent* harm. Used in this context, "assumption of risk" is a misleading misnomer. Some courts refer to this as the "primary" sense of the term, and the remaining cases (where defendant had a duty to exercise care for plaintiff's safety and was negligent) as its "secondary" sense.

Secondary assumption of risk: future negligence. In the second group are the cases where plaintiff voluntarily enters into some relationship with defendant with knowledge that there is a substantial risk that defendant will act negligently in the future. The passenger who consents to ride with an intoxicated driver is a typical example. It is sometimes said that one does not assume the risk of future negligence, but these cases constitute an exception and some courts will permit the defense to be asserted in this situation. While "assumption of risk" is the term used, the true basis of the defense is the unreasonable conduct of the plaintiff in proceeding to enter into the relationship, and thus it would be preferable to restrict these cases to the defense of contributory negligence. While plaintiff may have taken a bad risk, his conduct hardly manifests consent to excuse the defendant of responsibility if defendant does in fact negligently injure the plaintiff.

Secondary assumption of risk: preexisting negligence. The third group comprises cases where the plaintiff is fully aware of a risk that has already been created by the negligence of the defendant and voluntarily proceeds to encounter it. For example, the defendant furnishes the plaintiff, a painter, a scaffold with a badly frayed rope. Plaintiff, fully aware of the rope's condition, proceeds to use the scaffold and is injured. Or defendant, owner of a baseball stadium, is under a duty to furnish a number of screened seats. None are provided. Plaintiff, a spectator, chooses to sit in an area which ought to have been screened and is injured by a foul ball.

Analytically, a stronger case can be made for implying consent in this situation, since the plaintiff is confronted with negligence that has already occurred. Again, however, the "consent" is illusory.

Plaintiff may have chosen to take a risk, but his conduct hardly can be construed as manifesting consent to excuse defendant from liability if the risk is realized. In other words, plaintiff's conduct manifests *fault, not consent.* Plaintiff may be foolish, but he can hardly be said to have manifested consent to sustain injury without recompense.

Despite its questionable rationale, prior to the adoption of comparative fault the defense flourished, in part because it was not necessary to distinguish carefully between it and contributory negligence. Both were complete defenses. Even today, implied assumption of risk remains viable in certain contexts.

Elements: Consent, Knowledge, Voluntariness. Three criteria must be met to support a finding of implied assumption of risk. The conduct must (1) manifest consent, and the risk must be encountered (2) voluntarily and (3) with full knowledge and appreciation of the danger.

(1) *Manifestation of Consent.* The essence of the defense is consent to relieve defendant of liability, and therefore plaintiff's conduct must be capable of being interpreted as implicitly manifesting such consent. Not all conduct by which one voluntarily proceeds to encounter a known danger qualifies. For example, a pedestrian who dashes into the path of a speeding car, fully aware of the risk, does not thereby manifest his consent to relieve the driver of his obligation to exercise care for the pedestrian's safety, nor of his liability for failure to do so. Rather

the opposite is true; he is demanding that care be taken for his safety. He may be contributorily negligent, but he does not assume the risk.

(2) *Knowledge.* To excuse defendant's liability, the consent must be an informed one, and therefore defendant must show that plaintiff actually knew, understood and appreciated the risk. R. § 496D. Unlike contributory negligence, the test is a subjective one—what did plaintiff actually know, not what should he have known.

At the same time, plaintiff's knowledge may be proved circumstantially, and where the risk ought to have been obvious to him, he will probably be unsuccessful if he tries to deny the import of what he saw. Similarly, he is ordinarily charged with matters of common knowledge, such as the slipperiness of ice, and those things which ordinary observation of his surroundings would reveal.

(3) *Voluntary Exposure.* No consent can be inferred unless plaintiff's exposure to the risk was free and voluntary. R. § 496E.

In many cases, voluntariness may be inferred from his conduct in entering or remaining in the zone of danger, albeit reluctantly or under protest. But there are cases, usually involving employees, where the danger is not imminent, plaintiff protests and defendant then promises to remedy the risk-creating condition. Plaintiff's consent is then vitiated until so long a time has passed that he can no longer reasonably rely on the promise.

Evidence that plaintiff exposed himself to the risk under duress or compulsion will, of course, negate this element. There is an analogy between the *voluntariness* of plaintiff's conduct here and the *reasonableness* of his conduct on the issue of contributory negligence. If the plaintiff had no real or effective choice, or no better or safer alternative, his conduct in encountering the risk may be found not voluntary. Thus, a tenant does not assume the risk of his landlord's negligence in maintaining a common stairway that the tenant must use for access to his apartment. Nor is one required to surrender a valuable legal right (of which defendant has no right to deprive him) in order to avoid the zone of danger. For example, plaintiff is not required to forego use of a public railroad crossing because defendant railroad has failed to keep it in repair. And would-be rescuers do not assume the risk of their own injury by attempting the rescue, where the alternative is to permit the threatened harm to occur.

What about economic duress? Does an employee assume the risk of using negligently maintained equipment where the alternative is to be fired? Many courts have said yes, but the trend and better view is to permit such compulsion to be shown to defeat the defense.

Violation of Statute. As in the case of contributory negligence, assumption of risk is a defense to negligence based on violation of a statute, except for a limited group of statutes intended to protect a certain class of persons from dangers against which they are incapable of protecting themselves. R. § 496F. Some statutory torts (e.g., workers' compensation, F.E.L.A., structural work acts) expressly exclude the defense.

Limitation to Particular Risk. The assumption is, of course, limited to the particular risk which plaintiff freely and knowingly encountered.

Abolition of the Defense. Analytically unsound, misunderstood and thus misapplied, often confused with other tort concepts (such as duty and contributory negligence), and subject to some of the same criticisms that apply to contributory negligence, the defense of *implied* (secondary) assumption of risk is in similar disfavor. Many jurisdictions simply refuse to recognize the doctrine separate from contributory negligence; others refuse to apply it in certain classes of cases. To the extent that it survives at all, it is now a distinctly minority view.

As noted, there is a substantial—perhaps complete—overlap between implied assumption of risk and contributory negligence. The "voluntariness" requirement of the former has evolved to strongly resemble the "reasonable person" test of the latter. However, in the remaining area of difference— where the assumption of risk was reasonable under the circumstances and therefore not negligent— there remains room for disagreement. It can be argued that if it was reasonable (and therefore not negligent) to encounter the risk, the negligent defendant should not be exonerated. Many legal writers support this view. On the other hand, there are cases where plaintiff may *reasonably* elect to consent voluntarily to accept the consequences of a negligently created risk—in other words, to deliberately, freely and knowingly "take a chance" and accept the consequences. Thus, the courts may be required to continue to recognize a limited form of the defense, perhaps under another name.

Even where abolished as a defense in negligence cases, implied assumption of risk remains a defense to strict liability in some jurisdictions, but sometimes only as a damage-reducing factor.

To the extent one subscribes to the view that implied assumption of risk is fault-based, the doctrine has no justification as a complete bar in jurisdictions that have adopted comparative negligence, and most of those states have abolished it by merging it into the unified concept of comparative fault.

§ 5–5. Mitigation of Damages and Avoidable Consequences

Mitigation of Damages. An injured plaintiff must exercise reasonable care to seek treatment for his injuries, and he must follow reasonable directions from his health care provider. If his injury causes him to lose earnings, he must make a reasonable effort to find gainful employment of which he is now capable. If he fails to do so, he cannot recover those damages that flow from such failure; technically, those damages are the result of the plaintiff's own wrongful conduct, not the defendant's.

Plaintiff need only do what is reasonable, and in some jurisdictions he need not submit to major surgery if he prefers not to.

Avoidable Consequences. In a few situations, courts have held that a plaintiff who fails to exercise reasonably care *before* the accident to do something that would have mitigated his damages cannot recover for the damages caused by that failure. The most common example is a plaintiff injured in an automobile collision who failed to wear an available seat belt. Such conduct is distinguishable from contributory negligence, in that it does not contribute to the accident itself but merely serves to aggravate the damages. If the defendant can prove that some separable part of plaintiff's injuries was caused by such conduct, some courts will refuse to award damages for that part.

§ 5–6. Statutes of Limitations and Repose

Just as in all other areas of the law, tort law imposes time limits on bringing claims. The purposes of these limits are to protect defendants (1) from perpetual exposure to potential liability—to permit defendants (and their insurers) to "close the books" at a fixed time, and (2) from the evidentiary problems of defending against stale claims.

Such limitations take the form of two types of statutes: (1) statutes of limitations and (2) statutes of repose.

Statutes of Limitations. The statutory period of time in which a tort action can be filed generally starts to "run" when the cause of action accrues. Ordinarily, this is at the time of the injury. When the injury is caused by a single traumatic event, such as an accident, the statute begins to run on that date, whether or not the plaintiff knows that his injury was caused by tortious conduct.

If the injury is one that accrues over time, such as by exposure to an environmental pollutant, the statute does not start to run until the last exposure or until the injury is manifest (subject to the "discovery" rule discussed below).

If the injury is one that is not readily perceptible as having an external source, a special rule called the "discovery rule" may be applicable. For example, assume a two-year statute. Further assume that during plaintiff's surgery a foreign object (e.g., a surgical sponge) is left inside his body. The plaintiff may experience symptoms, but he may have no reason to suspect that they are the result of tortious conduct. By the time the plaintiff discovers the wrong, it may be more than two years after the surgery. In these types of cases, decisions or statutes usually provide that the action does not accrue for purposes of the statute of limitations until the plaintiff knew or in the exercise of reasonable care should have known that (1) he sustained an injury and (2) that injury may have been caused by someone's tortious conduct.

The statute of limitations is ordinarily tolled (1) during the time the plaintiff is a minor or mentally incompetent, and (2) when the defendant fraudulently conceals the facts from which the plaintiff could have determined that he had a cause of action.

Statutes of Repose. A fairly recent development, statutes of repose are now common. They are limited to specific classes of claims—medical (or other professional) negligence and strict product liability are two of the most common types.

Unlike statutes of limitations, statutes of repose start to run when the tortious conduct is complete, whether or not there has been an injury. Thus, a plaintiff's claim can be barred *before* his cause of action even arises. In addition, such statutes often run against minors and incompetents. The purpose of these statutes is to eliminate the possibility of claims which could arise many years—even decades—after the tortious act, for which the burden of maintaining records and insurance or otherwise providing for such contingent liabilities is thought to be too great. Despite their draconian consequences, most statutes of repose have been upheld against constitutional challenges.

CHAPTER 6

LIABILITY FOR INTENTIONAL MISCONDUCT

§ 6–1. Intent

The old common law actions of trespass and case evolved such that, so far as physical harm is concerned, the distinction between them was not whether the harm was direct or indirect, but rather whether the tort could be classified within the confines of the traditional trespass actions—battery, assault, false imprisonment, trespass to land and chattels—or whether the wrong involved mere negligence, for which case was the usual remedy. At the same time the courts came to require fault an element of the plaintiff's trespass cause of action—that is, some sort of wrongful intent. Thus, the trespass actions became what we now call the intentional torts.

Morally, greater blame attaches to intentional misconduct than to lesser degrees of fault, and that is reflected in the law of intentional torts. In general, to establish a prima facie case, plaintiff need only prove that defendant intentionally invaded a protected interest. The burden then shifts to defendant to show some justification or excuse. And, unlike negligence actions, actual damages need not be proved. If plaintiff cannot establish any actual harm (tangible or intangible), nominal damages can be awarded.

Traditionally, the intentional torts are those named and discussed in the sections which follow. However, there has come to be recognized a general principle of intentional tort liability, analogous to the general principle of negligence liability (see § 4–1), sometimes called "prima facie tort," which may be invoked when no particular intentional tort applies. See, e.g., *Nees v. Hocks* (Or. 1975) (wrongful discharge). Section 870 of the Restatement provides:

> One who intentionally causes injury to another is subject to liability to the other for the actual harm incurred, if his conduct is culpable and not justifiable. This liability may be imposed despite the fact that the actor's conduct does not come within one of the traditional categories of tort liability.

For a discussion of the elements and limits of this liability, see the Comments to this section; for authorities supporting it, see the Reporter's Notes. Of course, it must not be inferred from this that all unjustified intentional wrongs are actionable. But in a proper case, the courts need not and do not consider themselves bound by the traditional intentional tort pigeon-holes.

An intentional tort is an act committed (or omitted) with a particular state of mind. How is the actor's state of mind to be proved? Direct evidence—the actor's own statement of his actual intent—is rarely available. Indeed, after the fact he may claim to have had the best of intentions. Thus, as in all other cases where one's state of mind must be shown, it is usually proved by circumstantial evidence. His conduct, in the context of his surroundings and what he presumably knew and perceived, is evidence from which his intent may be inferred. We may infer that one intends the natural and probable consequences of his acts in light of the surrounding circumstances of which he may be assumed to be aware.

Intent, in the sense required here, must be distinguished from motive. *Intent* is usually defined as the desire to cause certain immediate consequences. One who throws a rock with great force against a glass window obviously intends that it will be broken. One who points a loaded gun at another and pulls the trigger surely intends that the bullet will strike and injure him. The actor's *motive* for his conduct—revenge, protest, punishment, theft, self-defense, or even a desire to be of help (e.g., the surgeon who operates without consent)—may, in certain cases, aggravate, mitigate or excuse the wrong. For example, malice may permit assessment of punitive damages; self-defense may be a complete defense to tort liability. But to establish a prima facie case, all that need be shown is the defendant's conduct, the invasion of a legally protected interest of the plaintiff, and the requisite intent.

Thus, certainty of the harmful consequences is the basis on which we distinguish intentional torts

from negligent or reckless ("willful and wanton")
ones. If the result is intended or substantially certain to occur, the tort is intentional. But if the
actor's conduct merely creates a foreseeable *risk* of
harm, which may or may not be realized, then the
conduct is negligent or reckless depending upon the
magnitude of the risk.

Unique to the intentional torts, borrowed from
the criminal law, the doctrine of "transferred intent" reflects the greater blame which attaches to
intentional misconduct. In effect, it is a broadened
rule of proximate cause. Thus, where *A* acts with
the intent to injure *B*, but at the same time or
instead injures *C*, his intent to injure *B* "transfers"
to *C* and *A* is deemed to have committed an intentional tort upon *C*, even though he was completely
unaware of *C*'s existence or of any risk of harm to
C. For example, *A* shoots at *B* and wounds or misses
him. The bullet strikes *C* who was hidden from view
and not known to be in the vicinity. *A* may be liable
to *C* in battery. In addition, the intent transfers
among the five progeny of the parent trespass action—battery, assault, false imprisonment, trespass
to land and trespass to chattels—so long as the
harm is direct and immediate. For example, *A*'s
intent to commit only an assault upon *B* such as by
shooting in his direction to frighten him may support liability for a battery to *C* who is unexpectedly
struck by the bullet.

Often the same act is both a tort and a crime.
This is especially true with respect to the intention-

al torts. But despite their common origins, tort and criminal law rules are now more different than similar, and analogies and comparisons between torts and crimes of the same name or having similar bases in conduct should be made only with the greatest caution.

Both a civil tort action and a criminal prosecution may be brought for the same wrongful conduct. The remedies are concurrent, and either a successful or unsuccessful result in one is ordinarily not a bar to the other. But the most common intentional torts are often committed by judgment-proof persons; intentional torts are usually uninsured and in most cases uninsurable; and vicarious liability for intentional torts is limited. Thus, intentional tort litigation is of relatively less significance in the day-to-day work of lawyers and courts.

§ 6–2. Battery

Battery is the remedy for an intentional and unpermitted physical contact with plaintiff's person by defendant or (now that the distinction between trespass and case has disappeared) by an agency defendant has set in motion. It reflects the basic right to have one's body left alone by others. Secondarily, it seeks to deter relatively minor but offensive contacts that can precipitate breaches of the peace.

Plaintiff's "person" includes his body and those things in contact or closely connected to it and identified with it, such as clothing, an object held in his hand, or an object so associated or identified with plaintiff that, considering the nature of the contact, a normal person would deem it an offense against his person.

The tort is the contact, and thus plaintiff need not have been aware of it at the time.

Two forms of contact are actionable. First and foremost are those which cause some *physical harm,* broadly defined to include any physical impairment of the condition of the body (such as a cut, a bruise, a burn, etc., however slight), even if beneficial; illness; and physical (but not emotional) pain. R. § 15. Second, battery also encompasses contacts which do not cause physical harm but are hostile, offensive, or insulting, such as poking with a finger in anger, angrily knocking off one's hat, dousing one with water, spitting in one's face, cutting hair, and even an unwanted kiss. R. §§ 18, 19. The gist of the action is contact without consent, resulting in harm to plaintiff's person or dignity.

The contact must have been intended (unless the doctrine of transferred intent applies); otherwise the action if any lies in negligence. But defendant need not have intended any harm. It is no defense that defendant intended only a joke or a compliment, or even to render assistance. Thus, where a doctor performs surgery without the patient's consent, a battery has been committed.

If plaintiff consents to the contact, defendant is privileged to make it and there is no tort. This is generally true of all torts. See § 7–2. So far as battery is concerned, consent may sometimes be assumed. In a crowded society, some unpermitted contact is inevitable, customary and reasonably necessary. Consent to certain kinds of contacts may also be assumed where there is some prior relationship between the parties. Thus, where reasonable and customary, given the time, place and circumstances of the contact and the relationship of the parties, a privilege will ordinarily exist, unless and until plaintiff gives notice to the contrary.

§ 6–3. Assault

An assault is an act that arouses in plaintiff a *reasonable* apprehension of an imminent battery. Like battery, the action (1) protects one's right to his bodily integrity, in this case against psychic harm, and (2) deters conduct that often leads to disturbances of the peace.

Apprehension, but not fear, is required. The tort is committed when plaintiff perceives the threat, even though he is too courageous to be frightened or intimidated. But since the essence of the tort is the apprehension, plaintiff obviously must be aware of defendant's threatening act at the time. R. § 22.

The contact must be perceived as imminent. R. § 24. There must be an apparent intent to carry out the threat immediately. Thus, it is often said that mere words, however strong, do not constitute an assault. R. § 31. There must be some overt act. Ordinarily this is true. But words may give character to an act. An otherwise innocuous or inoffensive movement (e.g., reaching into one's pocket) or perhaps even a stance may become an assault when coupled with threatening words such that a reasonable person would apprehend a battery. Conversely, a threatening gesture accompanied by words that negate any present intent of a tortious contact may not be an assault if a reasonable person in plaintiff's position would perceive no immediate danger of a battery. For example, if defendant's words indicate that he jests, or that the threat is for the future ("The next time I see you I will hit you") or conditional or hypothetical ("If it were not assizetime, I would not take such language from you"), there is no assault.

Similarly, there must be an apparent present ability and opportunity to commit the threatened battery. For example, if defendant is located or confined or otherwise under some restriction or disability so as to be physically incapable of immediately carrying out the threat, and plaintiff is aware of this, then there can be no reasonable apprehension of contact and therefore no assault. Conversely, if plaintiff reasonably apprehends a battery, there is an assault even though defendant (unbeknown to plaintiff) is in fact incapable of it (such as when the gun he points at plaintiff is not loaded).

To be liable for assault, defendant must intend to commit an intentional tort but need not intend to commit battery. He may have intended only an assault. Or, under the doctrine of transferred intent

(§ 6–1), his intent to commit one of the other trespassory torts will suffice, provided plaintiff reasonably apprehends an imminent battery.

Much confusion has arisen from the tendency of some to use the term "assault" as synonymous with battery, or as a shorthand expression encompassing both torts. While a battery and an assault are often parts of the same tortious event, either tort may be committed by itself and without committing the other. Be precise in the use of these two terms, and do not be misled by those who are not.

§ 6–4.   False Imprisonment

The action for false imprisonment enforces another basic personal interest, the right to be free from wrongful confinement.

The essence of the tort is the mental harm caused by the knowledge that one is not free to move about at will. Thus, where there is no other harm caused by the confinement, plaintiff must be aware that he is confined at the time or there is no tort. But he may also recover damages for physical harm and any other consequential damages caused by the confinement; and where such damages are incurred there is a cause of action even though, due to his mental incapacity or for some other reason, he is then incapable of realizing that he is confined. R. § 42.

Prima facie, the tort occurs when defendant confines plaintiff, intending to confine him or another, within boundaries set by defendant. R. § 35. The place of confinement may be much broader than the term "imprisonment" implies. It is enough that plaintiff is prevented from leaving a given area, such as a room, an automobile, a building, or perhaps even a larger area. Within that area, however, the confinement must be total, and plaintiff must have no reasonable or safe avenue of escape known to him. Merely to block one's path in one direction is not sufficient. R. § 36.

Thus, the restraint may be by means of actual or apparent physical barriers, or by physical force or threats of force, express or implied. R. §§ 38–40. It may be by duress sufficient to vitiate consent, such as where defendant threatens to harm another or plaintiff's valuable property, or restrains such property. R. § 40A. However, merely moral or social pressure is not sufficient. Thus, where plaintiff remains confined to clear his name, or to avoid attracting attention or public humiliation, there may be some tort, but it is not false imprisonment.

Confinement may be imposed under color of legal authority, in which case it is sometimes called false arrest. R. § 41. If defendant has or asserts the legal power to detain the plaintiff and purports to exercise it, plaintiff believes that defendant has or may have such power, and plaintiff submits to it against his will, there is confinement. If the arrest is in fact without legal authority, it is a false arrest and therefore false imprisonment.

An actionable confinement may occur when plaintiff, once properly restrained, is now entitled to leave the premises, and defendant intentionally fails to perform his legal duty to release plaintiff or to provide or show him a means of egress. R. § 45.

In order to be liable for false imprisonment, defendant must be an active and knowing participant in procuring or instigating the confinement, including its wrongful aspect. R. § 45A. It is not sufficient that he merely gives information to others who independently decide whether and how to confine plaintiff. Nor is he liable where he requests a proper arrest and some one else performs an improper one.

The requisite intent, however, is merely the intent to confine plaintiff, or another where plaintiff is confined instead or in addition. A mistake of identity is no excuse. Similarly, a good faith belief that the confinement is justified is no defense. Of course, the presence or absence of malice will aggravate or mitigate the damages.

Once the fact of intentional confinement is shown, the burden is on defendant to prove legal justification.

Detention of a suspected shoplifter is a recurring case. Where defendant acted in good faith, the courts have struggled to deny liability, frequently by finding that plaintiff voluntarily consented to remain or by creating a special privilege to detain him on the premises, without arrest. See R. § 120A. Given the magnitude of this problem, most states have enacted statutes which give the shopkeeper a limited privilege to detain such persons for a reasonable time to investigate.

The torts of false arrest and malicious prosecution are sometimes confused. Basically, malicious prosecution is the remedy for the institution of groundless criminal proceedings against the plaintiff for an improper purpose. Thus, if defendant complies with the proper formal requirements in procuring plaintiff's arrest and confinement, he is liable if at all, only in malicious prosecution for misuse of legal process to effect a valid arrest for an improper purpose, and not for false imprisonment.

§ 6-5. Intentional or Reckless Infliction of Emotional Distress

The common law has been slow to accept plaintiff's interest in freedom from emotional distress as entitled to independent legal protection. Such reluctance is incongruous in view of the fact that damages for mental trauma and its physical effects have long been awarded as adjunct to damages for other kinds of harm, such as bodily injury. Moreover, equally intangible harms—pain and suffering, for example—are regularly valued and compensated. And harms to purely mental interests have long been recognized in the actions for assault, false imprisonment, and to a lesser extent battery (in cases where the contact is slight but offensive). Thus, any difficulties inherent in proving and measuring damages for emotional distress are insufficient to justify nonliability.

The principal bases of the reluctance to allow a separate action for causing emotional distress are probably the fear of false claims and a feeling that the courts should not redress mere wounds to the ego. But where defendant's conduct is sufficiently outrageous to be likely to produce a strong emotional response in a normal person, there is a sufficient assurance that the alleged harm is real together with a strong public interest in deterring such conduct. Thus, it is in such cases that most courts (and the Restatement) have come to recognize a separate and distinct cause of action, apart from any other tort, for the intentional or reckless infliction of mental anguish.

To qualify for liability, defendant's conduct must be "extreme and outrageous" (R. § 46), intolerable, and not merely insulting, profane, abusive, annoying or even threatening. It must go beyond all reasonable bounds of decency. Unless defendant knows of some special sensitivity of the plaintiff, mere verbal abuse, name-calling, rudeness, insolence, and threats to do that which defendant has a legal right to do are generally not actionable, absent circumstances of aggravation. The courts cannot provide a remedy for bad manners, rough language, and other such acts, merely inconsiderate and unkind, which are a regrettably common occurrence in human interaction. But where, by community standards, the conduct may be characterized as shocking and indecent there may be liability in tort.

(There is, however, an exception to the foregoing rule in the case of innkeepers, common carriers, and other public utilities, who may be liable for profane, grossly insulting, or indecent language or conduct by their employees acting within the scope of their employment. See R. § 48. It has been suggested, so far with little success, that this rule might be extended to all possessors of land whose premises are held open to the public. And cf. statutes in Virginia, West Virginia, and Mississippi making actionable insulting words likely to provoke violence.)

A common fact situation involves the abuse by defendant of some relation or status that gives him actual or apparent power to damage plaintiff's interests. For example, actionable conduct has been found in threats (and other indignities) by bill collectors, insurance adjustors, landlords, school officials, police and those posing as police, and officials of a trade association, where such threats go beyond the ordinary means of persuasion or demands which they have a right to make and become flagrant abuses of power in the nature of extortion.

Intentional or reckless mishandling of a corpse may give rise to a cause of action in the next of kin who are thereby emotionally distressed. R. § 868.

As previously noted, the courts are unwilling to redress minor psychic harm. Therefore, not only must defendant's conduct be extreme and outrageous, but plaintiff's emotional response must be severe. A plaintiff who merely becomes unhappy, humiliated, or mildly despondent for a short time and spends a sleepless night or two cannot recover.

But if the emotional anguish is great, and especially if it is prolonged, most courts (and the Restatement, § 46) will allow the action whether or not there is any physical manifestation of the mental suffering, or bodily harm (such as a physical illness, heart condition, miscarriage, and the like) caused by it. A few jurisdictions seem to require such resulting bodily harm as a condition to liability.

Special scope of liability rules apply to this tort. Recall that the usual rule is that defendant takes his plaintiff as he finds him, and will be liable for all the physical consequences of his tort upon that plaintiff, however unforeseeable they are or especially sensitive that particular plaintiff may be. This is sometimes called the "thin-skulled" or "eggshell" plaintiff rule. See § 4–4, supra. However, in the case of the infliction of emotional distress, defendant is not liable to the extent that plaintiff's emotional response is not within the range of normal human reactions to that conduct. In other words, the distress must be such as a reasonable person of ordinary sensitivity would experience. And as a corollary rule, where defendant intended to inflict only severe emotional distress, he is not liable for greater harm (in the form of illness or other bodily harm) unless his conduct created a foreseeable risk of such aggravated harm. R. § 312.

Of course, if defendant has knowledge of a peculiar or special sensitivity of the plaintiff, he may be liable for conduct which is extreme and outrageous in light of that special vulnerability, even though the same conduct would not be expected to produce a severe response in a normal, healthy adult. The physically infirm, the mentally ill, children, and pregnant women are commonly held to be examples of such plaintiffs.

In most of the decided cases, the mental distress was inflicted intentionally—that is, defendant desired to cause it or knew that it was substantially certain to occur. However, most courts and the Restatement allow recovery where defendant is merely reckless ("willful and wanton"), in that there is a high probability that emotional distress will follow from his conduct and he goes ahead in conscious disregard of that risk.

The intent required for this tort may *not* be supplied by the doctrine of transferred intent (§ 6–1), at least so far as defendant's intent was only to commit some *other* tort. R. § 47. For example, the intent to commit a battery, or to harm plaintiff's property, is not enough. Defendant must intend to cause emotional distress, or at least act in conscious disregard of a high probability of such harm. However, there would seem to be no good reason why the doctrine of transferred intent may not be applied as between different *persons*. Thus, where defendant intends to inflict emotional distress upon A and takes steps to do so, but due to unforeseen events B is traumatized instead, B should have a cause of action.

Moreover, defendant's *acts* need not be directed at plaintiff, so long as he intentionally or recklessly causes plaintiff's mental anguish. He will be liable to plaintiff for shocking conduct directed at some third person, *provided* plaintiff's mental harm was also intended or recklessly caused. The courts have generally required that plaintiff have witnessed the conduct, and that defendant knew or had reason to know of plaintiff's presence. And according to the Restatement (§ 46(2)), if the third person is *not* a member of plaintiff's immediate family, plaintiff may recover only if the distress reasonably results in some bodily harm. These requirements are intended as safeguards against questionable claims and excessively broad liability, such as to a large number of persons who witness a shocking event or to one who merely hears of it second or third-hand. However, it would seem that liability may well be extended in favor of a close relative who was not present at the event when the circumstances of the case justify. See, e.g., *Knierim v. Izzo* (Ill. 1961) (defendant threatened to murder plaintiff's husband, and then did so).

If a statement is entitled to First Amendment protection, then it may not be the basis for a claim of intentional infliction of emotional distress if it could not (constitutionally) have been the basis for a libel action. *Hustler Magazine v. Falwell* (U.S. 1988).

§ 6–6. Trespass to Land

At common law every unauthorized and direct breach of the boundaries of another's land was an actionable trespass—trespass *quare clausum fregit* (wherefore he broke the close). For historical reasons already discussed (§ 1–3) plaintiff did not have to prove an intent to commit a trespass (or other fault). All that was necessary was that the act resulting in the trespass be volitional, and that the resulting trespass be direct and immediate. Nor did actual damage need to be shown. Any trespass justified at least nominal damages. The strictness of the common law trespass liability reflects the great importance in feudal times of the right to the possession of land and its incidents. It also reflects the fact that one of the chief functions of the action was to try the land's title, the technical trespass being merely a vehicle for doing so. (The action may also be a means to prevent the habitual trespasser from acquiring a prescriptive right.)

With the shift to fault as the principal basis of tort liability, almost all jurisdictions have come to require that the trespass be intentional, reckless or negligent to be actionable (R. § 166), except where the rules of strict liability for abnormally dangerous activities (§ 3–3) apply. However, *nota bene*—defendant need not intend a *wrong;* he need only intend to (or negligently) cause the *entry.* It is no defense that defendant acted under a mistaken belief (not induced by the possessor) that he had a privilege to enter. Of course, some entries are privileged, as will be discussed in later sections.

At common law, the action of trespass could be maintained only if the invasion of plaintiff's land was direct, immediate, and by some tangible or visible agent. Otherwise, the remedy was in case. Thus, trespass was the proper form of action where defendant threw water directly on plaintiff's land, but not where he merely constructed a spout or erected a dam such that water of its own accord eventually flowed onto plaintiff's property. Or if defendant discharged water onto *B*'s land that then flowed across to the land of *C*, he was liable in trespass to *B* but not to *C*. And there was no trespass liability where the damage on plaintiff's land was caused by vibration of the ground, or by invisible fumes, gases or microscopic particles suspended in the air. These distinctions have largely disappeared with the abolition of the forms of action, and today both direct and indirect entries are generally actionable under the rules applied to trespass to land. As to air-borne gases and particles, a number of courts have characterized them as a trespass, although most such cases seem to be brought under the alternative theory of nuisance (§ 8–18). Vibration or concussion waves, while still not technically a trespass, may cause damage that is actionable under principles of strict liability (§ 3–3) or nuisance.

It is still true that no actual harm need be shown where the trespass was intentional. However, where it was recklessly or negligently caused, there is liability only if and to the extent that some damage results.

Once trespass liability is established, the damages recoverable include all harm directly resulting from the trespass and a broad range of consequential damage. Thus, defendant will usually be liable for any physical harm occurring on the land caused by or during the entry, no matter how carefully he acts while on the land. For example, a trespasser who builds a fire, digs a hole, or merely leaves a door or gate ajar may be liable for resulting physical harm, at least to the premises and to the possessor and members of his household and their property, without any showing of negligence. Physical harm includes emotional distress.

The interests protected are those incident to the right to possession of the land. Thus, only the person(s) then in actual possession of the land may bring a trespass action. As to unoccupied land, the owner is deemed to be in possession. If the interests of someone *not* in possession (such as the owner who has leased the premises to another) are damaged by the trespass, that person must sue under some other theory. However, it is no defense that the actual possessor has no legal right to be there. Even a wrongful possession carries with it rights superior to those of a trespasser.

Now that the distinction between trespass and case is abolished, a trespass may consist of entering upon the land, or causing some thing or third person to do so; remaining on the land after one's right to be there has terminated; or failing to remove from the land a thing which one is under a duty to remove.

Where the trespass consists of the failure to remove something from the land, it is a continuing trespass. May plaintiff bring successive actions, or must she recover in one action for all damages, past and prospective? Case law provides no clear answer; the Restatement (§ 161) would give the plaintiff an option to pursue either remedy.

The boundaries of land extend vertically as well as horizontally. Thus, it may be a trespass to cross the plaintiff's property line beneath the surface of the land or to penetrate his airspace, at least so far as the zone infringed is close enough to the surface to potentially interfere with some conceivable use or enjoyment of the property. A bullet traversing the air above the surface, a mineshaft, utility wires, underground water, and the overhanging portion of a structure are illustrative.

Aircraft flights over private property present special problems. Several theories have evolved to balance the possessor's right to the peaceful use and enjoyment of his property against the needs of aviation. Under the "zone" theory, the landowner owns only so much of the airspace as is in his "effective possession," that is, the altitude up to which he might in the future make effective use of the airspace. The "actual use" theory denies any ownership of any airspace of which the owner of the land is not making some present use; there is no tort unless there is interference with the present enjoyment of the property. The first Restatement (§ 194) and a number of state statutes (based on the now-withdrawn Uniform Aeronautics Act) recognize unlimited ownership of upward airspace, subject to a privilege of flight similar to the public right to make use of a navigable stream which flows through private property. Finally, there is the "nuisance" theory, which ignores arguments about ownership of the air, and gives a remedy in the form of an action for nuisance, or possibly negligence, only when the flight results in actual interference with the use and enjoyment of the land.

In *United States v. Causby* (U.S. 1946), the Supreme Court held that continual low-altitude flights by military aircraft that ruined plaintiff's poultry business constituted a compensable "taking" of private property by the government. In doing so, it ruled that federal statutes and regulations had the effect of making the airspace above the prescribed minimum altitudes a public, and a federal, domain and highway, so there can be no trespass in flights at or above such levels. This, of course, invalidates all state law to the contrary. It is now generally agreed that there can be a "taking" (or creation of a compensable nuisance) by overflights, even above the statutory minimum altitudes, if the flights uniquely affect a particular landowner and substantially interfere with the owner's use and enjoyment of his property.

As to liability for falling aircraft or objects, or forced landings, see § 3–3.

§ 6–7. Chattels

Trespass to chattels and *conversion* are the two principal intentional torts against personal property.

Historically, the first remedy for interference with a chattel was the writ of trespass *de bonis asportatis* (for goods taken away). A direct descendant of the original trespass writ, it therefore required a direct, immediate and forcible interference with the chattel of another.

As the common law developed, case spawned the actions of detinue and trover. Detinue lay for the wrongful *detention* of a chattel where defendant's original possession was rightful. (In such cases, trespass was not the proper writ because trespass required that plaintiff have possession at the time of defendant's tort.) Trover, at first, was for the case where a finder of lost goods failed to return them to the person entitled to possession, and instead converted them to his own use or disposed of them to another. But trover had certain procedural advantages over the older forms of action, not the least of which was that defendant could not have trial by wager of law (oaths). Its popularity grew, and soon the necessary allegations of plaintiff's losing and defendant's finding of the chattel became mere formalities, fictions which could not be denied. Thus, trover came to be available for *any* intentional interference with another's chattel which was so substantial as to be inconsistent with ownership in another. In other words, defendant's interference was the equivalent of a conversion, and he could be forced to keep and pay for the chattel. Detinue fell into complete disuse, and trespass, while still a concurrent remedy with trover, came to be used only for harm which was *not* so substantial that defendant could be held to have appropriated the chattel to himself and therefore be compelled to pay plaintiff its full value and keep it. Thus, the main distinction between trespass and conversion is in the remedy. Trespass is available for any intentional interference, but damages are limited to plaintiff's actual harm. But if the interference is sufficiently substantial, plaintiff may bring an action for conversion and recover the full value of the chattel—in effect, require defendant to buy it—even though the actual damage to the chattel is less than total, or even nil. Hence, we see that all conversions are also trespasses, but all trespasses are not conversions.

Conversion is the name of the tort for which trover was the appropriate form of action. Now that the forms of action have been abolished, the term "trover" is rarely used. Plaintiff is said to bring a civil action for conversion.

Possession. In trespass to chattels and conversion, just as in trespass to land, the traditional common law rule has been that the action must be brought by the person who had actual possession of the property at the time of the tort, or at least by the person entitled to immediate possession (such as a bailor at will). Indeed, so strong has been the law's protection of possessory rights that it is no defense that plaintiff's possession is wrongful, so long as he holds the property under some colorable claim of right superior to that of defendant. In other words, the defense of *jus tertii*—that some one other than plaintiff has title or a superior right to possession—is ordinarily not available unless defendant can connect himself with that third person's right. It is this emphasis on possessory rights that gave rise to the old maxim "possession is nine-tenths of the law." But the idea was carried to absurd lengths, and at one time *only* the possessor could bring these actions. Therefore, if defendant harmed the interests of some one *not* in possession, such as the owner who had leased the chattel or a chattel mortgagee, that person might have a cause of action but it was not trespass or trover. Obviously, any rule which bars the true owner of goods from the preferred remedies for damage to them merely because he is not in possession places far too great an emphasis on possessory rights, and a good many courts (and the Restatement) will now permit such an owner to sue for trespass or conversion for the damage to his reversion.

The fact remains, however, that the person in possession of the chattel—be he lessee, bailee, mortgagee, pledgee, finder, or whatever—is always a proper plaintiff. Thus, the true owner could wind up empty-handed. If the possessor sues and is successful, he may recover far more than the value of his interest in the chattel, and the owner must look to him to account for the owner's share of the recovery, no matter how irresponsible he may be. Or the possessor may mishandle the suit to the prejudice of the owner's interests. Nevertheless, it is the owner who has parted with possession, and the possessor who must account to the owner for the chattel's return, and therefore there is something to be said for the rule that permits the mere possessor to sue for conversion or for the full amount of the damage caused by the trespass.

Types of Chattels. Originally, trover and trespass were available only with respect to tangible personal property. By now, most courts have extended the action for conversion to include intangible personal property which is represented by or merged into a document, such as a promissory note or stock certificate, and even to intangibles represented by documents which do not embody the right but are merely important to its exercise, such as a bank deposit book or an insurance policy. Theoretically, there is no logical reason why intangible rights unrelated to a document cannot be converted, but as yet the cases have not gone that far.

Trespass to Chattels. One commits a trespass to another's chattel by intentionally interfering with it. Interference may consist of damage, alteration, destruction, unpermitted use or movement, or of depriving the possessor of his possession or control of it, however briefly. Since the abolition of the distinction between trespass and case, it is no longer necessary that the interference be inflicted directly and immediately.

As in the case of trespass to land, there is no longer liability without fault. But there is no such thing as a "negligent trespass" to a chattel. Unlike trespass to land, this is exclusively an intentional tort. If a chattel is harmed by defendant's negligence (such as in an automobile collision), the action is in negligence and the rules of negligence law apply.

Note, however, that as in the case of the other intentional torts, no wrongful motive is necessary. The intent required is merely to act upon the chattel. Thus, defendant's good faith but mistaken belief that he owns the chattel or for some other reason is privileged to deal with it is no excuse.

While there is not much law on this point, it appears that (unlike trespass to land) there is no trespass to a chattel in the absence of some actual damage. For example, a defendant who merely handles the chattel or moves it or perhaps even uses it, without harming or affecting it or impairing its usefulness, has committed no tort. But the foregoing must be qualified by the rule that *any* dispossession is a trespass, for which at least nominal damages may be awarded. If the possessor is deprived of the chattel for even a short time, there is nevertheless a dispossession even though it is returned to or found by the possessor before there is any significant injury.

Given a trespass, the same broad damage rules apply as in the case of trespass of land, and defendant will be liable for all resulting damages to the chattel and to the plaintiff, however innocently caused, including bodily harm (which encompasses emotional distress).

Conversion. The concept of conversion is sufficiently broad to defy accurate definition. For most purposes, it may be thought of as a trespass to a chattel which is so serious, aggravated, or of such magnitude, as to justify forcing defendant to buy it. It is often defined as intentional conduct that deprives another of his property permanently or for an indefinite time or the intentional exercise of dominion or control over a chattel that is inconsistent with another's property in it.

When is the interference with another's chattel so aggravated or serious as to constitute a conversion? There is no simple test. The Restatement (§ 222A) deems the following factors to be important:

(a) the *extent* and *duration* of the actor's exercise of *dominion* or *control;*

(b) the actor's *intent* to assert a right which is in fact inconsistent with the right of control of another;

(c) the actor's *good faith;*

(d) the extent and duration of the *interference;*

(e) the *harm* done to the chattel; and

(f) the *inconvenience* and *expense* caused thereby.

It is a matter of degree, measured by the nature, extent and duration of the interference and defendant's motives and intentions.

As in the case of trespass, intent is required—there can be no negligent conversion—but again, no more is needed than an intent to act with respect to the chattel. Here, unlike trespass, defendant's motives may be *relevant* in determining whether the interference is sufficiently aggravated to constitute a conversion, but his good faith or honest mistake is no defense if the interference is otherwise sufficiently great. For example, one who steals my hat from a hat rack is liable for conversion even though he is immediately apprehended and the hat promptly tendered back. But so is one who by justifiable mistake takes my hat from a hat rack promptly discovers his error, and is about to replace it when the wind catches it and blows it down the sewer.

Trespass and its damages are premised on the concept that title to the chattel remains in its owners, and the possessor retains possession or is entitled to the chattel's return. Conversion, on the other hand, is a forced sale to defendant. Thus, its measure of damages includes the full value of the chattel at the time of the conversion, plus interest. The traditional view has been that plaintiff is never required to (although he may) accept a tender of the chattel's return in mitigation of the damages, but some recent authorities would require him to do so where the conversion was by innocent mistake, the chattel is undiminished in value, and no special damage resulted from the detention.

The following are illustrative of the various ways in which a conversion may occur.

(1) *Acquiring Possession.* One who wrongfully acquires possession of a chattel, as by theft, illegal levy or attachment, duress or fraud, converts it. The same is true, in most jurisdictions, of a bona fide purchaser, lessee, pledgee or donee from a thief or one who had no power to transfer it. Not so, however, a b.f.p. from one who acquired the chattel by fraud or duress, who takes without notice of the wrong. And, of course, a b.f.p. who is a holder in due course of a negotiable instrument is ordinarily thereby protected.

Even acquiring possession under the mistaken belief that one has a privilege to do so may be a conversion, unless the interference with plaintiff's rights is relatively minor as where the duration is brief and no significant harm is done.

A bailee who merely receives possession of a chattel for storage, safekeeping or transportation is not liable for conversion unless he has knowledge that another is then entitled to immediate possession. The same is true of an agent or employee who receives the chattel on behalf of his principal or employer, except where he himself directly negotiates the transaction in which he takes possession on his principal's behalf.

(2) *Removal.* Moving a chattel from one location to another may constitute a conversion, but only if

the interference with plaintiff's possession is significant or where defendant intends to exercise possessory rights or control over it inconsistent with those of plaintiff.

(3) *Transferring Possession.* The unauthorized transfer, delivery or disposal of a chattel to one not entitled to possession is normally a conversion, notwithstanding defendant's innocent mistake, unless the mistake is promptly rectified and no serious harm is done. Thus, an auctioneer who innocently sells stolen goods, or a carrier who by justifiable mistake misdelivers a chattel, are converters. Even involuntary bailees, such as a finder or one who acquires possession of the chattel by accident or mistake, are so liable.

Some protection is given to bailees, agents and employees, who may redeliver the chattel to their bailor, principal or employer or deliver it pursuant to his instructions without liability, provided they have no knowledge of plaintiff's right to possession. But even an innocent agent will be liable for conversion where he himself negotiates on his principal's behalf the transaction by which the chattel is transferred to a third person.

(4) *Withholding Possession.* Refusal to surrender possession of a chattel to one entitled to it is a conversion, again unless the tort was relatively insignificant as where the delay was short, the chattel was not harmed, and there was no intent to deprive the plaintiff of her right of control.

Where defendant came into possession of the chattel rightfully, there is no tort unless and until there is a demand and refusal to surrender. Moreover, not every failure to deliver the chattel upon demand is a conversion. Defendant is not liable in conversion where he no longer has the chattel, even though it was lost or destroyed through his own fault (in which case the remedy, if any, is in negligence), unless he converted it in some other way.

There is no conversion if the refusal is reasonably qualified. Defendant may insist on a reasonable time, place and manner of delivery, or upon a reasonable delay for a proper purpose (such as to verify title, charges, agency or other facts). Of course, the delay must be sought in good faith and for the reason stated.

(5) *Destruction or Alteration.* Obviously, there is a conversion when a chattel is intentionally destroyed; and also when, intentionally, its condition is materially altered or substantially damaged such that to repair or restore it would be impossible or unduly burdensome, or whereby plaintiff is thereby denied the use of it for a substantial period of time.

(6) *Use.* The casual and harmless use of a chattel, involving no intent to usurp the owner's right to dominion and control, is not a conversion. On the other hand, mere use may be a conversion where it is so substantial as to amount to the exercise of dominion and control over the chattel; or where the use, however brief, was with the intent to usurp dominion and control (e.g. a short joy ride in a

stolen car); or where the chattel is seriously damaged by or during its use.

Similar rules apply in the case of agents or bailees who are authorized to make some use of a chattel and exceed or deviate from the scope of their permission.

(7) *Asserting Ownership.* Merely to assert ownership of a chattel, without more, is not a conversion. But little else is required. Coupled with any interference with the owner's rights of possession or control, the tort is complete.

CHAPTER 7

DEFENSES TO LIABILITY FOR INTENTIONAL MISCONDUCT

§ 7–1. In General

"Privilege" is the general term applied to certain rules of law by which particular circumstances justify conduct that otherwise would be tortious, and thereby defeat the tort liability (or defense) which, in the absence of such circumstances, ordinarily would follow from that conduct. In other words, even if all of the facts necessary to a prima facie case of tort liability can be proved, there are additional facts present sufficient to establish some privilege, and therefore defendant has committed no tort. Privileges thus differ from other defenses, such as contributory negligence, which operate to reduce or bar plaintiff's recovery but do not negate the tortious nature of defendant's conduct. Conversely, plaintiff's privilege may defeat a defense that defendant otherwise might have had.

The term and concept of privilege apply primarily to the intentional torts, but also appear in other areas, such as defamation.

Privileges may be divided into two general categories: (1) consent, and (2) privileges created by law irrespective of consent. In general, the latter arise where there is some important and overriding social value in sanctioning defendant's conduct, despite the fact that it causes plaintiff harm.

Consent will be treated in the next section, and the remaining intentional tort privileges in the sections that follow.

Strictly speaking, consent is technically not a privilege in the case of the intentional torts that are invasions of plaintiff's interests in his person (assault, battery, false imprisonment) as opposed to his property interests, since lack of consent is an element of the tort and ordinarily plaintiff must establish it as a part of his prima facie case. However, the consent rules are similar as to all torts and for convenience are customarily treated as part of the law of privilege.

Except as noted in the last paragraph, privilege is an affirmative defense that must be pleaded and proved by defendant.

A word about mistake. As we saw in Chapter 6, defendant's mistake, in and of itself—even a non-negligent one—is per se no defense to an intentional tort, nor does it negate the requisite intent. One who intentionally (and without a privilege) enters upon plaintiff's land, or confines plaintiff, or uses plaintiff's chattel, or performs unauthorized surgery, is no less a tortfeasor merely because he quite reasonably (but erroneously) believed that he was entitled to do so. But as will be seen, mistake is often relevant in determining the existence of a privilege. Certain privileges are based on defendant's reasonable belief concerning some fact(s), even though it later turns out that he was mistaken. Generally, a mistake is privileged where it appears necessary for defendant to act quickly to protect some important interest that does in fact exist, or when defendant is under a duty to act for the protection of the public interest. In addition, it is a general rule that where plaintiff himself induced defendant's mistake, defendant is absolved of liability for the mistake so long as he did not act unreasonably.

§ 7–2. Consent

Consent is a defense to virtually any tort. The law ordinarily has no interest in compensating one who validly, knowingly and freely consents in advance to the invasion of the interest that the law would otherwise have protected. In the law of negligence and strict liability, consent goes by the name "assumption of risk," and a separate body of law has grown up around that concept which is described elsewhere (§ 5–4). While consent will be treated here in relation to the intentional torts, similar or analogous rules apply in other areas of tort law.

There is consent when one is, in fact, willing for conduct to occur. It is a matter of plaintiff's subjective state of mind, and assuming it can be proven, the fact that he failed to communicate his secret consent to anyone does not make it any less valid.

At the same time, people must rely on the overt words and acts of others, rather than their undisclosed thoughts. Thus, plaintiff's words or conduct manifesting consent are sufficient to create a privilege for defendant to act in light of the apparent consent, notwithstanding the fact that plaintiff's actual but undisclosed state of mind was to the contrary. R. § 50.

Consent may, of course, be communicated by assertive conduct as well as words, such as by beckoning defendant onto one's land or by holding up one's arm to be vaccinated without protest. Even silence and inaction may indicate consent, provided such conduct would ordinarily be so interpreted, as where a reasonable person would be expected to speak or move if he objected.

Consent may be inferred from custom and usage, from prior dealings between the parties, or from the existence between them of some relationship. For example, where there is a general custom to embrace friends upon meeting, and plaintiff and defendant are friends, consent to an embrace may be assumed, at least until defendant is given notice to the contrary. Participants in sporting events thereby consent to the physical contacts consistent with the understood rules of the game, and perhaps even to contacts resulting from rule violations during the course of play. Consent ordinarily does not extend, however, to intentional harm not incidental to the play, as when the game is not in progress (e.g., after the whistle has blown).

The consent must be given by one having the capacity to do so, or one authorized to consent for him. Infancy, intoxication, or mental incapacity, known or obvious to defendant, ordinarily will vitiate effective consent. Consent in such cases, if required (as for medical treatment), must first be obtained from some person empowered to give it on plaintiff's behalf, such as his next of kin.

Where an emergency actually or apparently threatens death or serious bodily harm and there is no time or opportunity to obtain consent, it is said that consent is "implied," which is to say that defendant is privileged because he has no reason to believe that plaintiff or some one acting for her would not consent if given the chance.

The consent is to defendant's conduct, and therefore plaintiff cannot complain of the consequences of that particular conduct even though unforeseen. One who plays football consents to ordinary tackles, even if one renders him quadriplegic. But defendant's privilege is limited to the conduct consented to or acts substantially similar. Consent to right ear surgery (if, indeed, such consents are ever so limited in medicine today) does not authorize surgery on the left (absent an unforeseen emergency). And consent to an operation does not create a privilege to perform it negligently. In addition, the consent may be conditioned or limited as to time, place, duration, area and extent, and defendant will be liable to the extent that she fails to conform to the conditions or limitations.

Even though plaintiff's consent is given pursuant to his material mistake, misunderstanding or ignorance as to the nature or character of defendant's proposed conduct or the extent of the harm to be expected from it, the consent is effective as manifested unless defendant knows of the mistake or induced it by his misrepresentation. Even here, the mistake must go to the essential character of the act or its consequences, and not merely some collateral inducement, in order for the privilege to be lost. Suppose plaintiff consents to permit defendant to punch him in the nose in return for fifty dollars. The consent is still effective even though the money is counterfeit and defendant knows it, but not if defendant is secretly wearing brass knuckles. In the former case there may be an action for deceit or upon the contract, but not for battery.

The doctrine of informed consent, applicable in professional negligence ("malpractice") cases, is derived from these rules. For example, if a physician misrepresents or fails to disclose the proposed treatment or consequences that he knows are certain to follow from it, knowing of the patient's ignorance of these matters, the patient's consent is ineffective. Some cases have gone beyond this and vitiated the consent, and thus found a battery, where the doctor merely failed to disclose known *risks* inherent in the treatment. The prevailing view is to treat the failure to disclose mere risks as collateral, and thus a matter of negligence only, which permits inquiry into the proper professional standards of disclosure, instead of making full disclosure mandatory in all cases.

Consent is not effective if it is given under duress, which of course includes actual physical force, but it is not entirely clear what kinds of threats are sufficient. Threats of immediate harm directed against plaintiff, his family, or his valuable property are usually enough, depending upon the nature of the tort. But it has been held that threats of future harm, such as arrest, or "economic" duress such as loss of employment, do not render the consent ineffective (although some other tort may have been committed).

There is a division of authority as to whether plaintiff's consent is effective if the conduct consented to is a crime. At least in battery cases, the prevailing view seems to be that it is not, apparently on the theory that to hold otherwise would condone violence and lawlessness. However, a strong minority and the Restatement (§§ 60, 61, 892C) reject the notion that the specter of tort liability has any effect whatsoever on the parties' decision to engage in the conduct and hold that the consent in such cases is nevertheless effective, *except* in the case of statutes making conduct criminal in order to protect a certain class of persons irrespective of their consent—for example, statutes fixing the age of consent to sexual intercourse or prohibiting boxing matches because of the danger to the participants. The cases involving criminal abortions are divided, some holding the consent valid and denying recovery on the ground that the statute making the abortion illegal is for the benefit of the unborn child and the public and not the woman.

§ 7–3. Defense of Self and Others

Self–Defense. The basic instinct to defend one-self against the threat of harm together with the fundamental ethic that one has a right to do so justify the law's privilege to commit in self-defense an act that otherwise would be a tort. "Self-preservation is the first law of nature." It is a kind of self-help remedy, where there is no time to resort to the law. More often the threatened harm is battery, but there is also a privilege to use appropriate and reasonable force to defend against an unlawful confinement or arrest, and even against the threat of negligently caused harm. The defensive conduct may take the form of an assault, a battery, or a confinement, as appropriate to the situation.

The privilege exists not only where the danger to defendant is real, but also where defendant reasonably (but mistakenly) believes that self-defense is necessary. Thus, where plaintiff reaches into his pocket for the apparent purpose of retrieving a weapon, defendant may be privileged to act accordingly even though no weapon in fact existed. The reasonableness of defendant's belief, frequently a jury question, is judged by the objective standard of the reasonable person of average courage, and will depend, in part, on the circumstances of the event and the past history of the relationship, if any, between the parties.

Defendant may use only as much force as is or reasonably appears to be immediately necessary to protect himself. When he becomes the aggressor he exceeds the scope of the privilege, which does not encompass retaliation or revenge, and will be liable to the extent of the damage caused by the excessive force. Thus, he may not use violence after plaintiff is subdued, disarmed or helpless, or has clearly withdrawn from the fray or terminated the immediate threat. Nor may defendant use violence in response to verbal abuse, insults, threats for the future, or other mere provocation. Only defensive force is permitted.

Defendant may use force likely to inflict death or serious bodily harm *only* where (1) he reasonably believes that he is in danger of similar harm, and (2) it is not required that he retreat or escape. As to the latter, there is a division of authority. Some jurisdictions *never* require retreat, permitting defendant to defiantly stand his ground. However, others and the Restatement (§ 65) hold that defendant is not privileged to cause death or serious bodily harm, even in defense of a threat of similar harm, if he has some reasonable means of escape. Of course, retreat will be required only when it is obviously safe and expedient to do so, and if there is any reasonable doubt he need not flee. Moreover, there is an exception to the rule requiring flight, which is that one need not retreat if he is attacked within his own dwelling place, based apparently on the traditional sanctity of the home.

When in the course of defending himself defendant *accidentally* injures a third person, ordinary principles of negligence law apply and liability will depend on the reasonableness of defendant's conduct under the circumstances. However, if he *intentionally* causes harm to another (whose conduct was not the cause of defendant's jeopardy) because to do so is or seems necessary to save himself from harm, there is no privilege and defendant will be liable for at least compensatory damages for the harm he caused, unless it was relatively minor compared to the harm with which he was threatened. For example, where defendant kills an innocent person to save his own life, or uses another person as a shield to absorb a bullet meant for him, or intentionally runs down another and seriously injures him in order to escape his peril, he is liable; but not where the harm to the innocent bystander is merely offensive or slight, such as knocking him down or confining him against his will for a short time.

Defense of Others. In general, consistent with the Good Samaritan principle, the modern view seems to be that one is privileged to come to the defense of any third person. Absent mistake, he stands in that person's shoes and acquires that person's privilege of self-defense with the same rights and limitations.

Here, there is disagreement as to the effect of a mistake as to the actual necessity of intervention or the extent of the force required. Some courts hold that in such cases defendant assumes the risk that he is mistaken, and is privileged only if and to the extent that the third person was. However, other courts and the Restatement (§ 76) hold that a reasonable mistake does not negate the privilege.

§ 7–4. Defense and Recovery of Property

Defense of Property. One's interest in the peaceful possession and enjoyment of his property justifies a limited self-help privilege to defend it against imminent intrusions. However, the social value of property is considerably less than that of the safety and bodily integrity of human beings, and therefore the privilege is more limited than that of self-defense.

A possessor is privileged to use *reasonable* force to expel another or a chattel or to prevent another's intrusion upon his land or chattels, even though such conduct would otherwise be an assault, battery, false imprisonment, or trespass to the chattel.

There must be an actual intrusion or a threat of an immediate interference with defendant's possession.

Unless it would clearly be in vain or there is no time or opportunity, the possessor must first request that the intruder leave or desist. If he does not, defendant may use a threat of force or reasonable force itself, but it must be such as is minimally required to prevent or terminate the intrusion. Force or the threat of force calculated to cause death or great bodily harm is not permitted. But if the intruder persists, greater force may be used. The intruder, of course, has no privilege of self-defense, and if the intruder threatens bodily harm to defendant, ordinary principles of self-defense apply, and defendant may use any force required to defend his person, including the infliction of death or serious bodily harm if he is threatened with similar harm. But such force is never justified solely in defense of the property. Even the traditional notion that one may kill in defense of his dwelling house has been replaced in most jurisdictions by the more humane rule that such force is not permitted unless the intrusion threatens the personal safety of the occupants or the commission of a forcible felony.

Clearly, defendant may not do indirectly what he himself could not do. Spring guns, concealed traps and other mechanical devices, and vicious animals, calculated to cause death or great bodily harm, are used at the possessor's risk. He will be liable to the intruder for any harm that he would not have been privileged to inflict if he were personally present, in most cases notwithstanding posted warnings of the device or animal. R. § 85.

The same rules of apparent necessity apply here as in the case of self-defense. Note, however, that a mistake concerning the intruder's actual status is not privileged. Thus, where the intruder in fact has a privilege to intrude upon the land or chattel, the possessor's ignorance or mistake concerning the existence of that privilege is no defense to the tort he commits upon the intruder, unless the intruder himself was responsible for that mistake. Conversely, the intruder's mistake does not defeat the possessor's privilege unless the mistake was caused by the possessor's fault.

There are a number of rules that govern privileges to enter upon land and to invade interests in chattels. See R. §§ 167–215, 252–278. Except as discussed in the remainder of this section, or mentioned collaterally elsewhere, they are beyond the scope of this book.

Forcible Retaking of Chattels. Where plaintiff has wrongfully and forcibly taken defendant's chattel from his possession, even under claim of right, or obtained it by fraud or duress, the law recognizes a limited self-help privilege to recapture it by the use of force or threats of force.

Defendant must begin his recapture efforts promptly after his dispossession, or at least immediately upon learning of it, and must continue his efforts without interruption. He must be in "fresh pursuit." Where the chattel rightfully came into plaintiff's possession and he merely wrongfully detains it, or though wrongfully acquired defendant acquiesces in his possession for any period of time, defendant has no privilege and must resort to his legal remedies.

Ordinarily, where feasible, defendant must first demand return of the property. If plaintiff refuses, necessary and reasonable force may be used. Again, force calculated to cause serious bodily harm is not privileged. Of course, plaintiff is not privileged to resist, and if he does and thereby threatens defendant's person, defendant may use any force required to defend himself.

Unlike self-defense, defendant's mistake as to the existence of the privilege is no defense, unless knowingly induced by plaintiff.

Under certain circumstances, the privilege includes a privilege to enter upon another's land in pursuit of the chattel without liability for trespass, such as where the land is the plaintiff's or the possessor is aware of the facts and still refuses defendant reasonable entry, or is otherwise at fault. In other cases there may be a right to enter the land but liability for any damage caused thereby. But where the chattel is on the land with defendant's consent or through his fault, he must resort to legal process. A conditional seller of goods, by a clause in the contract, may acquire an irrevocable license to enter the buyer's premises upon his default and remove the property, but even this permits him only to enter peaceably, at a reasonable time and in a reasonable manner, and he will be liable if he uses any force to break in. A clause in the contract authorizing him to use force is probably void as contrary to public policy.

A special application of this principle of recapture is found in court decisions and statutes authorizing a shopkeeper to detain a suspected shoplifter for a reasonable time to investigate the suspected crime without liability for false imprisonment. See § 6–4.

Forcible Repossession of Land. One who as owner is entitled to the immediate possession of land may, if she can, peaceably enter the land and retake possession without liability for trespass, and may thereafter maintain her possession as discussed in the first part of this section.

The next question is, when is she privileged to use force to enter and evict the occupant without liability for assault, battery or some other tort.

If the occupant qualifies, he may be entitled, even as against the owner, to the protection of a forcible entry and detainer statute. These statutes are designed to prevent just such self-help remedies.

Assuming no such statute applies, defendant may use reasonable force to enter and take possession where:

(1) He (or his predecessor in title) was tortiously dispossessed, either without claim of right or under claim of right but by fraud, duress, or breaking and entering; or the occupant holds the land for the defendant.

(2) Plaintiff was the one who tortiously dispossessed defendant, or else plaintiff acquired custody or possession from someone who he knows or should know so dispossessed him.

(3) Defendant is in fact entitled to immediate possession.

(4) Defendant enters promptly after his dispossession or after he learns or should know of it.

Unless it would be useless, dangerous, or counterproductive to do so, defendant must first demand that plaintiff surrender possession. If he refuses, defendant may then use such reasonable force (short of that likely to cause serious bodily harm) as he reasonably believes necessary to effect the entry.

Here, as in the case of recapture of chattels, defendant's mistake as to the existence of his privilege is no defense unless knowingly induced by plaintiff.

§ 7–5. Necessity

The privilege of necessity may be invoked when defendant, in the course of defending himself or his property or others or their property from some threat of imminent harm for which plaintiff is *not* responsible, intentionally does some act reasonably deemed necessary toward that end that results in injury to plaintiff's property and that would otherwise be a trespass or a conversion.

Thus, it is analogous to the privileges of self-defense and defense of property, with the important difference that here plaintiff did not put defendant or his property in jeopardy and therefore plaintiff is entitled to greater protection. Hence, this privilege is more limited. In essence, an innocent plaintiff's property interest is necessarily sacrificed for a worthy cause. This may excuse the tort, but in some cases at least defendant will still be required to compensate plaintiff for his loss.

Frequently the decided cases have involved threats of harm from forces of nature, such as fires, floods, storms, disease, and the like. But the potential sources of harm are not so limited; all that is required is that the necessity arise from some independent cause not connected with the plaintiff.

The law distinguishes between "public" and "private" necessity. Where the danger affects the entire community, or so many people that the public interest is involved, most cases have held that the privilege is complete and defendant is entirely excused from liability. Thus one who dynamites a house to stop the spread of a fire that threatens the entire town, or destroys animals having an infectious disease to prevent its spread, or in time of war destroys property to prevent it from falling into enemy hands, is completely privileged and is not liable to the owner, provided the emergency is sufficiently great and defendant acted reasonably under the circumstances. This seems fair enough where defendant is a private individual, who ought not to have to pay out of his own pocket for acts that benefit the public. But most courts have held that the privilege is complete even where defendant is a governmental unit and the act was done by its employee or under its specific direction for the benefit of its citizens. (Moreover, the destruction of private property under such circumstances is generally construed not to be a "taking" under constitutional provisions requiring compensation where private property is taken for public use.) Such decisions would appear to be open to question.

Where no public interest is involved and the defendant acts only to protect a private interest, his own or that of another, it is deemed a "private necessity" and the privilege is properly more limited. Again, the emergency must be sufficiently great, and defendant must have acted reasonably under the circumstances. Defendant will not be liable for mere technical torts, such as a trespass on private land to escape a danger, and the possessor is not privileged to resist or expel him. But where the act causes actual damage, as where a boat is saved by being kept moored to a dock during a storm causing damage to the dock, defendant is required to compensate plaintiff for the injury. *Vincent v. Lake Erie Transp. Co.* (Minn. 1910); R. § 263.

As in the case of self-defense, defendant's reasonable mistake as to the existence of the privilege does not negate it.

§ 7–6. Authority of Law

There is, of course, a privilege to do that which is authorized or required by the law. The difficult problems here are in determining (1) what is the law, and whether it is valid, questions that often vex the best of lawyers, and (2) the effect of the actor's good faith mistake as to his legal authority. The execution of legal process by a public official is a common situation in which this privilege may be invoked.

The law commonly distinguishes between "discretionary" and "ministerial" acts. Where the law is such that a measure of judgment or discretion is required to be exercised in order to determine whether or how to act, such as to seek an indictment or to close a public street, the act is privileged so long as done honestly and in good faith. Ministerial acts (those requiring little or no personal judgment as to whether or how they shall be done—for example to close an office at five o'clock or to record a deed) are not privileged if done improperly, regardless of the actor's good faith. As might be expected, it has been found exceedingly difficult to distinguish one from the other, and the cases are in hopeless confusion.

Another such distinction is between acts done without jurisdiction, which are not privileged because not official acts at all, and acts that are merely "in excess of" the official's jurisdiction— that is, within the scope of the general subject matter of his power but outside his authority on the particular facts—which are privileged if done in good faith. Here also the distinction has been hard to make, and where the officer takes action under a law that later is declared unconstitutional, there is a tendency to hold that the act if done in good faith is privileged.

Arrest. Arrest of the person is one of the more common acts under authority of law. It may be with or without a warrant, which is simply a court order directing the arrest.

An arrest under a warrant, or the seizure of goods under civil process (to which the same rules apply), is generally regarded as a ministerial act, which means that the officer is not privileged unless his acts in fact conform to law. As noted above, there is no privilege if the warrant was issued by a court without jurisdiction to issue such warrants. But if the court has the general power to issue arrest warrants, the arrest is privileged if the warrant appears valid and proper on its face, even though there were errors or irregularities in its issuance that would be regarded as divesting the court of jurisdiction of this particular case.

In addition, the officer must properly carry out the order given her in the proper manner, and if she does not there is no privilege even where her act is based on an entirely reasonable good faith mistake. For example, if the warrant commands the arrest of *A*, but the officer arrests *B* instead, there is no privilege even though she reasonably believed that *B* was *A*.

Under certain circumstances, either a police officer or a private citizen may make a lawful arrest without a warrant. The common law developed an elaborate set of rules governing such arrests, which have now been largely superseded by statute. Again, such arrests are privileged, but only when in actual conformity to law.

Trespass ab Initio. The common law developed a fiction that where an act or series of acts was properly commenced under authority of law, and subsequently that authority was exceeded and a tort thereby committed, defendant's abuse of his authority "related back" and he was deemed to be a wrongdoer, without privilege, from the very beginning—ab initio. The result was that he was liable not merely for the subsequent tort, but as though his entire course of conduct, including the initial entry, seizure or arrest, had been tortious.

The doctrine has long been thoroughly discredited and disapproved, and has rarely been invoked except occasionally in cases of arrest. The Restatement (§§ 136, 214(2), 278(2)) has rejected it entirely, and most writers consider it doubtful that it will ever again be applied.

Immunity. In addition to the foregoing, one must remember that public officials and governmental entities are sometimes immune from tort liability for certain of their official acts. See § 11–1, infra.

§ 7–7. Discipline

Within certain relationships, as a matter of custom and necessity, one party is privileged to discipline the other by the intentional use of threats, physical coercion, corporal punishment, and restraint, which would otherwise constitute assault, battery, false imprisonment, and perhaps even the infliction of emotional distress.

The privilege of a parent, or one standing in the place of a parent, to use force and restraint in the control, training and education of his child, is the most common example. The privilege also extends to a school teacher, to the extent necessary to maintain order in and about the school, and when necessary for this purpose may even extend to discipline for the pupil's conduct away from the school premises.

Only the force reasonably necessary to accomplish the permissible purpose is privileged, and the teacher or the parent (if not otherwise immune; see § 11–3) may be liable to the extent that the force used is excessive. The reasonableness of the force used is a question of fact that depends upon a variety of factors, such as the nature of the offense and its apparent motive, the age, sex and physical and mental condition of the child, his past behavior, and the like. An external standard applies; the parent or teacher cannot be permitted to judge for himself what is reasonable. It must be administered in good faith for a proper purpose and without malice, and may not be unnecessarily degrading or calculated to cause serious or permanent harm.

Military officers have a privilege of discipline over their subordinates that is governed largely by military law. And the master of a ship may exercise reasonable discipline over his crew and passengers.

CHAPTER 8

SPECIAL LIABILITY RULES FOR PARTICULAR ACTIVITIES

§ 8–1. Introduction

To the general rules of tort liability for physical harm discussed in Chapters 3 through 7 there must be added a number of special liability rules that apply in particular fact situations. Chief among these are the rules discussed in this Chapter 8 that govern the liability of (and to) those engaged in certain activities with respect to those activities: owners and occupiers of land; sellers of products; employers, employees and contractors; owners and drivers of vehicles; and others.

In some cases, these special rules are merely specific applications of (and are consistent with) the general rules of tort liability previously discussed; they have evolved as separately stated rules because the recurrence of common fact situations has led the courts to generalize about them. In many cases, however, these special rules contract or expand the duty that would otherwise exist in response to felt considerations of social policy.

The trend of U.S. tort law during the twentieth century was to expand the scope of potential tort liability, especially as to business and property owners, mainly by: (1) abolishing duty limitations and immunities in negligence cases and moving toward a general duty of ordinary care under the circumstances for all activities; (2) abolishing special limitations on the class of persons to whom defendant's duty is owed (i.e., privity limitations) and applying ordinary rules of proximate cause to all; (3) making sellers of products strictly liable in tort for product defects; and (4) creating new liability rules by statute (e.g., workers' compensation, F.E.L.A., and auto compensation acts).

This chapter will provide an overview of the most important of these special liability rules.

A   OWNERS AND OCCUPIERS OF LAND

§ 8–2.   Liability to Persons Off the Premises

Until the late nineteenth century, real property was of dominant importance in the economics of England and America. Important social values included individualism and the sanctity of private property. Thus, predictably, the value of the rights to ownership, possession and use of land weighed heavily in the law's balance of competing interests, and special tort liability rules emerged that reflect this balance. So strong was the land ethic that it was not until the last third of the twentieth century that the special duty limitations favoring land owners and occupiers were restricted, if not entirely eliminated.

The term "owners and occupiers" reflects the fact that in general these special rules may be invoked only by (or against) the possessor of the land—the person who occupies it or, if it is not occupied, its owner who is then deemed to be in possession. The benefits and burdens of the rules stated in this Subchapter A ordinarily extend (1) to activities carried on by members of the possessor's household (R. § 382) and (2) to activities conducted and conditions created on the land by another who is acting for the possessor (R. §§ 383, 384). If one who conducts an activity or creates a condition on land does not fit one of these categories, then the special liability rules discussed in this subchapter do not apply to him and he is liable or not according to the usual rules of tort law (R. § 386).

In the main, the special liability rules applicable to possessors of land take the form of limitations on the duty of landowners and occupiers to take affirmative precautions for the safety of persons who enter upon the land for nonbusiness purposes, with or without permission. These are discussed in the sections that follow.

As to persons *outside* the premises, however, no social policy operates in favor of a limited duty rule. Even under the view that a possessor of land ought to be free to do as he pleases within the confines of his own property, it is agreed that his special domain ends at its boundaries and he must exercise reasonable care to see that activities and possessor-created conditions on his premises do not harm his neighbors or passers-by on adjacent ways. R. §§ 364, 365, 366, 370, 371.

Liability to persons off the premises is, of course, not limited to negligence. It may be based upon principles of intent, negligence, or strict liability as discussed in the preceding chapters, or in accordance with the law of nuisance discussed in § 8–18, infra. But where the theory of the action is the possessor's negligence, the courts have articulated a number of rules. For the most part, these are but special applications of the general principles of negligence in fact situations that frequently recur.

Adjacent Public Ways. Many cases have involved dangers to persons traveling on public ways (highways, streets, alleys, sidewalks) adjacent to defendant's land. The possessor's duty to them is one of reasonable care, and thus he may be liable where he obstructs a public way, allows a sign or structure to fall upon it, or conducts an activity upon his land so as to create a foreseeable and unreasonable risk of harm to travelers. R. § 368.

His duty may require him to foresee slight deviations from the public way upon his land, and so to exercise reasonable care not to cause or allow unsafe artificial conditions (e.g., an excavation) so close to the public way as to create an unreasonable risk of harm to those who so deviate. This includes both inadvertent deviations (e.g., where a pedestrian slips and falls off the sidewalk and onto defendant's land) and even in a proper case one who deviates intentionally for some purpose connected with his travel (e.g., a pedestrian who stops momentarily in defendant's doorway to tie his shoelace).

Intentional deviations by children may be quite foreseeable (see § 8–4, infra). R. § 369. But where the adult traveler leaves the public way, enters upon defendant's land, and temporarily ceases his journey (e.g., to rest or to chat with a friend), he ceases to be a traveler and becomes a trespasser with all the consequences of that status (see § 8–3, infra).

While most cases have involved deviations of only a few feet, what is important is not so much the distance as the foreseeability that a normal user will deviate so as to encounter the danger. Cf. R. § 367 (possessor maintains a part of his land so that it appears to be a public highway).

Natural Conditions. The traditional rule has been that reasonable care does not require the possessor of land to alter its natural condition so as to prevent harm—however foreseeable—to persons outside the premises or to adjoining land. R. § 363(1). Typically, these cases involve harm caused by (1) the natural flow of surface water off the land, (2) natural accumulations of ice and snow on adjacent public sidewalks, and (3) trees that die and fall upon adjacent ways.

This principle is strictly limited. If the possessor or anyone else has ever altered the natural condition of the land so as to create or aggravate the risk, the possessor is subject to liability—for example, where he or another erects or maintains a structure such that water, snow or ice is discharged or unnaturally accumulates on a public way, or plants a row of trees next to a highway, or landscapes so as to change the natural flow of water, or dams a stream, or piles sand where it will blow. And, of course, the occupier may be liable if he undertakes to remove snow or ice from his premises or an adjoining public way and does so negligently.

Moreover, it must be remembered that the "natural conditions" rule developed in a predominantly rural society where tracts of land were large and it might indeed be an unreasonable burden to require the possessor to take affirmative action to alter the natural state of his property when he was making no use of the land that would itself require him to do so. There are indications that the courts may be willing to modify the rule with respect to land in urban areas when ordinary principles of negligence compel a different result. For example, it is now generally agreed that an urban property owner may be liable for his negligence in failing to inspect and maintain his trees so as to prevent an unreasonable risk of harm to passers-by on adjoining public ways. R. § 363(2).

§ 8–3. Trespassing Adults

When plaintiff's injury occurs *on* premises occupied by defendant, a different situation is presented. Except in the rare case where the visitor enters under a privilege conferred by law, a possessor of private property may, of course, determine whom he will allow to enter upon it, and the conditions of the visit. Therefore, the amount of care that the possessor may *reasonably* be required to exercise to make the premises safe for plaintiff's visit (or to discover dangers and warn of them) depends on (1) the extent to which his entry is foreseeable, (2) the scope and other conditions of his privilege to enter, if any, and (3) the purpose of his visit. The latter is relevant on the theory that the greater the benefit or potential benefit of the visit to the possessor, the greater should be his obligation to take precautions for the visitor's safety.

The common law might have simply left the question whether the possessor exercised reasonable care with respect to each plaintiff—that is, acted as a reasonably prudent occupier of land under the same or similar circumstances—to a case-by-case determination, as in other negligence cases, using the foregoing factors as guides to the trier of fact or as standards by which to review its decision. It did not. Perhaps the courts did not trust juries to give adequate protection to land owners. Instead, it divided entrants upon land into three rigid categories—(1) trespassers, (2) licensees, and (3) invitees—and then established fixed limitations on the possessor's duty with respect to trespassers and licensees.

As in the case of other duty limitations, these arbitrary classifications have proved increasingly unsatisfactory, and the courts have been required to change the definitions and to create exceptions to the duty limitations in order to do justice in the infinite variety of fact situations that occur. Dissatisfaction with this approach has now reached the point that courts and legislatures have begun to overthrow it and impose instead the prevailing general duty of ordinary care under the circumstances—one of those circumstances being the status of the entrant. This movement will be discussed in § 8–6.

Nevertheless, the traditional common law system of classifications and duty limitations is still the law in many jurisdictions. What, then, are these classifications and limitations?

Adult Trespassers. The law subdivides trespassers into (1) adults and (2) children, recognizing that the latter sometimes require special protection (§ 8–4 infra). Thus, the rules discussed in this section apply only to (1) trespassers who are of legal age and (2) trespassing children who do not meet the qualifications for special treatment.

A trespasser is a person who enters or remains upon land in possession of another without a privilege to do so. R. § 329. In the usual case, the privilege, if any, arises from the possessor's consent. See §§ 6–7 and Chapter 7, supra, and R. §§ 10 and 167–215 for discussions of such privileges. (While there are few cases, these same principles apply to one who trespasses upon a chattel (e.g., a motor vehicle).)

The general rule is that with respect to a trespasser, a possessor of land is under no duty to exercise reasonable care (1) to make the premises reasonably safe for him (or to warn him of hidden dangers) or (2) to carry on activities on the premises so as not to endanger him. R. § 333. So far as the possessor is concerned, one who is wrongfully on the premises must watch out for himself and take the premises as he finds them, concealed dangers and all. He has no right to expect ordinary care for his safety.

As to portions of the premises where no visitor is permitted to go, this rule is perhaps justifiable on the ground that in the usual case it leads to the same result as if general principles of negligence were applied. Generally a reasonably prudent possessor can safely ignore portions of the premises where visitors are prohibited. But the rule is not so limited. It applies, for example, to a portion of the premises as to which there is an open invitation to the public or which is otherwise frequently used by invitees (to whom the possessor would owe a duty of ordinary care), and despite the fact that there is an equally strong probability that either trespassers or invitees may be present. And it bars recovery by a technical trespasser who was on the premises in the good faith (but erroneous) belief that he had a privilege to be there and who meant no harm. One can even imagine a trespasser and an invitee standing side by side, both injured by the same negligent act of the possessor, the former being barred and the latter recovering a judgment. In other words, the possessor's limited duty to trespassers may sometimes prevent recovery where ordinary principles of negligence would not.

One might suppose that the rule could be justified in part on the ground that a trespasser is a wrong-doer whom the law will not assist. Not so; a trespasser injured while on the land by the negligence of anyone other than the possessor is not barred. R. § 386. The rule can only be understood as a special privilege possessed by the occupier of land solely by reason of his right to exclusive possession and control of the premises.

As in the case of other duty limitations, the law has been forced to recognize exceptions in situations where the equities favoring plaintiff outweigh the policies underlying the rule. Generally, these are cases where (1) the foreseeable probability of trespassers and (2) the nature and extent of the foreseeable harm to such trespassers outweigh (3) the burden to the possessor of taking precautions and (4) the value of his right to exclude others at will.

Intentional and Reckless Misconduct. Naturally enough, the possessor's privilege does not extend to intentional torts. Trespassers may not be shot merely for trespassing.

In addition, most jurisdictions have adopted the blanket rule that a possessor of land is subject to liability to a trespasser for harm caused by the possessor's "willful and wanton" or reckless misconduct. (This concept is discussed in § 4–7, supra. Some jurisdictions have rather generous interpretations of this concept in premises liability cases.) On the other hand, some courts (and the Restatement) do not recognize a general rule of liability for reckless misconduct; but almost all jurisdictions have embraced the rules discussed in the remainder of this section protecting (1) discovered trespassers and (2) frequent trespassers on a limited area. These special rules cover the most common fact situations in which reckless misconduct may be committed by a possessor against a trespasser, and in addition go further and subject the possessor in such situations to liability for ordinary negligence.

Frequent Trespassers Upon a Limited Area. When the possessor knows (or from facts within his knowledge ought to be aware) that trespassers constantly intrude upon a limited area of his premises, he is subject to liability for ordinary negligence with respect to them in two situations: (1) in the conduct of active operations on the premises that create a risk of harm to them (R. § 334); and (2) when he has created or maintains a dangerous artificial condition that he has reason to believe they will not discover, and he fails to warn them of the condition and the risk (R. § 335). For example, a railroad that knows that the public habitually crosses its tracks at a particular spot, albeit as trespassers, must exercise reasonable care for their safety in the operation of its trains at that point, and would have a duty to exercise reasonable care to warn them if it decided to electrify one of the rails. (In fact, many of the decided cases have involved railroad defendants.) Liability is justified on the ground that the frequency of the trespasses makes the presence of intruders highly foreseeable, and the limited area reduces the burden to defendant of protecting them. Although the cases mostly have involved activities or conditions that created risks of serious bodily harm or death, which would further justify liability, the rule need not be limited to such activities or conditions. R. §§ 334, Comment *b.*, and 335, Comment *b.*

Discovered Trespassers. From the rule that a possessor will be liable for intentional harm to a trespasser there evolved the rule that he will also be liable for willful and wanton misconduct with respect to a discovered trespasser. A few courts have still not yet gone beyond this point. Some have broadened the rule to include *all* reckless conduct, whether the trespasser's presence is known or not. But almost all courts now go further and hold that once the possessor discovers the presence of the plaintiff-trespasser on his premises, the possessor's duty to him is similar to that stated in the preceding paragraph, with equal or greater justification. If he has reason to believe that a discovered trespasser is unaware of a danger arising from active operations on the premises, he must exercise reasonable care to warn him of that danger, or if it is apparent that a warning is not enough, he must exercise reasonable care to conduct or control these activities so as not to injure him (R. §§ 336, 338). And while there is older authority to the contrary, modern authority holds that he must exercise reasonable care to warn the known trespasser of a dangerous artificial condition to which the trespasser is in dangerous proximity if the possessor has reason to believe that the trespasser will not discover the danger or appreciate the extent of the risk (R. § 337). In these cases, the presence of a trespasser is no longer merely foreseeable, it is a known fact; and the burden of protecting him is less than the burden of protecting merely foreseeable trespassers because it is now focused on a particular person in a particular situation. Therefore the equities justify a duty of ordinary care. Again, the cases have mainly involved risks of serious bodily harm, but the principle need not be so limited. R. §§ 336, Comment *b.*, and 337, Comment *b.*

A corollary rule is that the possessor may have a duty to exercise reasonable care to rescue or aid a trespasser who is injured or in peril on his premises even though the possessor is not legally liable for the trespasser's condition. *Pridgen v. Boston Housing Auth.* (Mass. 1974).

Note that the possessor's duty to even a discovered trespasser is *not* a general duty of reasonable care; he is not obligated to make the premises reasonably safe for the trespasser, but merely in the first instance to exercise reasonable care to warn him of proximate dangerous conditions and activities, and as to active operations to conduct or control them for the trespasser's protection only when it is apparent that a warning is insufficient.

§ 8–4. Trespassing Children

By custom and tradition, all adults have a special responsibility for the physical safety of children, and this is no less true of possessors of land. Children at play instinctively wander and explore, more or less oblivious to property lines. It is neither customary nor practical for their parents to confine them or to supervise them closely at all times. And by reason of their immaturity, lack of judgment, and inexperience, they often do not recognize nor fully appreciate the dangers in their surroundings.

Thus, it is generally agreed that the arbitrary and rigid limitations on the possessor's duty to trespassers would lead to especially unjust results in many cases if they were applied across the board to trespassing children. Accordingly, most courts have held that these considerations alter the balance of competing interests in such cases, and have adopted special liability rules that impose on landowners and occupiers a greater duty of care as to children.

These special liability rules are equally applicable to children who are trespassers, licensees, and even invitees (R. § 343B). But the cases almost always involve youngsters who are trespassing and so the doctrine is invariably discussed as to them.

The doctrine is sometimes called the "turntable doctrine" because it originated in two cases, both of which involved a trespassing child injured while playing on a railroad turntable. *Sioux City & P. Ry. v. Stout* (U.S. 1873); *Keffe v. Milwaukee & St. P. Ry.* (Minn. 1875). In *Keffe,* the court rationalized its result on the theory that the turntable had attracted the child onto the defendant's land and thus defendant, having induced the trespass, would not be permitted to set it up as a defense. This theme was picked up in subsequent cases, and from this idea the doctrine acquired the unfortunate misnomer "attractive nuisance," a label that persists to this day. It cannot be taken literally, since the courts have now largely rejected the notion that the child must be attracted by that which injures him, and whether or not the condition is in fact a "nuisance" (see § 8–19) has nothing at all to do with defendant's liability to the child.

Despite its apparent equity, the doctrine has not had universal acceptance. A number of jurisdictions initially rejected it as too soft on trespassers, and while most of these have since reversed themselves and adopted it in some form, there are still a few states where it is not recognized as such.

Among the jurisdictions that do accept the concept, there are important differences in its component liability rules. However, the courts have increasingly relied upon the Restatement's formulation of the doctrine in § 339, and it now represents the most widely held version. Under § 339, "A possessor of land is subject to liability for physical harm to children trespassing thereon caused by an artificial condition upon the land" if the following requirements are met.

(a) [T]he place where the condition exists is one upon which the possessor knows or has reason to know that children are likely to trespass. . . .

It is not enough that trespasses by children are merely foreseeable. But neither does the possessor have to have actual knowledge that children are entering upon his premises. This requirement is met if he has such knowledge, or if he has actual knowledge of facts from which he ought to infer that such trespasses are likely to occur. In other words, he need not inspect the premises to determine whether children are present or whether the conditions are conducive to their trespasses, but he is held to what he actually knows about his premises and what he can reasonably anticipate based upon that knowledge.

In most jurisdictions, it is not necessary that the child be attracted onto the premises by the condition that injures him. This was once a fairly common requirement, derived from the "attraction" justification for the rule that originated in the *Keffe* case and given impetus by a much-criticized opinion by Mr. Justice Holmes in *United Zinc & Chemical Co. v. Britt* (U.S. 1921); but this limitation has now been largely abandoned. It is enough that children who do trespass for whatever reason can be expected to encounter the condition. Thus, it is not necessary that the condition be an open and obvious one, or that the child intermeddle with it or even discover it prior to his injury.

(b) [T]he condition is one of which the possessor knows or has reason to know and which he realizes or should realize will involve an unreasonable risk of death or serious bodily harm to such children. . . .

The doctrine applies only to *conditions* on the land, not to activities. Of course, as to the latter the child has the same protection given to all other trespassers (see § 8–3, R. §§ 334, 336).

The possessor need not have created the condition; it is sufficient that he maintains it or permits it to exist. However, it is generally held that the doctrine applies only to "artificial" (i.e., man-made) conditions (e.g., structures, excavations, swimming pools, machinery and equipment) and not to natural conditions such as trees, land formations, and bodies of water (including, however, man-made lakes and ponds that resemble those that exist in nature).

This limitation is derived from the broader rule that the hazard must be an unusually dangerous one. The key phrase is "unreasonable risk." Some critics of this doctrine have failed to observe that it is not every condition on the land that presents a foreseeable risk of harm to a child that will subject the possessor to liability. The condition must create a risk of serious bodily harm to a child that is unreasonable in light of the utility of the condition and the burden to the possessor of reducing or eliminating the danger to the child. In addition, the risk is not unreasonable if the child whose trespass is to be anticipated can be expected to observe and fully appreciate the danger and avoid it. There are a number of cases denying liability where a child trespasser injures himself or another while engaged in recklessly making some hazardous use of an object or condition that, in and of itself, presents no unusual danger. Quite apart from any issue of contributory negligence, the possessor is not liable because the risk was not unreasonable, provided the possessor could expect the child to perceive and appreciate the consequences of his reckless misuse. The possessor is not required to make his premises "child-proof."

Fears that this doctrine will be abused have led some courts to create arbitrary categories of conditions for which there is no liability. It is sometimes said that a possessor is not liable for "common hazards," or is liable only for "dangerous instrumentalities." Thus, some courts have held that any child old enough to be allowed to wander about will be held as a matter of law to be capable of appreciating such dangers as fire, falling from a height, drowning in water, ordinary visible machinery in motion, piles of lumber, and so forth. But like all such rigid rules, they have tended to break down in particular cases, as where the possessor knows or has reason to know that the children who are likely to trespass are so young that they cannot appreciate the danger, or where there is some unusual or enhanced danger associated with the condition that is *not* apparent to the child. The trend is to abandon such arbitrary rules.

Here lies the true basis for the rule excluding liability for natural conditions of the land. In the typical case the hazards presented by such conditions do not create *unreasonable* risks, because almost all children may be expected to appreciate them and the burden of altering or guarding them usually is disproportionately great. Cases may arise, however, in which the risk even of a natural condition might be an unreasonable one under the circumstances, and hence the Restatement leaves open the possibility of liability in such cases. R. § 339, Caveat and Comment *p*.

In addition, the risk must be one of serious bodily harm or death to the child; but if it is, the possessor will of course be liable for any lesser injury that the child in fact sustains.

The possessor must know, or have reason to know, (1) of the existence of the condition and (2) that the condition presents an unreasonable risk of serious harm to a child of the class whose trespass he knows or should know is likely. Here, also, there is no duty to inspect the premises, but the possessor is charged with the facts he actually knows and logical inferences from those facts.

(c) [T]he children because of their youth do not discover the condition or realize the risk involved in intermeddling with it or in coming within the area made dangerous by it. . . .

It must be proved that the child did not recognize and fully appreciate the risk—that is, did not assume the risk (§ 5–5)—by reason of his age and inexperience. This is, of course, to be distinguished from contributory negligence, which is unreasonable conduct. The child may have been too young to be capable of contributory negligence, or may have acted reasonably for a child of his age, but he cannot recover if he knew of the condition and fully understood the danger and proceeded to encounter it anyway. And plaintiff has the burden of proof on this.

As might be expected, most of the cases have involved rather young children, usually under twelve. A few courts have established an arbitrary age limit for the doctrine, such as fourteen. In theory, however, there is no reason why it should not apply to children as old as sixteen or seventeen if the hazard is a particularly sophisticated one, and the Restatement no longer limits the doctrine to "young" children. But obviously, the older the child the fewer the dangers which it may be found he did not understand and appreciate.

(d) [T]he utility to the possessor of maintaining the condition and the burden of eliminating the danger are slight as compared with the risk to children involved, and

(e) the possessor fails to exercise reasonable care to eliminate the danger or otherwise to protect the children.

Clauses (d) and (e) are somewhat duplicative of each other, since (d) is essentially Judge Learned Hand's classic test for negligence and (e) merely reiterates that the possessor must have been negligent. It would appear that the purpose of clause (d) is to give the court an additional opportunity to rule that the risk was not unreasonable as a matter of law since the question whether defendant was negligent (clause (e)) is ordinarily one of fact for the jury. The term "slight" in clause (d) could be interpreted as imposing a greater burden upon plaintiff than in other negligence cases, where plaintiff need only establish that the utility and burden to defendant were "less than" the risk, but there is no indication in the authorities that any such greater proof is required. Nor is there anything to suggest that the term "eliminating the danger" should not include *warning* of the danger, as it would in other cases, assuming of course that a warning would have been a reasonable and effective means of protecting the child against the risk.

It will be seen that the duty created by § 339 is not very far removed from the one that would be imposed if we simply said that a possessor of land must exercise reasonable care for the safety of foreseeable child trespassers. But the practical difference is that questions of negligence are for the jury but questions of duty are for the court, and thus by stating these rules as duty limitations, the courts retain greater control over the outcome of these cases.

§ 8–5. Licensees and Invitees

One who enters upon the premises of another with a privilege to do so is either a licensee or an invitee. Actually, the term "licensee," strictly speaking, encompasses *all* such entrants, including invitees. However, in this branch of the law it is customary to use "licensee" in a narrower sense to mean those who enter with a privilege but not as invitees.

Much controversy and confusion has surrounded the classification of particular entrants upon land, especially as between licensees and invitees, a subject that will be discussed later in this section. At the outset, however, it must be noted that the term "invitee" can be confusing unless it is remembered that not all persons who come upon the premises at the invitation of the possessor are invitees. In a nutshell, the distinction is this. An invitee is one *invited* by the possessor to enter or remain upon his land *for a particular purpose;* traditionally, that purpose had to be one that involved some *economic benefit* to the possessor. Thus, the term "business invitee" was often used to describe the entire class of invitees. The typical example is a customer in a store. Most courts today have broadened invitee status to include persons on land as a member of the *public* for a purpose for which the land is held open to the public—for example, a visitor to a public park or beach. R. § 332. Absent one of these purposes, however, one who is invited and even encouraged to come or remain upon another's land is in many states merely a licensee. A typical example is a social guest in one's home. Licensee status also includes those who enter merely with the possessor's express or implied consent, and usually also those who enter pursuant to some other privilege. Compare R. §§ 330, 345.

Duty to Licensees. Traditionally, the duty owed to a licensee has been very close to the duty owed to a trespasser. The possessor is under no general duty to exercise reasonable care for his safety. The possessor must not injure him intentionally or by reckless or "willful and wanton" misconduct. He must conduct active operations on the premises with due care for his safety once his presence is discovered, and if the presence of licensees at a particular place is to be expected he must conduct such operations with a view toward the possibility of their presence. R. § 341. As to such operations, however, he may assume that the licensee will watch out for himself to the extent that he can and that the licensee will not expect the possessor to alter his customary activities for the licensee's benefit.

As to static conditions, the licensee, like the trespasser, must take the premises as he finds them. He is not entitled to have the premises made safe for his visit, nor is the possessor required to inspect the premises for the benefit of the licensee.

The principal difference between the duties to licensees and trespassers is that the licensee is entitled to be *warned* of *concealed* dangerous conditions of which the possessor has *"actual knowledge"* and the licensee does not, and which the licensee is not likely to discover. R. § 342. (The Restatement says "knows or has reason to know," but the cases generally have required something very close to actual knowledge.) The duty here is to exercise reasonable care to *warn,* and hence whether a warning is required and when and how it should be given will be judged by what a reasonably prudent possessor would have done under the same or similar circumstances, knowing what he actually knew about the condition, the foreseeability of the licensee's presence, and the likelihood that the licensee would encounter it without discovering it first.

Duty to Invitees. The duty owed to an invitee can be stated very simply; it is to exercise reasonable care for his safety. R. §§ 341A, 343. The possessor must take the precautions that a reasonably prudent possessor of land would take under the circumstances to make the premises reasonably safe for his invitees. This may, in a given case, require that he inspect the premises to discover dangerous conditions, keep the premises in safe repair, remove hazards where invitees are likely to walk, obviate slippery conditions, anticipate foreseeable activities and uses by invitees and others (R. § 344), and, of course, conduct active operations on the premises with reasonable care for their safety. And when a hazard cannot reasonably be reduced or eliminated, he must exercise reasonable care to warn invitees of the danger. Of course, the possessor is not a guarantor of his invitees' safety; his duty is only to exercise *reasonable* care. For example, he may reasonably expect that invitees will avoid known or obvious dangers if they can, and he will not be liable unless the patent danger is such that injuries to invitees exercising proper care for their own safety can be anticipated. R. §§ 343(b), 343A. As in all other negligence cases, the question whether the possessor has exercised reasonable care is ordinarily for the jury.

The possessor's duty to invitees is, of course, nondelegable, and he will be liable if his employee or an independent contractor whom he has hired to perform it for him fails to perform it properly.

An interesting question that arises from time to time is the extent of the possessor's duty to a business invitee to protect him against criminal violence by third persons on the premises. The authorities are divided. Some courts have held on particular facts that there is no duty, for example, to accede to criminal demands even at the risk of harm to an invitee (e.g., *Boyd v. Racine Currency Exch.*, Ill. 1973); but in other cases the possessor's negligence has been held a question of fact for the jury.

Classifications of Entrants. The most difficult and controversial problems in this area involve attempts to define the categories of entrants and to apply the definitions in particular cases.

As between licensees and trespassers, the line is not too hard to find. In the usual case the issue is whether the entrant had a privilege to enter arising from the possessor's manifestation of consent that he do so. Such consent may be express, or implied from words or conduct. A recurring question is whether the possessor's mere failure to object to entry may be interpreted as a manifestation of consent; the answer is that it may or may not, depending upon all the facts. The test is whether, in light of all the surrounding circumstances, a reasonable person would interpret the possessor's words or conduct as manifesting that he is in fact willing for another to enter or remain upon his land. For example, when the possessor constructs or maintains a path or roadway across his premises, or permits another to do so, he may have manifested consent to entry, especially if he then tolerates some public use of it; but not if he erects a gate or barrier or posts a "no trespassing" sign. But when discouraging or prohibiting trespassers would be unduly burdensome (e.g., pedestrians who walk along defendant's railroad tracks), mere tolerance of such entries ordinarily may not reasonably be interpreted as manifesting permission for them. Consent may also be implied from customs of the community, at least in the absence of a locked gate or posted notice to the contrary. Thus, a traveler in need of assistance, solicitors and canvassers, and friends paying a social call may ordinarily infer consent at least to enter and knock upon the occupier's door unless otherwise informed.

Typical licensees include persons on the land solely for their own purposes, members of the occupier's household, and social guests. (Servants and paying lodgers are invitees.) Classifying social guests as licensees has been justified on the ground that they should stand in no better position than members of the possessor's own household and must take the premises on the same terms. However, there is a good deal of dissatisfaction in placing the possessor's friends, who usually have been expressly invited and even urged to visit, in the same class as canvassers and bill collectors and only slightly ahead of trespassers, and in preferring the possessor's business visitors (who may be strangers) to his friends who provide him the important benefits of friendship and companionship. Thus, as will be noted, there is a trend to merge the licensee and invitee categories, or to broaden the invitee category to include those with an express invitation.

Incidental services performed by the guest do not transform her into an invitee. The visitor's gratuitous services must be sufficiently substantial that she could reasonably expect additional protection in return for them before she can be deemed an invitee. Nor does the existence of a business motive lurking in the invitation (as where the boss is invited to dinner) transform a social guest into an invitee.

By analogy to social guests, some jurisdictions used to treat guest passengers in automobiles as the equivalent of licensees upon real property. See § 8–16, infra. These special "guest passenger" rules have now been almost entirely abandoned.

As previously noted, invitees traditionally have included at least persons invited to enter the premises for a purpose which involves some economic benefit to the possessor. His greater duty is justified as the quid pro quo for that benefit. Customers of stores and patrons of theaters, banks, places of amusement, and the like are all invitees. So are persons making or receiving, deliveries of goods, and employees and independent contractors of the possessor doing work on the premises. The list is, of course, endless.

At one time, the "economic benefit" test was the sole test in most jurisdictions. So confined, the courts displayed considerable ingenuity in finding the requisite economic benefit when required to reach a just result. Thus, persons entering a place of business merely to browse or use a public telephone or public rest room or entering a bank to change a bill, and friends or children accompanying a customer to the store or other place of business all have been held to be invitees on the somewhat specious ground that the economic benefit may be merely potential, indirect, or remote in time.

The fact that the courts have had to stretch the economic benefit test past the logical limits of its underlying rationale is a good sign that there is something wrong with the test. It is too narrow to encompass the entire spectrum of cases in which invitee status is justified. Accordingly, the courts have gradually developed a second test, called the "public invitation" test, which supplements and expands it, and is now recognized in most jurisdictions. It extends invitee status to members of the public where (1) defendant invites the public (or some segment of the public) to enter his premises and (2) plaintiff enters for a purpose for which the invitation was extended. Under this test, invitees include persons attending free public meetings, lectures, church services, and college reunions, spectators at free public amusements, and those using public or private land held open to the public for a recreational or social purpose, absent any economic benefit whatsoever to the possessor. (Statutes in most states have modified this rule as to recreational land. See page 234, infra.)

The Restatement codifies both tests in § 332:

(1) An invitee is either a public invitee or a business visitor.

(2) A public invitee is a person who is invited to enter or remain on land as a member of the public for a purpose for which the land is held open to the public.

(3) A business visitor is a person who is invited to enter or remain on land for a purpose directly or indirectly connected with business dealings with the possessor of the land.

What is the element common to all these persons that justifies their classification as invitees? Such entrants are entitled to expect that the premises have been made reasonably safe for them. In these circumstances, the invitation may be construed as carrying with it an implied representation by the possessor that reasonable care has been exercised for their safety during their visit, upon which representation they are entitled to rely. The courts have now come to recognize that this reliance is justified, and ought to be protected, not only where the possessor derives some economic benefit from the visit, but also where the premises are opened to the public for whatever purpose.

Thus, consistent with this rationale, a person is an invitee only when the possessor expressly or impliedly invites or encourages his entry, and not when his presence is merely tolerated or permitted. This is true even though he enters for a purpose of mutual economic benefit. Thus, a salesman who calls at a private home or place of business without an invitation or appointment is ordinarily a licensee unless and until he is invited to remain and discuss his business, unless custom would imply the invitation. And a property owner who merely permits neighborhood children to play on his vacant lot does not make them invitees unless he somehow encourages such use, as by improving the premises for them.

By the same token, a visitor is an invitee only when he is upon the area of the premises within the scope of the invitation, which in turn depends upon the physical character of the premises and the purpose that makes him an invitee. It extends, of course, to any portion of the premises to which the purpose of his visit may be expected to take him and which gives the appearance of being open to him, including entrances and exits, public rest rooms and telephones, and other common areas. As to portions of the premises normally maintained for the private use of the possessor and her employees (e.g., storerooms, private rest rooms and private telephones), plaintiff may be an invitee, licensee, or trespasser, depending on whether he was invited or encouraged to go there for a purpose consistent with the purpose of his visit, or goes there as a social guest or on his own initiative and with the possessor's mere consent, or goes there without permission. Similarly, a visitor's status as an invitee may be limited in time, either expressly or by the purpose of the visit.

Public Employees. Persons who enter upon defendant's premises without invitation or even consent but pursuant to some other privilege, such as to recapture a chattel or in pursuit of a felon (see R. §§ 191–211 as to such privileges) are ordinarily classified as licensees. R. § 345(1). But the courts have had considerable difficulty with one group of such persons: public employees who enter on official business involving the occupier.

Publicly-employed sanitary and safety inspectors, garbage collectors, meter readers, postmen, and even revenue collectors are generally held to be invitees on the theory that their visits, while not always an economic benefit, are at least an economic necessity. A better rationale is that such visits are required by law and definitely foreseeable, and the visitor may reasonably rely on the fact that the portion of the premises where he is to be expected has been made reasonably safe for him.

Firemen and policemen present the greatest problem. Traditionally they have been classified as licensees, the best justification being that they arrive at unexpected times and go to unexpected places and thus it might be an inordinate burden on the landowner to provide for their safety. Nevertheless, this is not invariably true; and even when it is true, ordinary principles of negligence and proximate cause arguably would provide adequate protection to the occupier when the time or place of entry is unforeseeable.

Accordingly, there is something of a trend to broaden the landowner's duty to them. Some courts treat them as a special separate category, more than licensees but less than invitees; for example, some hold that they are invitees in certain situations, as when a policeman routinely and thus foreseeably makes an after-hours security check of defendant's business premises (*Cameron v. Abatiell*, Vt. 1968) or when a fireman or policeman is injured by an unsafe condition on a portion of the premises held open to the public (R. § 345(2)). At least one court has held that they are always invitees. *Dini v. Naiditch* (Ill. 1960). And other courts are beginning to reach the same result by abolition of the classifications and substituting a general duty of reasonable care under the circumstances, either as to public employees (*Spencer v. B. P. John Furniture Co.*, Or. 1970) or generally, as discussed in the next section.

Note that even if he owes the fireman a duty of reasonable care, the possessor is not liable to him for injuries caused by the fire itself notwithstanding the fact that the fire resulted from the possessor's negligence.

Recreational Entrants. All but a few states now have statutes that limit the liability of a landowner or possessor to visitors whom he invites or permits to come upon his land for recreational purposes, provided he makes no charge to, or receives no "consideration" from, the visitor. The occupier's duty varies and the individual statute must be consulted, but in general the visitor's status is similar to that of a licensee or trespasser.

§ 8–6. Rejection of Categories

There has long been an undercurrent of dissatisfaction with the rigid categories of trespasser, licensee, and invitee, and increasingly with the proliferation of rules and subrules and exceptions necessary to administer them. In addition, there is strong sentiment to the effect that in our increasingly urban and crowded society, land owners no longer need or deserve special protection. Many legal writers have urged that the categories be abolished and replaced with a single duty applicable to possessors in all premises liability cases: a duty to exercise reasonable care under the circumstances, one of those circumstances being the status of the plaintiff. Premises liability cases would thus be treated the same as other negligence cases, and the foreseeability of the entrant's presence, the purpose of his visit, and the extent to which he could reasonably expect the premises to be made safe for him would be subsumed under the general principles of negligence, proximate cause, contributory negligence, and assumption of risk.

England abolished the distinction between licensees and invitees by statute in 1957, substituting a single duty of care owed to all lawful visitors (i.e., everyone other than trespassers) and enumerating various factors to be considered. In 1959, the U.S. Supreme Court did the same for purposes of admiralty jurisdiction, holding that the ship owes a duty of reasonable care to all persons lawfully on board. *Kermarec v. Compagnie Generale Transatlantique.*

The first state to abolish the categories was California. In the oft-cited *Rowland v. Christian* (Cal. 1968), the court held that whether plaintiff was an invitee, licensee or even trespasser makes no difference as to the duty owed to him—henceforth the general duty of reasonable care—but may be considered on the issue of what was reasonable care under the circumstances.

Since then, about half the states have modified their classifications, either by legislation or judicial decision, but most of these have retained the trespasser status and the traditional rules that go with it. These jurisdictions have either included social guests (or others with an express invitation) in the invitee category, or simply merged the invitee and licensee categories. Only a handful have merged all three categories.

Although it is likely that more states will follow this trend, it is doubtful that the states will ever be unanimous on this. The greatest disagreement concerns the trespasser category. The decisions following *Rowland* usually include dissenting opinions, and some cases expressly disapprove it, even while imposing a greater duty on the possessor with respect to lawful visitors.

The reasons advanced for retaining the categories include: (1) they make sense; (2) they have been painstakingly developed and should not be discarded without compelling justification; (3) they work sufficiently well; (4) in general, they have evolved to keep pace with changing social policy, and can continue to do so; (5) they reflect judgments on matters of social policy, which are for the courts and not for the jury; and (6) juries are notoriously sympathetic to plaintiffs and cannot be trusted to give proper weight to the interests of the landowner. The latter is most likely the most important justification.

§ 8–7. Lessors

The general rule is that a lessor of real property is not liable to his lessee or anyone else for physical harm sustained by such persons during the term of the lease as a result of a condition of the premises, even though that condition existed at and before the time the lessee took possession. R. §§ 355, 356. Traditionally, as a matter of property law a lease is the equivalent of a sale of the premises for a term. During that period of time the lessee becomes the owner and occupier and he is entitled to exclusive possession of the premises, even against the lessor (unless the lease provides otherwise). Absent a contrary provision in the lease, he alone has the right and the responsibility to keep the leased premises in repair and otherwise to determine how they shall be maintained and used.

However, to this general rule there are several important exceptions. The trend has been to enlarge the number and scope of these exceptions, mainly in recognition of the changing nature of the landlord-tenant relationship and the economic realities of life. In today's society, the typical lease is not a demise of a plot of ground but a contract for the use of space in the lessor's building. Especially in the case of residential leases, the landlord often has the superior bargaining power and can virtually dictate the terms of the lease. And it is he who receives the rent and who has the greater incentive, opportunities and resources to maintain the premises; he is the one who can allocate and distribute maintenance costs and best insure against the risks inherent in the condition of those parts of the premises which are there when the tenant takes possession and will be there when he leaves. Thus, his tort liability increasingly tends to reflect these factors. The exceptions also cover cases where he retains actual control over the premises or some aspect of them or fails to disclose a latent hazard.

Exception: Latent Hazards. When the lessor knows or has reason to know of a concealed unreasonably dangerous condition (artificial or natural) existing on the premises at the time the lessee takes possession under the lease, but says nothing to the lessee about it, he has committed a species of fraud that subjects him to liability for physical harm sustained prior to the time the lessee discovers or should have discovered the danger. R. § 358.

Jurisdictions vary as to the extent of the lessor's knowledge of the condition required for liability.

Almost all agree that there is no duty to inspect the premises to discover such conditions, but neither does the lessor have to have actual knowledge of the danger. Most require that she have knowledge of facts that would put a reasonable person on notice that a dangerous condition may exist—in the words of the Restatement, that she "know or have reason to know of the condition" and that she "realizes or should realize the risk involved."

In addition, the condition must create a latent danger, in the sense that it may be expected that the lessee will not discover the condition or the extent of the risk. The duty is only to disclose the existence of the condition, and therefore there is no liability for open and obvious hazards, however dangerous.

Liability extends to the lessee and all persons on the premises with his consent or by his right, since the lessor's concealment of the danger from the lessee has deprived those persons of the opportunity to have the lessee protect them from it.

Exception: Persons Outside the Premises. If there is a condition on the land that the lessor realizes or should realize unreasonably endangers persons outside the premises, the lessor's liability to such persons survives the transfer of possession to the lessee just as though the lessor remained in possession. R. § 379. He cannot escape liability for such hazards by leasing the premises. Thus, as to such persons it is immaterial that the lessee is aware of the condition or even that he has promised to alter or repair it, or that there is a clause in the lease exonerating the lessor from liability for such conditions, although this may affect rights as between the lessor and lessee. Of course, the lessor's liability is not exclusive; the lessee may in certain cases be jointly liable.

Generally, the lessor is not liable for conditions on the premises that come into existence after the lessee takes possession (R. § 377) or for the lessee's activities on the premises. But if the lessor knows at the time the lease is executed that the lessee intends to conduct an activity on the premises that will necessarily subject persons off the premises to actionable harm, and nevertheless consents to this activity or fails to require proper precautions, the lessor is subject to liability for foreseeable harm that results to those persons. R. §§ 379A, 837.

Exception: Public Admission. When the lessor leases his premises for a purpose that involves the admission of the public, he has a duty to them to exercise reasonable care to inspect for and remedy unreasonably dangerous conditions that exist when possession is transferred. R. § 359. Here, too, the lessee's agreement to alter or repair the dangerous condition does not absolve the lessor of liability unless the lessee agreed not to admit the public until this was done, and the lessor could reasonably expect him to keep that promise.

The first cases recognizing this exception involved the admission of large numbers of persons, but it is now well established that the rule is not so limited and encompasses any place, however small, where the public may enter. And it is not necessary that admission be charged or that the visitor be a business invitee of the lessee or the lessor; any purpose involving public admission is sufficient. But, of course, the lessor's liability is limited to those parts of the premises which, under the express or implied terms of the lease, are to be open to the public, and to visitors entering for the contemplated purpose. And the lessor is not liable for the lessee's negligence after possession has been transferred, as to conditions that were not unreasonably dangerous at that time.

Exception: Retained Control. Most leases today involve the rental of an apartment, suite of offices, or similar space within a building such that the lessor retains control over portions of the premises not exclusively possessed by any tenant. These portions include: (1) common areas for use by the tenants and their visitors, such as approaches, entrances, hallways, common stairways, elevators, yards, garages, common rooms, and basements; (2) appliances and other appurtenances necessary to the use of the premises, such as heating and air conditioning systems, water and water heating systems, electrical systems, and common laundry facilities; and (3) structural components, such as foundations. Since he retains control over these portions of the premises, the lessor must exercise reasonable care to keep them in a reasonably safe condition. R. §§ 360, 361.

Liability extends to the lessee, members of his family, his employees, and to all lawful visitors on the premises, even though as to a tenant a particular visitor may be only a licensee. The landlord is in the business of providing these facilities for the benefit of all such persons, and therefore as to him they may be regarded as invitees. But his liability does not extend to areas of the premises where tenants and their guests are forbidden, or to visitors of a tenant who intrude upon areas that have nothing to do with the proper purpose of their visit.

The lessor's duty is one of reasonable care, and he must inspect, repair or warn as circumstances and that duty require. The fact that the danger is apparent does not affect his duty, but of course may be relevant on plaintiff's contributory negligence or assumption of risk. And most courts extend liability to unreasonably dangerous natural, as well as artificial, conditions.

A clause in the lease exonerating the lessor from this liability may or may not be effective as to the tenant (see § 5–5) but of course it is always ineffective as to third persons not parties to the lease.

Is a lessor liable to residents in his building for criminal violence by third persons occurring in common areas, if the lessor negligently failed to provide adequate security devices or personnel? The cases are divided, some holding that there is no duty as a matter of law and others finding an issue of negligence for the jury.

Exception: Agreement to Repair. Where the lessor has contracted, in the lease or otherwise, to repair certain defective conditions or to keep the premises in safe repair generally, may he be held liable in tort if he fails to perform his promise with the result that a tenant or another is injured?

The law here is in transition. At one time the general rule was that there was no tort liability for the mere failure to perform a contractual promise. See Chapter 10, infra. This limitation is being abandoned, and a majority of jurisdictions now follow the Restatement § 357 (which represented a distinctly minority position when it was first adopted) and hold that such a promise by a lessor creates a duty that runs not only to the tenant but to others on the premises with the tenant's consent. Reliance by the lessee upon the promise is reasonable and ordinarily will induce him to forego undertaking the repairs himself, to the detriment of himself and all others who enter with his consent.

The promise to repair must be enforceable; liability may not be based on the failure to perform a gratuitous promise to repair. Hence, if not a part of the lease agreement, as where it is made after the lease has been executed, there must be a separate or new consideration for it.

The lessor's duty is defined by the contract. And ordinarily his duty is only to exercise reasonable care to make the repairs after he has notice of the need for them. He need not inspect the premises unless he is required to do so by the lease.

By analogy, there may be liability for failure to provide a service required by the lease (e.g., heat, light) where the premises cannot be safely used without it.

Exception: Negligent Repairs. As a general rule, one who undertakes to perform a task, even gratuitously, must perform it with reasonable care. See § 4–5, supra. Logically this principle can be applied to a lessor who undertakes to repair the premises. However, in some jurisdictions the lessor is not liable when he negligently makes gratuitous repairs unless (1) he increases the danger that existed before he undertook the repairs or (2) a concealed danger remains and his repairs create a deceptive appearance of safety or (3) the danger is a latent one and the lessor assures the lessee that the repairs have been made when in fact they have not been. R. § 362. The lessor is liable only if the danger (or enhanced danger) is such that the lessee neither knows nor should know that the repairs were not made or were made negligently. Thus, the lessor's liability is based on a theory of deceit.

This restrictive view seems to be giving way to the rule that the lessor is liable for negligent repairs on the same basis as any other tortfeasor.

Independent Contractors. In general, the lessor cannot escape his responsibilities by delegating the work to an independent contractor, and he is liable for the contractor's negligence to the same extent as if the contractor were his employee. R. §§ 419–421.

General Duty of Reasonable Care. Here, as elsewhere, we see some courts rejecting this system of classifications and duty limitations in favor of imposing upon the lessor a general duty of reasonable care under the circumstances. However, this remains a distinctly minority view.

Most states now recognize an implied warranty of habitability in short-term residential leases, but so far the damages for breach of that warranty have not included damages for physical harm.

Statutes. All of the foregoing are common law rules. Statutes and ordinances in many jurisdictions impose duties on certain lessors that may have the effect of expanding their tort liability, typically with respect to their duty to keep the premises in repair.

§ 8–8. Vendors and Vendees

Vendors. When a landowner transfers title and possession of his property to another, unlike the lessor he has no continuing or reversionary interest in the premises. Thus, as would be expected, the general rule is that his responsibility for the condition of the premises and the tort liability accompanying it pass to the buyer upon completion of the transfer. However, there are two exceptions.

Exception: Latent Hazards. At one time, consistent with the principle of caveat emptor, the land's vendor was not even liable for injuries resulting from concealed dangers of which he was actually aware and that he failed to disclose to his buyer. However, most states now impose liability in this situation in favor of the vendee and others upon the land with his consent, provided (1) the vendee did not know or have reason to know of the condition or the risk involved; (2) the vendor knew or should have known of the condition, realized or should have realized the risk it created, and could anticipate that the vendee would not discover the condition or appreciate the risk; and (3) the risk is an unreasonable one. R. § 353. As in the case of the similar liability of a lessor, it is based upon the vendor's deceit under circumstances where the burden of imposing a duty to speak is small compared to the risk of harm created by his failure to do so.

The vendor's liability continues until the vendee has had a reasonable opportunity to discover the condition (or if the vendor actively concealed the condition, until actual discovery) and a reasonable time thereafter to correct it.

Exception: Persons Outside the Premises. When a vendor transfers land that has on it an artificial condition unreasonably dangerous to persons outside the premises such that he would have been liable as possessor for harm caused by it (see § 8–2, supra), his liability for the actionable consequences of that condition continues for a reasonable time after the transfer, until the vendee has had a reasonable opportunity to discover the condition (or actually discovers it, if it was actively concealed by the vendor) and a reasonable time to correct it.

According to the Restatement (§ 373), this liability is limited to conditions created or negligently permitted to remain on the land by the vendor.

Builder–Vendors. As to buildings sold new by the person who built them, the courts are increasingly basing liability for injuries caused by defects in them upon ordinary principles of negligence (by analogy to manufacturers of chattels), or upon principles of strict liability for breach of warranty by creating an implied warranty of habitability. And a few courts have even imposed strict liability for unreasonably dangerous defects by analogy to principles of strict product liability (see § 8–9, infra), at least where the builder-vendor is a mass-producer of homes.

Vendees. When a transferee of real property acquires possession, he will have a reasonable time to discover and remedy actionable conditions on the premises before he will be held liable for them, although undoubtedly he must exercise reasonable care to warn of them or take such other temporary precautions as he reasonably can (where his duty is one of reasonable care) until that time.

Where the condition is one that creates an unreasonable risk of harm to persons or property *outside* the premises (typically a private or public nuisance, see § 8–18, infra), the rule is no different, except that where the condition constitutes a private nuisance he may in certain circumstances be entitled to assume that it exists with the consent of the adjoining landowners (or that compensation has been paid for it) and so he will not be liable until he is on notice that it is in fact an actionable nuisance. However, if the condition constitutes a public nuisance, no such notice is required, since the vendee is required to know that the public cannot consent to it, and therefore he must take immediate steps to abate it. R. § 366.

B. PRODUCTS LIABILITY

§ 8–9. An Overview of Products Liability

In recent decades the law governing liability for injuries caused by defective products has undergone rapid growth and dramatic changes. "Products liability" law has moved from caveat emptor to strict liability, and at present is one of tort law's most important areas.

Products liability law has become so specialized and complex that it is properly the subject of a separate Nutshell (J. Phillips, PRODUCTS LIABILITY IN A NUTSHELL (6th ed. 2003)). Therefore, this section will be confined to a brief overview of this area, merely to place product-caused injuries in perspective in the general scheme of the law of liability for physical harm.

Theories of Liability. When physical harm to plaintiff or his property is causally related to the unsafe condition of a "product," he may have a cause of action against the person(s) who designed, manufactured, sold, or furnished that product. (The scope of the concept "product" is a separate and interesting issue. It is not confined to manufactured goods purchased by consumers; but for simplicity's sake that is the prototype that will be used here.)

In most jurisdictions, plaintiff's cause of action may be based on one or more of three different theories: (1) negligence; (2) breach of warranty; and (3) strict tort liability.

Negligence. There are many ways in which the manufacturer of a product (or of one of its component parts) may have negligently created an unsafe condition. For example, he may have chosen an unnecessarily dangerous *design.* Some one may have been negligent during the *manufacturing* process, as by using defective materials, or omitting a part or a step. Perhaps there was negligence in the testing and inspection of the product. Sometimes the product's container or packaging is inadequate. Or he may have failed to furnish adequate *warnings* and directions for use with the product.

Moreover, after the product has left the manufacturer's hands, subsequent sellers or furnishers (e.g., a wholesaler, distributor, retailer, or lessor) may also have been negligent in failing to discover or failing to warn of the unsafe condition.

The usual principles of negligence apply. Thus, the issue is whether the burden of conduct that would have prevented the harm is greater or less than the foreseeable probability and gravity of that harm, and this is a question of fact.

Breach of Warranty. "Warranty" is a general concept. The law recognizes a variety of warranties besides those with which we are concerned here. Basically, warranties are certain kinds of express or implied promissory representations of fact that the law will enforce against the warrantor. Most warranties arise in transactions involving transfers of real or personal property.

Products liability law is concerned primarily with three of these warranties, as they concern the product's quality or fitness for use: (1) *express* warranties; and the *implied* warranties of (2) merchantability and (3) fitness for a particular purpose. While these warranties are now regarded as a branch of sales or commercial (i.e., contract) law, their roots are in the old law of wrongs (see § 1–3) and for a long time the remedy for their breach was in tort. These warranties are of interest to us because the remedies for their breach include damages for physical harm. These and other warranties are now codified in the Uniform Commercial Code; comparable warranties existed under the Uniform Sales Act and the common law.

An *express warranty* (U.C.C. § 2–313), as the term implies, is simply a promissory assertion of fact about the product that the seller made as a part of the sales transaction and which was a "basis of the bargain"—for example, that "this widget is guaranteed to be free from defects for one year from date of purchase."

The *implied warranties* are those created and imposed by law, and accompany the transfer of title to goods unless expressly and clearly limited or excluded by the contract. (With respect to damages for personal injury, any such contractual limitations or exclusions are "prima facie unconscionable." U.C.C. § 2–719(3).)

The implied warranty of *merchantability* (U.C.C. § 2–314) requires that the product (and its container) meet certain minimum standards of quality, chiefly that it be fit for the ordinary purposes for which such goods are sold. This includes a standard of reasonable safety.

The implied warranty of *fitness for a particular purpose* (U.C.C. § 2–315) imposes a similar requirement in cases where the seller knows or has reason to know of a particular purpose for which the goods are required and that the buyer is relying on him to select or furnish suitable goods; he then warrants that the goods are fit for that particular purpose.

The action for breach of one of these warranties has aspects of both tort and contract law. Its greatest value to the injured product user lies in the fact that liability for breach is *strict;* no negligence or other fault need be shown. However, in addition to the privity limitation (to be discussed), certain contract-type defenses have impaired the remedy's usefulness. These include: (1) the requirement that the seller receive reasonably prompt *notice* of the

breach as a condition to his liability; (2) the requirement that the buyer have *relied* upon the warranty;
and (3) the ability of the seller to *limit* or *disclaim*
entirely the implied warranties. Obviously, these
defenses are most appropriate in cases of commercial loss (economic loss caused by the product's
failure to perform as expected), and there has been
a trend away from strict enforcement of these defenses in personal injury cases where the action has
more of a tort flavor.

Privity Limitations. The history of the law of
products liability is largely a history of the erosion
of the privity limitation, which severely constricted
the seller's liability in both negligence and breach of
warranty actions

In negligence, the seminal case is *Winterbottom v.*
Wright (Exch. 1842), which established the rule
that liability for injuries caused by a negligently
made or maintained product is limited to the parties to the contract (see Chapter 10, infra). In other
words, defendant's duty of reasonable care arose
only from the contract and only a party to that
contract could sue for its breach. This meant that a
negligent manufacturer who sold his product to a
retailer, who in turn sold it to plaintiff, was effectively insulated from liability; and the plaintiff was
usually without a remedy in tort, since it was the
manufacturer and not the retailer whose negligence
caused the harm.

Gradually exceptions to the *Winterbottom* rule
emerged. Soon privity of contract was not required

(1) where the defect was fraudulently concealed by the seller (based on a deceit theory) and (2) for products "inherently" or "imminently" dangerous to human life or health, such as poisons and guns. The decisions then began to expand these exceptions. Some courts dropped the fraud requirement; a concealed defect coupled with some sort of "invitation" by defendant to use the product was enough. And a few cases construed the term "imminently dangerous" to mean especially dangerous by reason of the defect itself, and not necessarily dangerous per se—for example, products intended for human consumption, a defective scaffold, and a coffee urn that exploded.

Finally, *MacPherson v. Buick Motor Co.* (N.Y. 1916) (Cardozo, J.) broadened the category of "inherently" or "imminently" dangerous products so as effectively to abolish the privity requirement in negligence cases. It held that lack of privity is not a defense if it is foreseeable that the product, if negligently made, is likely to cause injury to a class of persons that includes the plaintiff. Since this is essentially the test for negligence anyway, the exception swallowed the rule. The *MacPherson* case quickly became a leading authority, and the privity rule in negligence cases soon was history.

In warranty, a similar privity limitation was imposed, in part because warranties were thought to be an integral part of the contract of sale. Beginning in 1913, an exception developed for cases involving products intended for human consumption (food, beverages, drugs, etc.) and eventually also for products intended for "intimate bodily use" (e.g., cosmetics), so that the warranty in these cases ran all the way to the ultimate consumer. In the case of *express* warranties which could be said to be made to the public generally, such as a statement by a manufacturer in literature distributed with an automobile that the windshield was "shatterproof," the privity requirement was quickly abandoned following *Baxter v. Ford Motor Co.* (Wash. 1932). But with respect to *implied* warranties, there was almost no extention beyond food, drink and similar products until *Henningsen v. Bloomfield Motors, Inc.* (N.J. 1960) abolished the privity limitation generally and held that the implied warranties run to the foreseeable ultimate user or consumer of the product. (*Henningsen* also invalidated the manufacturer's attempted disclaimer of implied warranty liability.) *Henningsen* has been followed in almost all jurisdictions.

Strict Tort Liability. During the 1930's, '40's, and '50's various legal writers and an occasional judge proposed the creation of strict liability in tort for defective products. The best known judicial exposition of this view was Justice Traynor's concurring opinion in *Escola v. Coca Cola Bottling Co.* (Cal. 1944). The principal justifications advanced for strict product liability are: (1) negligence is often too difficult to prove; (2) res ipsa loquitur has been stretched to nearly this point anyway; (3) strict liability can be accomplished already through a series of actions for breach of warranty; (4) strict liability provides needed safety incentives; (5) the manufacturer is the one best able to either prevent the harm or insure or spread the cost of the risk; and (6) the manufacturer of a product by placing it on the market induces justifiable consumer reliance on the expectation of the product's safety, and since reputable manufacturers do in fact stand behind their products all should do so. In addition, after *Henningsen* the last major barrier to direct strict liability was removed, leaving only the remaining contract defenses to warranty liability that most felt were inappropriate to personal injury cases.

Finally, in *Greenman v. Yuba Power Products, Inc.* (Cal. 1963), California became the first jurisdiction to adopt strict tort liability for defective products. At about the same time, work was underway on the Restatement (Second) of Torts, and its Reporter was Dean Prosser, an advocate of strict product liability. Relying only on *Greenman* and a New York warranty case (*Goldberg v. Kollsman Instrument Corp.*, N.Y. 1963), the American Law Institute approved § 402A which embodied strict liability as follows:

(1) One who sells any product in a defective condition unreasonably dangerous to the user or consumer or to his property is subject to liability for physical harm thereby caused to the ultimate user or consumer, or to his property, if

(a) the seller is engaged in the business of selling such a product, and

(b) it is expected to and does reach the user or consumer without substantial change in the condition in which it is sold.

(2) The rule stated in Subsection (1) applies although

(a) the seller has exercised all possible care in the preparation and sale of his product, and

(b) the user or consumer has not bought the product from or entered into any contractual relation with the seller.

Strict product liability, almost always in the form provided in § 402A, promptly swept the country and became the law in all but a few states. At the same time, negligence and breach of warranty remain alternative or concurrent theories of recovery. In fact, some writers and a few judges have been unable to understand how the courts could simply bypass the warranty provisions of the U.C.C. (which purport to legislate liability rules for exactly the same fact situations) and adopt common law tort rules different from the Code. But the simple answer is that the courts have regarded the U.C.C. as contract or sales law which does not affect their traditional role as makers of the common law rules of tort law. As a practical matter, the differences between strict tort liability and liability for breach of warranty are now slight; but differences do exist in certain cases.

Other Issues. The emergence of strict product liability has raised a host of new issues. The principal questions are as follows.

Defect. What is a "defective condition unreasonably dangerous"? In negligence cases, the focus is upon defendant's conduct. In strict liability (whether warranty or tort) the focus shifts to the condition of the product; but there is still an element of fault, in the sense of placing on the market an unsafe product. Many cases have had to deal with this question. As in negligence cases, the defect may be in the design (in which case a balancing test similar to that used in negligence cases must be used), in manufacture, or in the failure to warn or to provide adequate directions for use.

The most difficult problem has been to determine when a product is "defective" in its design. One of the first tests, derived from the language of the Restatement § 402A, is the "consumer expectation" test. Under this test, a product is defective if it is "dangerous to an extent beyond that which would be contemplated by the ordinary consumer who purchases it, with the ordinary knowledge common to the community as to its characteristics." This test may be adequate for certain products, but it soon became apparent that there are many products for which the average consumer does not have sufficient knowledge to have safety expectations. In addition, this test tends to eliminate liability for observable defects, so that the manufacturer who makes his product manifestly hazardous escapes liability.

To supplement the consumer expectation test, the courts have developed the "risk-benefit" test and the "presumed seller" test. Under the latter, a product is defective if a manufacturer would be negligent in placing the product on the market, presuming that he had full knowledge of the product's harmful or dangerous propensity. The risk-benefit test (much like the Hand test for negligence) balances the gravity and probability of the risk on the one hand against the benefit and utility of the actual design versus the benefit and feasibility of an alternative design that would have prevented the injury.

Most courts have realized that no one single test is adequate by itself, and will utilize the one that is most appropriate to the facts of the particular case. It must be remembered, however, that design safety is not an absolute concept; a product need not be designed to be perfectly safe. It is always a matter of balancing safety against other considerations. In this sense, design defect liability resembles negligence liability, with the important difference that in strict product liability, the focus is on the product itself and not on the conduct of the manufacturer.

Informational Defects. Section 402A makes no special rules for informational defects (warnings and directions for use). Such defects are really just a specific type of design defect. Thus, in theory, a manufacturer could have a duty to warn of a defect of which he was unaware. While this was indeed the case at one time, the courts, beginning with prescription drug cases, have now generally retreated from strict liability for informational defects and require plaintiff to prove that the manufacturer knew or should have known of the risk about which the plaintiff claims he should have been warned or instructed. This shift is reflected in the new Restatement (Third) of Torts: Products Liability § 2(c).

Type of Harm. What kinds of harm are compensable under § 402A? With an occasional exception, the courts limit § 402A damages to physical harm (personal injury and property damage to other than the product itself) on the ground that warranty law is better suited to govern merely economic or commercial loss. *Seely v. White Motor Co.* (Cal. 1965) is a leading example. Contra, *Santor v. A & M Karagheusian, Inc.* (N.J. 1965). The issue that has divided the courts is whether strict products liability is applicable to accidental damage to, or destruction of, the product itself caused by a defect. The new Restatement (Third) of Torts: Products Liability § 21 (1998) concludes that it is not.

Plaintiffs. Who may be a plaintiff? Section 402A speaks of the "user or consumer" of the product, but in a Caveat the Institute leaves open the possibility that liability may be extended in favor of others. The courts have generally allowed recovery by "bystanders" (i.e., persons other than the purchaser, user or consumer) whose exposure to the risk of injury was foreseeable (e.g., a third person injured in a crash caused by a defect in the vehicle).

In contrast, the U.C.C. (§ 2–318) provides three alternative provisions; each state is free to choose the one it likes best. Alternative A includes personal injuries to members of the purchaser's family or household and household guests. B covers personal injuries to all those who foreseeably may be expected to be users, consumers, or "affected by" the goods; and C covers all compensable harm (personal injury, property damage and economic loss) to those in group B.

Defenses. What defenses are available? At first, it was generally agreed that plaintiff's assumption of risk (§ 5–5) is a defense to strict liability, but not ordinary contributory negligence (§ 5–1). With the advent of comparative fault the authorities are divided, some courts now allowing any form of comparative fault to offset defendant's strict liability.

In addition, plaintiff's "misuse" of the product is sometimes said to be a complete defense, at least if that misuse was objectively unforeseeable. It would appear that this is merely another way of saying that the product was not defective (or if it was that the defect was not a cause in fact of the injury), since the manufacturer need only make the product reasonably safe for foreseeable uses. At the same time, if plaintiff's use, while not an *intended* use, is a *foreseeable* and not an uncommon one (e.g., standing on a chair, an infant drinking furniture polish), the manufacturer may have a duty to design his product in light of the foreseeable misuse. On this basis, the trend of authority is to hold manufacturers of automobiles strictly liable if the vehicle is unnecessarily dangerous to the occupants in the event of an accident (the so-called "crashworthiness" doctrine), since motor vehicle accidents are a rather common and foreseeable "misuse" of the product.

Defendants. Finally, who may be a defendant? Strict liability under § 402A extends to the manufacturer of the product, and in most jurisdictions to the supplier of the component part that was defective. It also encompasses all those in the distribution chain—wholesalers, distributors, retailers, and commercial lessors and bailors. Defendant must be "engaged in the business" of dealing in that product, but such products need not be her principal business; it is no defense that furnishing the product was merely an incidental part of her business (see R. § 402A, Comment f). But if defendant is primarily engaged in rendering services, some (but not all) courts have refused to impose strict liability for defective products incidentally supplied. And the courts have so far refused to impose strict liability on dealers in used products.

A few cases have extended strict liability for personal injury to a mass developer-builder-vendor of new homes (e.g., *Schipper v. Levitt & Sons, Inc.*, N.J. 1965).

The Restatement (Third) of Torts: Products Liability. Although realizing that it may be time for an update of the Restatement of Torts, the American Law Institute concluded that such a project was simply too large to be accomplished in one fell swoop. Accordingly, it first undertook to revise the product liability provisions, and in 1997, after much controversy, it promulgated the Restatement (Third) of Torts: Products Liability. (The next volume, the Restatement (Third) of Torts: Apportionment of Liability, was published in 2000.)

The new product liability provisions, which supersede § 402A, now explicitly recognize the three categories of product defects: manufacturing defects, design defects, and informational defects (warnings and directions for use). Sellers remain strictly liable for manufacturing defects, but the Restatement reverts to something close to a negligence standard for design defects, imposing liability only for "foreseeable risks of harm" that could have been avoided by the adoption of a "reasonable alternative design" (§ 2(b)) or by "reasonable instructions or warnings" (§ 2(c)). Thus, as a general rule, under this provision a product is not defectively designed unless the plaintiff can prove that there was a feasible alternative design at the time the product was manufactured, and that the risk created by the product as designed was known or should have been known by the manufacturer. Similarly, there is no duty to warn under this provision unless the plaintiff can prove that the manufacturer knew or should have known of the risk about which the plaintiff claims he should have been warned.

As an alternative, plaintiff can recover if he can prove that the product as design, or the warning, failed to comply with an applicable safety statute or administrative regulation (§ 4(a)). On the other hand, as evidence that the product was not defective, defendant can prove the product's compliance with an applicable safety statute or administrative regulation, although such compliance is not conclusive on the issue of defectiveness. (§ 4(b))

It is also recognized that plaintiff need not prove a specific defect, and therefore that a defect can be proved circumstantially, if the product causes harm that is of a type that is ordinarily caused by a product defect and the plaintiff can eliminate other possibilities as the sole cause of the occurrence. § 3.

The Restatement (Third) further restricts liability for defective prescription drugs and medical devices. Under § 6(c), a prescription drug or medical device is not defective in design unless the foreseeable risk of harm is so "great in relation to its foreseeable therapeutic benefits that reasonable health-care providers, knowing of such foreseeable risks and therapeutic benefits, would not prescribe the drug or medical device for any class of patients." Under § 6(d), warnings need only be given to "health care providers" unless the manufacturer "knows or has reason to know that health-care providers will not be in a position to reduce the risks of harm in accordance with the instructions or warnings." In that case, but only in that case, an adequate warning is owed to the patient.

It is too early to tell what influence the Restatement (Third) of Torts: Products Liability will have in the courts. Product liability law is now rather well settled, and proof of a feasible alternative design is not a universal requirement in design defect cases. Therefore, it seems quite possible that the Restatement (Third) provisions dealing with product liability will not have an impact on tort law comparable to that of their predecessor, § 402A of the Restatement (Second). The cases to date have not uniformly embraced this new formulation of products liability law.

C.   EMPLOYERS, EMPLOYEES AND CONTRACTORS

§ 8–10.   Vicarious Liability

Vicarious liability is a form of strict liability by which A is held liable to another for the tort of B for no other reason than that there exists some relationship between A and B and B was acting within the scope of that relationship when he committed the tort. The overwhelming majority of vicarious liability cases arise from the employer-employee[1] relationship, but the principle extends to other relationships such as a partnership, a joint venture or enterprise, and in some instances principal-agent and employer-independent contractor relationships.

Basically, if the requisite relationship exists, a third person (C) may sue A for injuries caused by

---

1. Traditionally, the terms "master" and "servant" have been used to designate the parties to an employment relationship, and these terms still appear in the cases and other authorities, and particularly in digests and indexes. "Employer" and "employee" are more modern and descriptive, and will be used instead herein.

the tort of B, even though A was entirely innocent of personal fault so far as C's injuries are concerned.

Often this is characterized as an instance of *imputed negligence*. That term is inaccurate for two reasons. First, there is vicarious liability for many torts besides negligence. It applies to all forms of strict liability, and as a general rule to intentional torts committed by B in the scope and furtherance of A's business. Second, it is not the negligence or other fault that is imputed, but the *liability*.

Various justifications have been advanced for the vicarious liability of an employer, and by analogy of others. These include: (1) he has a measure of control over the conduct of his employee; (2) it is he who initiated the activity out of which the tort arose; (3) he selected the employee; (4) vicarious liability is the price of the privilege to employ others; and (5) he is, frankly, more likely to have the means to compensate the plaintiff than is his employee.

Obviously, none of these standing alone is a sufficient reason. Perhaps the best justification is that torts are a more or less inevitable byproduct of the conduct of such activities, and thus tort liability should be treated as a cost of the enterprise as a whole. It is a cost of doing business (using that term in a broad sense). The enterprise functions through its employees; their acts may be said to be the acts of the enterprise. In addition, the enterprise is better able than either the innocent plaintiff or the employee to absorb the loss, plan for it, insure against it, and allocate the cost in the last instance to those who do business with it and partake of its benefits. Further, there is some merit to the argument concerning control. Employer liability does provide an incentive to exercise care in the selection of employees and the conduct of the activity, and thereby promotes the injury-prevention function of tort law.

For these and other reasons, the principle of vicarious liability is well established and there is no tendency at all to retreat from it.

§ 8–11. Employees

Let us first clarify some terms—principal, agent, employer, employee, and independent contractor. The following are not intended as definitions, and must not be relied upon as such.

The terms *principal* and *agent* encompass a variety of relationships, some of which may be subclassified as *employer-employee* and some as *employer-independent contractor.*

An *agent* is one who, by mutual consent, has undertaken to represent or act for another, the *principal,* subject to the latter's right to exercise some degree of direction and control over the former.

An *employee* is a particular kind of agent. Unfortunately, there is no one satisfactory definition of that term. Instead, the status question is resolved by considering the combined effect of all of the facts surrounding the actor's relationship to the other for whom he acts. By far the most important factor is the degree of *control* possessed or exercised by the latter. As a general rule, if the principal controls, or by custom or agreement has the right to control, the physical details (time, place, method, etc.) of the performance of the work, then the agent is very likely an employee and therefore his principal is his employer. If this degree of control does not exist, the relationship is very likely something else, but not necessarily. There are other relevant factors, and where they point strongly enough in the direction of an employment relationship, such may be found to exist notwithstanding the absence of control over the manner of performance of the work. These factors include (1) the skill required of the worker; (2) the term of the employment; (3) whether the work is part of the principal's regular business; (4) whether the worker has a separate business of his own; (5) who supplies the tools and other requisites of the job; (6) where the work is performed; (7) the method of payment; (8) the intent of the parties; and (9) so on. See Restatement (Second) of Agency § 220.

Note that since all employer-employee relationships necessarily involve *some* degree of control by the employer over the employee, all employers are also principals and all employees are also agents; but of course the converse is not true.

As the term implies, an *independent contractor* is one who is engaged to perform services for another (who in this instance is also termed an *employer*) but remains independent of the employer's own work force. It is a looser relationship; she retains a separate identity. It is commonly said that an independent contractor is one who is paid primarily to accomplish certain results (as opposed to an employee, who is paid for his time), with the manner of performance being left to the contractor's own discretion. This is usually true, but not always; one may be an independent contractor when the factors mentioned above so indicate, even though the employer possesses or exercises some significant control over how and when the work shall be done. If the employer retains some degree of control (as opposed to contracting solely for the result), he is also deemed to be a *principal* and the independent contractor is also his *agent* to that extent. If not, then no principal-agent relationship exists, but merely employer-independent contractor.

By way of illustration, a lawyer may be any of the three. A salaried associate of a law firm, or one who is on the payroll of a corporation or governmental unit (including, for example, a law professor), is ordinarily an employee (even though he is highly skilled and performs his work autonomously.) An attorney in private practice who is retained by a client to perform legal services on his behalf is customarily an independent contractor, and also the client's agent. But a lawyer who merely contracts to write a law book is an independent contractor, and not the publisher's agent.

It must be remembered that status is always a question of fact, and while the parties' own characterization of their relationship is one factor to be considered it is never determinative.

Given the absence of definitive tests and clearly visible lines, the courts have had difficulty with these status questions, and the cases are not always consistent. Perhaps after all is said and done, the customs, common sense, and experiences of the community are as reliable a guide as any.

The rules alluded to above are a part of the law of agency, to which reference must be made for further guidance. But these issues have important tort law consequences. As noted in the preceding section, an employer is liable to third persons for torts committed by his employee while acting within the scope of the employment. However, the general rule (subject to a number of exceptions) is that an employer is *not* vicariously liable for the torts of his independent contractor. (And deciding whether or not one is an employee will be necessary to determine whether he is entitled to certain other remedies, such as workers' compensation.)

Once it is determined that the tortfeasor was an employee at the time he committed the tort, his employer is vicariously liable if his conduct was within the "scope" (or sometimes the "course" or "course and scope") of his employment. This is also a question of fact for which no very useful test has been devised. All of the surrounding circumstances must be considered, including (1) the employee's job description or assigned duties, (2) the time, place and purpose of the employee's act, (3) the similarity of his conduct to the things he was hired or authorized to do, or which are commonly done by such employees, and (4) the foreseeability of his act. In general, "course" and "scope" have not been narrowly construed. Acts not strictly necessary to the work or authorized by the employer are included, so long as they bear a reasonable relation to the employment.

The employee was not necessarily beyond the scope of his employment merely because he did some act that his employer had expressly prohibited him to do, or did a permitted act in a forbidden way. For example, a gun salesman is within the scope of his employment when he inserts a live cartridge into a gun that he is demonstrating to a prospective purchaser, despite the fact that his employer expressly told him never to do this. An employer cannot limit his own liability merely by instructing his employee to act carefully. The forbidden act is within the scope of the employment if it is reasonably necessary in order to accomplish the assigned tasks, or if it is naturally to be expected that the employee will do such an act in performing the assigned work. On the other hand, an employer may limit an employee's duties as he sees fit, and thus one employed exclusively as an airplane pilot *may* be outside the scope of his employment when, contrary to specific instructions, he undertakes to make repairs on the airplane. (In such a case, there still might be vicarious liability, but on some other ground.)

Relatively minor deviations from the acts necessary to accomplish the assigned work usually will not take the employee outside the scope of his employment. Personal acts of an incidental nature, such as going to the toilet, lighting a fire to keep warm, going outside to smoke, and even taking a coffee break are ordinarily held to be within the scope, even though such acts are not among those the employee was hired to do. But he goes beyond the scope where the deviation is more substantial— constituting, to use the classic phrase, a "frolic and detour" for the employee's own purposes. The distinction is between major and minor departures from the tasks and methods authorized or reasonably foreseeable by the employer, and the principal variables are (1) the length of time of the departure, (2) the physical distance of the departure from the place or route assigned or expected to be used, and (3) the extent to which the employee was, at the same time, secondarily accomplishing a purpose of his employment. Thus, a deviation of a relatively short time and distance for a purely personal errand is not beyond the scope. A greater deviation is permissible if there is an employment purpose incidental to the personal one, as where a deliveryman varies from his assigned route in order to favor a customer who gives him presents. But a deliveryman with hours from eight to five who is assigned a delivery at four p.m. but goes home instead for personal reasons does not reenter the scope of his employment when he makes the delivery at ten p.m.

An employer's vicarious liability includes torts negligently or recklessly committed. It even extends to intentional torts committed in the scope of the employment and at least in part in furtherance of the employer's business. For example, a bill collector who commits assault, battery, false imprisonment, or intentionally inflicts emotional distress or maliciously prosecutes or defames the plaintiff in an effort to extract payment of a bill subjects his employer to liability for the intentional tort. Going a step further, some courts (a growing minority) will visit vicarious liability on an employer for intentional torts committed during a fight that ensued when the employee lost his temper during an argument that arose out of the employment. And it is generally agreed that where there is some special relationship between plaintiff and the employer such that the employer owes plaintiff a duty of protection (such as in the case of a carrier, an innkeeper, or a hospital) the employer is subject to vicarious liability to plaintiff for his employee's intentional tort even though the tort is committed for entirely personal reasons.

Ordinarily, an employer is not vicariously liable for harm caused by the employee's use of an instrumentality (such as an automobile) entrusted by him to the custody of the employee, when not then being used in the scope of the employment. However, a few courts have held otherwise where the instrumentality is a particularly dangerous one.

Bear in mind that all of the foregoing applies only to the employer's *vicarious* liability. There are many situations in which an employer may be held responsible for harm caused by the acts of his employee on the basis of the employer's *own* conduct, in which case the liability is direct and not vicarious and the foregoing limitations do not apply. Thus, an employer may be liable for his own negligence in the selection or instruction of the employee, or for failure to properly supervise him, or even for failure to fire him. Or he may be held liable under usual principles of agency law where he has commanded, authorized or ratified the employee's tortious act.

For purposes of tort liability to third persons, partners can be regarded as employees of the partnership, or of each other, and therefore all partners are jointly and severally liable for the tort of one, committed while acting within the scope of the partnership business. The same is true of the principals in a joint venture, which for almost all purposes is the legal equivalent of a partnership, the main difference being that a joint venture is more limited in its scope.

§ 8–12. Independent Contractors

As to agents who are *not* employees, the general rule is that the principal is *not* vicariously liable for their torts, even where committed within the scope of the agency, since such agents are not a part of the principal's enterprise, and therefore the most important justifications for vicarious liability (§ 8–10) do not apply. Restatement (Second) of Agency § 250. There are, however, exceptions, chiefly involving wrongful statements or representations that the agent has actual or apparent authority to make and the institution of legal proceedings that the agent was authorized to bring. (Here, too, the principal may be *personally,* not vicariously, liable where he commanded, authorized or ratified the agent's tortious act, or for his personal negligence in the selection, instruction or supervision of the agent.)

The same general rule of non-(vicarious) liability applies, for the same reasons, as to torts committed by those classified as independent contractors. (Recall that there may or may not be an agency relationship between an employer and one with whom he has contracted. See § 8–11, supra.) But as to independent contractors, the general rule has been ravaged by exceptions, to the point that it "is now primarily important as a preamble to the catalog of its exceptions." The Restatement states the general rule in one section (§ 409) followed by twenty-four sections that set forth the exceptions (§§ 410–429). Seven of those (§§ 410–415) involve liability based on the employer's own fault, and therefore are not, strictly speaking, exceptions to any *vicarious* liability rule; however, they are exceptions to the rule of nonliability for harm caused by the acts of the independent contractor, and all such exceptions may conveniently be treated together.

The various exceptions may be grouped into three general categories:

(1) The employer was negligent in selecting, instructing, or supervising the contractor;

(2) Out of some special relation to the public or to the plaintiff, there arises a duty that is of sufficient importance that defendant cannot escape responsibility for the proper performance of that duty by hiring an independent contractor to perform it;

(3) Work that is particularly or inherently dangerous.

(1) Employer's Own Negligence. Apart from any rule of vicarious liability, the employer of an independent contractor will be liable under ordinary principles of negligence for his own negligence in dealing with the contractor. Thus, he must exercise reasonable care to select a reasonably competent, experienced, careful, and properly equipped contractor. If the work will create a foreseeable danger to third persons, ordinary care may encompass a requirement that the employer insist (in the contract or otherwise) that the contractor take the necessary safety precautions, and then see that he does so. Reasonable care may also require inspections of completed work.

To the extent that the employer retains, by contract or in fact, authority to supervise and control the contractor's work, he will be liable for physical harm to others caused by his failure to exercise such supervision and control with reasonable care. This principle is important, since it is a common practice for employers to retain some such authority. Of course, his authority must be such that he could have acted with respect to the danger. A mere general right to supervise, receive reports, make suggestions, or alter the plans and specifications is usually not sufficient where such powers relate solely to the quality of the work and compliance with the plans. The control must involve the right to influence the manner of performance of the details of the work or otherwise to affect its safety.

(2) Nondelegable Duties. Where the safe performance of some duty is of sufficient importance to the community, the law will not permit the obligor to delegate his responsibility to an independent contractor and thereby insulate himself from tort liability for physical harm caused by its misperformance. Thus, one who does employ an independent contractor to perform such a duty will be vicariously liable for physical harm resulting from his contractor's negligence, even though the employer was himself entirely without fault.

The list of such duties is long, and there is as yet no general definition or test. They may be imposed by law (statutory or common), contract, franchise, or charter. What such duties seem to have in common is a substantial safety purpose underlying them. Examples include the duties owed by a common carrier to its passengers, the duty of a municipality to keep its streets in repair, the various duties owed by the owner or possessor of land to lessees and business visitors, the duty of an employer to provide his employees a safe place to work, the duty of the lessor or bailor of a chattel to maintain it in a reasonably safe condition, the duty of an auto owner to maintain adequate brakes, and the duty of one who deals with highly dangerous instrumentalities to construct and maintain them with care (e.g., a power company's duty to maintain its wires). Duties imposed by a statute or regulation requiring specific safeguards or precautions for the safety of others are nondelegable.

(3) Inherently Dangerous Work. Another important exception to the general rule is that there may be vicarious liability for the tort of an independent contractor where the work contracted to be performed involves some special, out-of-the-ordinary danger.

If the activity is one that may be classified "abnormally dangerous" such that one who engages in it will be subject to strict liability (e.g., blasting: see § 3–3), this exception clearly applies and the employer will be vicariously liable. But it is not so limited; "inherently dangerous" is much broader than "abnormally dangerous." A typical case involves the construction, repair or maintenance of a structure, which often will create special dangers to those in the vicinity. An independent contractor who hauls potatoes creates no *special* danger by the operation of his truck, and therefore there is no vicarious liability when he does so negligently; but one hired to transport explosives or huge logs that will be unusually dangerous if not securely fastened may subject his employer to vicarious liability under this exception when he is negligent with respect to the unusual risk.

While the risk must be a special or unusual one, it need not be an inevitable or unavoidable one. It is enough that the danger is one that is likely to arise in the normal course of the activity as that work is customarily done. Perhaps it is not strictly necessary to stack bricks on a public sidewalk in order to construct an adjoining building, but if it is to be anticipated then it is sufficiently inherent and this exception may be applied.

It will be observed that there is substantial overlap between the "nondelegable duty" and "inherently dangerous work" exceptions, since the employer's nondelegable duty is often based on the existence of some special danger to others. Many cases apply more than one of these exceptions.

Collateral Negligence. As a general rule, the employer's vicarious liability is limited to the particular risk or risks that give rise to the exception. In other words, the employer is *not* liable where the contractor's negligence pertains to or creates a risk that is collateral—not one of those inherent and foreseeable in the dangerous activity that creates the employer's liability. For example, there may be vicarious liability for physical harm caused when a bricklayer negligently drops a brick onto a passerby or negligently constructs a wall, but not where he negligently drives a truck en route to the brickyard.

Liability to Contractor's Employees. While the general rule seems to be that the employer's liability under these exceptions extends to injured employees of the contractor, there is a view that hold that the employer is not liable for injuries to the contractor's employees where the injuries arose out of those risks created by the conditions upon which the contractor was hired to work. In other words, suppose a contractor is hired to demolish an antiquated building (inherently dangerous work) and due to his failure to furnish certain safety equipment one of his employees is injured. There are those who would say that since the contractor is hired because of his (and his employee's) expertise in handling these risks, an owner, while perhaps liable to third persons who are strangers to the work, ought not to be liable to the contractor's own employees for injuries resulting from the very risks for which the contractor's expertise was sought.

Where the employer's liability is solely vicarious (as under the "nondelegable duty" and "inherently dangerous work" exceptions), an interesting and unresolved question is whether the contractor's immunity from tort liability to his own employee under the workers' compensation act would inure to the benefit of the employer of the contractor.

§ 8–13. Employer's Liability to Employee; Workers' Compensation

As commerce and industry flourished during the late nineteenth and early twentieth centuries, injuries to workers proliferated and became a major social problem.

In theory, if the accident was due to the employer's fault, the employee had his common law negligence action against his employer. But in practice, only a minor fraction of industrial injuries were compensated; limitations on the employer's duty and potent defenses often created insurmountable barriers to the employee's recovery.

In essence, the employer's basic common law duty is to exercise reasonable care to provide his employee with reasonably safe working conditions, and to warn of unsafe conditions that he should anticipate will not be discovered by the employee. It is analogous to the duty of a land owner or occupier to business invitees. Broken down into more specific components, this duty would include (1) a duty to provide safe premises, tools, equipment, structures, appliances and instrumentalities for the work; (2) a duty to provide a sufficient number of competent fellow servants so as not to create an unreasonable danger; (3) a duty to promulgate and enforce plans and rules for the conduct of the work and of the employees so as to make the work safe; (4) a duty to provide adequate supervision; (5) a duty to properly instruct the employee and to give him suitable work; and (6) so on. See Restatement (Second) of Agency §§ 492–520.

But even if it can be proved that the employer breached this duty (and such proof is often not easy, since ordinarily the other witnesses to the occurrence will be co-employees), the employee must circumvent the so-called "unholy trinity" of defenses—the fellow servant rule, contributory negligence, and assumption of risk.

The scope of the employer's liability is greatly constricted by the so-called "fellow servant" rule, which is both a duty limitation and a defense. Generally, the employer is not vicariously liable for an injury to an employee caused solely by the negligence of a fellow servant in the performance of the operative details of the work. The distinction is this. To the extent that a fellow servant is charged with responsibility to perform some part of the employer's duty to provide a safe place to work, the employer will be vicariously liable for that servant's negligence in executing that responsibility. It is sometimes said that the employer's duty to provide a safe place to work is nondelegable, and therefore he is vicariously liable for the negligence of anyone—employee or independent contractor—engaged to perform that duty on his behalf. Such an employee is sometimes called a "vice-principal," but this term is a little misleading since it does not matter whether the employee is superior or subordinate to the plaintiff. But when the fellow servant is doing work that is *not* in furtherance of the employer's duty to provide a safe place to work but rather is engaged in performing the "operative details" of the work of the enterprise (the ordinary tasks of production), the employer is not vicariously liable for his negligence that results in injury to plaintiff, a fellow employee. Thus, an employer may be liable for the negligent repair of a machine but not for its negligent operation.

In addition, the employer's defenses include contributory negligence and assumption of the risk. The usual rules of contributory negligence apply, even though they are especially inappropriate to a work environment, so that the employee's momentary lapse of care will bar or mitigate the employee's recovery. And where assumption of risk is still a complete bar, the employee is held to assume the risk of even negligently-created unsafe conditions of which he is (or is presumed to be) aware when he enters upon or continues his employment, even though under protest or economic duress. See § 5–5. It was once even held in some states that the employee could assume the risk of his employer's violation of safety statutes passed for his protection.

Decisions in some states have limited or abolished these defenses in certain cases. But, in general, these defenses were rather vigorously applied in favor of the employer. The result was that, absent legislation, most victims of industrial accidents bore the loss themselves as best they could, which was not very well.

During the late nineteenth century, as industrialization proceeded apace, the pressure to provide compensation for injured workers grew. In response, a number of states enacted a variety of employer liability statutes. Most retained common law tort principles of liability but limited or abolished some or all of the employer's defenses. Many of these applied exclusively to railroads. Other statutes created safety standards for particular kinds of work (e.g., structural work, mining) and provided the employee with a civil remedy for their violation. Most of these have now been rendered obsolete or have been superseded by workers' compensation, but occasionally such remedies survive.

Still, at the turn of the twentieth century, the statutory and common law remedies available to workers and their survivors were far from adequate, and interest mounted in the enactment of workers' compensation legislation along the lines of that then being adopted in Europe. It was urged on both humanitarian and economic grounds, as witnessed by the slogan, "the cost of the product should bear the blood of the workman." And it was correctly assumed that such legislation would create much-needed incentives to make greater provision for the safety of workers.

A workers' compensation act for federal employees was enacted in 1908, followed by the first state statute in New York in 1910. By 1921, most states had such a law, and today all do.

While there are important differences among the various statutes, the basic pattern is similar. Liability is strict. No employer negligence need be shown, and the "unholy trinity" common law defenses are not available. If a covered employee is injured in a work-related accident, his injury or his death is compensated according to a fixed schedule of benefits, irrespective of anyone's fault or lack thereof. Ordinarily benefits are payable weekly for a fixed number of weeks, and are computed as a percentage of the employee's weekly wages subject to a maximum limit. Compensable injuries usually include temporary and permanent disability (partial or total), fractures, total or partial loss of use of various specified parts of the body, disfigurement, and sometimes other permanent injuries. Death benefits are payable to designated dependents. And the employee is entitled to all necessary medical care. Many occupational diseases are compensated under the act or a related statute.

To obtain compensation, the employee must file his claim with the appropriate administrative agency. Usually an arbitrator initially determines whether the injury is compensable and what the award should be. An administrative board reviews or rehears the case and makes the award, approving, disapproving, or modifying the arbitrator's recommendation. Judicial review similar to that afforded other administrative rulings is then available.

Although the overwhelming majority of all employee injuries are compensable under some act, certain coverage issues remain. Due to early doubts about the constitutionality of such legislation (which were reinforced when the first New York act was held unconstitutional in 1911 because it imposed liability without fault), most acts were made wholly or partly elective, the latter making coverage mandatory only in the case of certain specified "hazardous" occupations. Often coverage was not required as to farm or domestic servants, or as to businesses employing less than a certain number of employees. However, no act since New York's first has been held invalid, and today there is little doubt that virtually any required coverage is permissible. Thus, there has been a strong trend to broaden coverage in most states. (Of course, as will be seen in the next two sections, most railroad and maritime employees are beyond the jurisdiction of state compensation legislation.)

Nearly all statutes require that the injury occur "by accident"; sometimes this is held to exclude damage that develops gradually over a period of time. The tendency has been to give this requirement the broadest possible interpretation, if indeed such injuries are not otherwise compensable under the occupational diseases act.

The injury must occur "in the course of" the employment, a concept similar to that discussed in § 8–11, supra. And the injury must also be one "arising out of" the employment, which roughly means that it must have at least some minimal connection with the risks of the employment.

If for some reason an injured employee is not within the coverage of a compensation act, then he may pursue any remedies otherwise available to him, including his common law negligence action against his employer. But if he is within the coverage of an act (whether or not his injury is compensable), workers' compensation is made his exclusive remedy against his own employer. His right to the full common law measure of damages for his injury has been exchanged for a reduced but relatively quick and certain compensation. However, he retains the right to bring any and all actions otherwise available to him against third persons who may have some common law or statutory liability for his injury. (In some states this does not include fellow servants, and in a few jurisdictions any third party who also happens to be covered by the compensation act is also immune.) For example, if he is injured by a defective punch press, he may collect compensation from his employer and then sue the press manufacturer in a product liability action. Of course, if his third party action is successful, his employer is entitled to reimbursement for his compensation payments, and in fact may bring such a third party suit if the employee fails to do so.

§ 8–14. Railroad Employees

If at the time of his work-related injury, an employee is lucky enough to be in the employment of a common carrier by rail, and if his work has a sufficient nexus with interstate commerce (i.e., di-

rectly or closely and substantially affects it), he is
under the benign protection of a special federal
statute: the Federal Employers' Liability Act (45
U.S.C.A. §§ 51–60).

The Act, adopted in 1908 (a 1906 version was
invalid), is based upon the same considerations that
were simultaneously generating the pressure that
would lead to the widespread enactment of workers'
compensation legislation. But railroading was then
a dominant and vital national enterprise, largely
interstate in character, and uniquely dangerous and
notorious for the carnage visited upon its workers.
Thus, there was thought to be a special need for
federal legislation directed solely at this industry,
and since it predated the general movement to
workers' compensation, the remedy was fashioned
by modifying traditional tort law doctrine. (Note
that a number of states had enacted employers'
liability acts of various types during the preceding
fifty years; many of them applied only to railroads.)

In essence, the F.E.L.A. preserves the railroad
employee's common law negligence action against
his employer while abolishing assumption of risk
and the fellow servant rule as defenses. The pure
form of comparative negligence is applied. Damages
are computed in accordance with the usual common
law rules.

One might speculate that the burden of proving
the railroad's negligence would reduce the remedy's
effectiveness and leave a number of injured workers
uncompensated. But, in keeping with the strong

trend of the courts to favor a compensation-oriented approach to the law of work-related injuries, special negligence rules have evolved. Following a series of cases in which the plaintiff's case was allowed to go to the jury even though evidence of negligence was weak, the Supreme Court in *Rogers v. Missouri Pac. R.R.* (U.S. 1957) declared that:

> Under this statute the test of a jury case is simply whether the proofs justify with reason the conclusion that employer negligence played *any part, even the slightest,* in producing the injury or death for which damages are sought. [Emphasis added.]

Thus, proof of only a very slight departure from ordinary care, or entirely circumstantial and somewhat speculative evidence of causation, will support a jury's verdict for plaintiff, even though in an ordinary (non-F.E.L.A.) negligence case the same evidence would require a directed verdict for defendant.

The Act preempts the employee's resort to any state law remedies that he might otherwise have had *against his employer.*

Certain statutes, which were formerly known as the Federal Safety Appliance Act (now Chapter 203 of Title 49 of the United States Code, 49 U.S.C.A. §§ 20301–20306) and the Boiler Inspection Act (now Chapter 207, "Locomotives," 49 U.S.C.A. §§ 20701–20703), impose absolute requirements with respect to certain parts of the train—locomotive, brakes, automatic couplers, grab irons, sill steps, ladders, running boards, etc. If the employee (or for that matter anyone else) is injured as a result of a violation of one of these statutory requirements, the railroad is strictly liable. Plaintiff need not prove that the violation was negligent, and his contributory negligence is no defense and does not mitigate his damages.

There has been a good deal of discussion, pro and con, as to whether F.E.L.A. is an effective remedy and whether railroaders and seamen (see § 8–15, infra) should be singled out to receive its benefits. However, such workers have generally resisted any efforts to shift them to a system of workers' compensation and thus appear reasonably satisfied with the present system.

§ 8–15. Maritime Employees

The maritime employee is in a class by himself because he is usually subject to the federal law of admiralty, a separate body of law with roots deep in the history and tradition of the law of the sea.

In general, if the employee is within federal maritime jurisdiction, the remedies for his work-related injuries or death are provided for by federal maritime law (including common law and statutory rules), which preempts pro tanto all state tort law. For this purpose, federal maritime jurisdiction includes all injuries or deaths occurring on board a vessel or caused by a vessel in navigable waters, as well as injuries occurring ashore that have some appropriate nexus to a vessel in navigable waters.

"Navigable waters" is a term of art that roughly means all waterways, including those inland, navigable in fact, which will support interstate or foreign commerce, either themselves or by connection with other waters.

A "vessel" is any floating structure capable of transporting something over the water.

There are two principal classes of maritime employees.

(1) *Seamen.* A seaman is a more or less permanent member of the ship's company (master, officer, or crewman) of a ship that is "in navigation," that is, capable of operation as a vessel (as opposed, e.g., to a floating restaurant that cannot leave the pier by itself).

(2) *Harbor workers* are all those (excluding seamen) who service the ship, such as longshoremen and maintenance and repair personnel, whether on board or dockside, and whether employed by the ship or by an independent contractor.

Very briefly, the principal remedies available to maritime workers include:

Maintenance and Cure. Any seaman who falls ill or is injured while in the service of his ship (whether on board or ashore and whether or not then actively engaged in the performance of his duties) is entitled to "maintenance and cure," an ancient form of workers' compensation consisting of wages to the end of the voyage (or other period of time for which he signed on) and subsistence, lodging and care until he reaches the maximum cure attainable. Liability is absolute, irrespective or anyone's fault or lack thereof, except that he may not recover for certain injuries caused by his own willful misconduct.

Seaworthiness. A *seaman* has a common law tort action against the ship or its owner for injuries caused by its being "unseaworthy." Traditionally, this form of strict liability involved a nondelegable duty to keep the ship and its appurtenances in good working order, and to supply sufficient proper and non-defective tools and equipment. But the concept has been broadened to include a duty to employ a sufficient and reasonably competent crew, and even to transitory unsafe conditions, such as an oil slick on the deck or the misfeasance of other ship personnel. Thus, it now amounts to a warranty of the fitness of the ship, its appurtenances and crew, irrespective of anyone's negligence and of the exercise of reasonable care by the other seamen on board. It is, therefore, a very potent remedy, particularly since the usual common law measure of damages applies.

Until Congress took it away from them in 1972, this remedy had been judicially extended to most harbor workers on the ingenious theory that they were doing work that seamen had historically done.

Jones Act (Negligence). The seaman's common law negligence action against his own employer was subject to the same limitations and inadequacies that had prompted workers' compensation legislation and the F.E.L.A. The seamen persuaded Congress to give them the latter, and in 1920 the Jones Act (46 App. U.S.C.A. § 688) extended the benefits of the F.E.L.A. to seamen by merely incorporating most of its operative provisions by reference.

Defenses. The obligation for maintenance and cure is absolute (except for certain injuries caused by the seaman's own willful misconduct). As to unseaworthiness and the Jones Act, the traditional maritime rule of pure comparative negligence is applied, and assumption of the risk is no defense except to the extent that it also constitutes contributory negligence and accordingly mitigates the award; the fellow servant defense is also unavailable.

Concurrence of Remedies. Maintenance and cure, unseaworthiness and the Jones Act are concurrent remedies, and the seaman (depending on which court he selects) may sue his employer for all three in the same lawsuit. Of course, these remedies are not cumulative; there is considerable overlap in the measure of damages and no double recovery is permitted. In addition, if his injury was caused in whole or in part by the fault of some third person, he may bring any tort action otherwise available to him against that third person, often in the same lawsuit, again with the proviso against double recovery.

Harbor Workers. If a harbor worker's work brings him within the scope of federal maritime jurisdiction, he is for that reason beyond the reach of state workers' compensation laws. Not being a seaman, he does not receive maintenance and cure. And his common law negligence action against his own employer is subject to the same difficulties previously discussed (§ 8–13).

However, for some reason the harbor workers never persuaded Congress to bring them under the Jones Act, although clearly it could have done so. It opted instead for workers' compensation and twice attempted to bestow upon the harbor worker for the benefits of the appropriate state compensation law. The Supreme Court scotched both attempts as unlawful delegations of federal power to the states. When the Court in 1926 held that a harbor worker could be a "seaman" under the Jones Act, Congress enacted the Longshoremen's and Harbor Workers' Compensation Act (33 U.S.C.A. §§ 901–950). It is similar to the state compensation acts, and in fact was patterned after the then New York Act. It compensates work-related injuries or deaths of most harbor workers within the scope of maritime jurisdiction, *except* where the work is deemed "local" in nature—that is, only incidental to navigation and commerce. In such cases, the appropriate state's compensation act applies, if the worker is otherwise covered by such an act. If the work falls within what is called the "twilight zone" where it cannot be determined in advance of trial whether or not the work is local in nature, the worker may choose either state or federal compensation.

Compensation under the Act is the exclusive remedy against the harbor worker's employer (be he ship owner or independent contractor), but does not bar any tort actions otherwise available against third persons, such as a common law negligence (but *not,* recall, Jones Act or unseaworthiness) action against a ship owner not his employer, or a products liability case. In such actions, if the harbor worker is within the scope of maritime jurisdiction, any appropriate admiralty law rules (e.g., comparative negligence) will apply to such third party suits.

Limitation of Liability. By statute (46 App. U.S.C.A. § 183), a shipowner may in certain cases limit his maximum *personal* liability for injury or death to the value of his interest in the vessel after the occurrence (but not less than $420 per ton), if he was without "privity or knowledge" of the cause of the loss. Generally, this means that he was without personal fault in the matter and had no prior knowledge of the situation or condition that caused the injury.

D.   AUTOMOBILES

§ 8–16.   Special Automobile Liability Rules

Automobile accidents are another important social problem, and it is not surprising that there are some special tort law rules applicable to this activity. For the most part, such rules' main purpose is to insure a financially responsible defendant so that plaintiff's loss will be compensated. They developed at a time when automobile liability insurance was not so prevalent nor so broad in coverage as it is

today, and thus they are not nearly so important
now as they once were. In particular, they have
been rendered largely unnecessary by the so-called
"omnibus clause" in auto policies that makes anyone driving the auto with the insured's permission
an additional insured. Nevertheless, they remain a
part of the fabric of our tort law, and therefore
must be noted. And in some cases they will provide
an additional defendant whose own insurance policy
may be "stacked" on top of the driver's policy to
increase the available limits.

Joint Enterprise. As previously noted (§§ 8–10
and 8–11), partners and the principals in a joint
venture are vicariously liable to third persons for
each other's negligence within the scope of the
business activity. The doctrine of joint enterprise is
a unique creation of U.S. courts that, under analogous circumstances, extends the same principle to
the operation of an automobile, so that all participants are vicariously liable to third persons for the
negligence of the driver.

Basically, a joint enterprise is founded upon an
express or implied agreement among two or more
persons to use an automobile for a common purpose, with all participants having a mutual right of
direction and control over its operation. At one
time, some courts held that *any* common purpose
was sufficient; but today, most require some business, financial or pecuniary interest in the objective
of the journey. The mutual right of control requires
that all have an equal voice; thus, there will usually

be no joint enterprise when an employee is riding
with his employer, even though for a common business purpose. Even joint ownership or possession of
the vehicle, or the sharing of the driving or expenses, are ordinarily not conclusive proof of the
mutual right of control, although they may be some
evidence of that right. In the final analysis, it is the
express or implied understanding of the parties that
is determinative, which is of course a question of
fact for the jury.

Owner–Passenger. At one time, some courts
held that an automobile owner who was a passenger
in his own car was *vicariously* liable for the negligence of the driver on the theory that by virtue of
his ownership alone he had the right to exercise
control over the driving. Most courts, however,
went no further than to create a rebuttable presumption that the driver is the agent of the owner-
passenger. Of course, an owner-passenger who *in
fact* retains the right to control the operation of the
auto is *personally*—not vicariously—liable for his
negligence in the exercise of that control.

Owner Not a Passenger. In the absence of a
statute or the family purpose doctrine, an owner-
bailor who merely permits another to use his automobile is not vicariously liable for the driver's negligence unless the driver was then his agent acting
within the scope of his employment. (In most jurisdictions there is a rebuttable presumption that such
an agency exists.) The single exception is Florida,
which has declared an automobile to be a "danger-

ous instrumentality" and thus the owner is vicariously liable when another person negligently operates it.

Family Purpose Doctrine. About half the states have accepted the "family purpose doctrine," under which the owner of an auto that he makes generally available for personal (noncommercial) use by members of his immediate household is vicariously liable for its negligent operation by such persons within the scope of the express or implied permission. In effect, the family unit is treated as a "business," and a member of that unit who uses the vehicle within the scope of that "business" subjects its owner to vicarious liability as if she were the owner's agent.

Consent Statutes. About one-fourth of the states have a form of statutory vicarious liability making the owner of an automobile vicariously liable for the negligence of anyone operating it on a public highway with the owner's consent, within the scope of the express or implied permission.

Imputed Contributory Negligence. The foregoing rules were designed for the protection of third persons injured by the driver's negligence. An interesting question often arises as to whether these various vicarious liability rules may be used in reverse, imputing the driver's negligence to the owner or other principal so as to bar his recovery under the rule of contributory negligence for harm he himself sustains as a result of the driver's negligence. As a matter of principle the answer should be no, but courts have sometimes held otherwise. See § 5–2, supra.

Guest Passengers. Guest passengers in an automobile have a status that was once thought to be analogous to that of a licensee upon real property. Based on this idea, statutes in some states (and judicial decisions in a few others) limited the auto owner's or driver's duty to guest passengers.

The statutes usually restricted liability to cases where the driver's conduct was reckless ("willful and wanton misconduct") or where the injury was caused by the driver's intoxication. Absent such a statute, some jurisdictions, by judicial decision, hold the driver liable for her negligent operation of the car and for harm caused by known defects, but not for injuries caused by defects in the vehicle of which the driver has no knowledge; the guest is said to "assume the risk" of such defects, and the owner or driver has no duty to him to inspect and discover them. Occasional cases and statutes, by analogy to the law of bailments, limited liability to the driver's "gross" negligence.

The difficult problem, of course, is to determine when the passenger is a "guest." Generally, he is not only if there is some direct or indirect pecuniary benefit to the host, as where the passenger pays for the ride or where some business interest of the host is being served by the passenger's presence (e.g., he is a prospective customer). Sharing the expenses of the trip may be sufficient, at least if agreed upon in advance (as opposed to the passenger, as a matter of courtesy, merely insisting upon paying for a tank of gasoline). Usually an owner cannot be a guest in her own car, nor can a child too young to understand his status be a guest. And a guest ceases to be such when his demand to be allowed to leave the vehicle is refused.

The guest statutes were passed largely at the urging of insurance companies who feared collusive lawsuits. But the possibility of fraud is now seen as greatly outweighed by the injustice of arbitrarily denying legitimate claims. No state any longer applies the rule as a matter of common law, and most states' guest statutes have been repealed. In some states, following the lead of California in *Brown v. Merlo* (Cal. 1973), guest statutes have been declared unconstitutional as arbitrary denials of the equal protection of the laws. Today, only a handful of jurisdictions still have such laws, and in some of those the statute's application is limited (e.g., to hitchhikers, members of the driver's family, or to particular types of vehicles).

§ 8–17. Automobile Accident Compensation

Motor vehicle traffic ranks high as a major source of injuries and deaths in this country, and indeed in all prosperous countries. Until very recently, tort law, as enforced through the litigation process, has had to shoulder a large share of the responsibility for compensating traffic accident victims in order to reduce the economic disruption that these losses cause.

From the advent of the automobile, there have been those who have suggested that all those who engage in the activity should share the costs of the inevitable traffic accidents. If one accepts this premise—and the number who do is increasing—then it is immediately obvious that there are much better and more efficient mechanisms for accomplishing this than the traditional tort litigation process. Indeed, recalling our discussion of the functions of tort law (§ 1–2), we saw that it was never intended to compensate every injured plaintiff; for the most part, it is designed to shift the loss from a more or less innocent plaintiff to a defendant who was somehow at fault in causing plaintiff's injury. Thus, tort law requires a fairly elaborate litigation process in order to determine fault and whether plaintiff is or is not entitled to compensation—in other words, whether he *qualifies* to have the law command another to reimburse him for his losses. Today, many want to abolish fault as a necessary qualification for compensation—and thereby eliminate the need for litigation to assess fault—and simply compensate all who are injured, at least for their basic economic losses, and distribute these costs more or less evenly among all who own or operate motor vehicles as a part of the price of ownership or operation.

Clearly, the widespread acceptance of automobile liability insurance was an important intermediate step in the retreat from the fault ethic. Since most defendants are insured, the losses of those plaintiffs who *are* compensated are in fact already being spread among the motoring public as a group. The impact of liability on any one defendant is slight, usually consisting, at most, of a manageable increase in his insurance rates. Thus, as to each motorist, we have assessed as a cost of his driving not the full cost of his *individual* fault, but merely his proportionate share of the total fault of the *entire group* (insured motorists). Having divorced individual fault from personal liability as to *defendants,* it now seems somewhat arbitrary and unjust to require a *plaintiff* to establish an individual defendant's fault in order to qualify for a share in the common compensation fund.

Those who favor some sort of "no-fault" compensation system for traffic accident victims have supported their view in large part by leveling a number of criticisms at the existing tort-litigation system. In essence, these criticisms may be groups as follows:

(1) *Not all traffic victims are compensated and those who are, are frequently over-or under-compensated.* This is certainly true. Of course, in some cases compensation is reduced or denied because the victim was contributorily negligent, or denied because defendant was not negligent. Those who support the fault requirement would not consider this a defect in the present system.

However, there are other reasons why some plaintiffs receive too little or too much. Some defendants are uninsured or underinsured. Insurance policy defenses occasionally permit the insurer to escape liability for plaintiff's judgment. Some needy plaintiffs are forced to settle too cheaply. Juries, for reasons that may or may not be apparent, sometimes return excessive or inadequate verdicts. Lawyers' fees and costs reduce most awards, but benefits paid from collateral sources (e.g., health, accident and disability insurance, wage continuation plans) do not. Damages for lost income are not taxable. Large verdicts for punitive damages or noneconomic losses (e.g., pain and suffering, humiliation) may amount to a windfall. But damage awards, when finally received, are paid in a lump sum (instead of periodically as required to replace lost income or future medical expenses) which too often is quickly dissipated.

Many of these problems, and particularly those involving insurance, could be solved through modifications of the existing system. For example, most states require *all* drivers to have liability insurance, and a few states have an unsatisfied judgments fund. All could. Most states also have some type of financial responsibility law, requiring either (a) one involved in an accident that injures another or (b) one who has an unsatisfied judgment against him resulting from such an accident, to furnish proof that he can satisfy claims arising from *future* accidents up to some relatively modest amount in order to retain his license. (They are notoriously ineffective, except as an inducement to purchase minimal insurance.) Insurance against injuries caused by an uninsured motorist is universally available, but of course it pays only when it can be proved that the uninsured motorist was negligent. And a surprising number of drivers manage to evade compulsory liability insurance laws.

Nevertheless, potential reforms of the *liability* insurance system do not meet the basic criticism that liability ought not to be required as a condition of compensation in the first place.

(2) *"Fault" is difficult and uncertain of proof, or else is easy to falsify.* To some extent this is true of every injury claim, including those not arising from a traffic accident. But certainly it is especially true of many vehicular accidents, where often little hard evidence of any value is available on the fault issue and the claim must be proved or disproved by the oral testimony of witnesses (the most important of whom are interested in the outcome) based on their memory of events that occurred during a traumatic few seconds, months or years earlier.

(3) *Litigation is too slow, cumbersome, involved, elaborate, costly, and wasteful of precious resources, especially as to relatively small claims.* The preparation and trial of a lawsuit certainly can be a time and resource-consuming process, involving investigation, pre-trial discovery (interrogatories, depositions, etc.), preparation of exhibits and witnesses, and the trial itself, which even in the simple case requires a number of hours of the time of lawyers, a judge and other court personnel, jurors, witnesses, and various other supporting staff. Cases often take a year or more to prepare for trial, and delays of several years are not uncommon on metropolitan dockets; meanwhile the victims do without. And

while the overwhelming majority of such cases are settled without trial, most are not settled until at least the fact-gathering process is complete, many not until suit is filed, and some not until the trial itself. Lawyers' fees and other costs are high. According to some studies, only about forty-four cents of every auto insurance premium dollar reaches the victim's pocket; the remainder pays for the cost of operating the compensation system, not counting the public funds that support the court, its personnel and facilities.

Nevertheless, it is no indictment of the litigation process merely to say that it is costly and time-consuming, and does not invariably reach the ideal result. One must ask (1) does it do substantial justice, and (2) is it worth the cost—that is, are sufficient benefits received in return or are community values sufficiently realized to justify the time, money, and effort expended in the process.

So far as the automobile accident case is concerned, fairminded persons can and do differ in their answers to these questions. Most trial lawyers are of the opinion that the present negligence litigation system can be modified so that it will produce substantial justice. Reforms suggested by plaintiffs' lawyers include universal adoption of comparative negligence (a goal now nearly reached), compulsory auto liability insurance with realistically high mandatory limits (or no limits), compulsory "medical payments" coverage expanded to include some payment for disability, expanded court facilities, and better unsatisfied judgments funds. Lawyers who customarily represent defendants (i.e., insurers) would regulate the contingent fee, abolish the "collateral source" rule and require plaintiffs to credit their judgments with medical and disability benefits received from other sources, regulate compensation for pain and suffering, provide for arbitration or small claims, and punish fraudulent claims.

Critics of the present system charge that trial lawyers' opinions are consciously or unconsciously biased by their obvious self-interest. In their view, no amount of tinkering with the present system will remedy its inadequacies. The fault requirement will still produce erratic and inconsistent results; dishonest plaintiffs will too often prevail and honest ones suffer; costly and painful delays will still occur; and too many victims who are no less deserving of compensation than the successful plaintiffs will get nothing at all. And they believe that the litigation process is an expensive luxury that the U.S. motorist can no longer afford, especially since it does not operate to sort out deserving and undeserving claimants.

Out of the heated debate that has raged over these issues a realistic compromise seems to be emerging. Compensate *all* victims' basic economic losses—medical and hospital expenses, and lost wages or services—and thereby eliminate the small cases where the litigation process is most inefficient; and preserve the tort claim (based on fault) for the more serious injuries, which are a small fraction of the total number of cases.

A variety of "no-fault" auto compensation plans, too numerous and varied to catalog here, have been put forth. Most prominent among them are the Columbia (University) Plan (1932), the Saskatchewan Plan (1946), Prof. Ehrenzweig's "Full Aid" Plan (1954), Prof. Conard's "social insurance" plan (1964), and the well-known Keeton–O'Connell Plan (1965). These have spawned countless other plans, all variations on the same basic themes, some of which have reached the legislative arena. Accurate generalization is difficult, but the various plans have some common features.

(1) *No-fault compensation.* The heart of all plans is some form of compensation for personal injuries and deaths which is paid to all victims of automobile accidents, irrespective of fault. Most are funded by private first-party insurance—that is, the benefits are paid to the victim by his own insurer, as opposed to third-party or liability insurance where the victim is paid by the insurer of the person (other than himself) who was responsible for the accident. In this respect it is similar in form to other kinds of health or accident insurance, and to the optional "medical payments" coverage commonly offered with most present auto liability policies. Under a few of the plans, none of which have so far been adopted in this country (except in Puerto Rico), the government collects and administers the compensation fund. (Occasional proposals call for

financing through the social security system or even general tax revenues. But unless financed by a tax on motorists, such a system is subject to the criticism that the activity (automobile traffic) does not bear the costs it generates.)

Under most plans, a certain basic coverage is mandatory. One cannot register or operate an automobile without it.

Benefits usually include medical, hospital and funeral expenses, lost wages, physical rehabilitation and (in the case of victims who are not wage earners) the cost of replacing his or her domestic services, all subject under most plans to maximum limits, either on each category of benefits or on total benefits. Occasionally benefits of a certain type are unlimited, as in the case of medical expenses in a few plans.

Sometimes optional broader coverages are available, including damages for noneconomic losses (e.g., pain and suffering).

Under some plans, the benefits payable must be credited with reimbursement received from other sources, such as other medical or disability insurance, social security, workers' compensation, etc.

(2) *Tort liability.* It is generally recognized that the cost of no-fault compensation would be prohibitive, absent an offsetting decrease in the frequency of liability claims under the tort system. There are two schools of thought on the best method of achieving this.

(a) Most plans expressly abolish the tort cause of action, making the no-fault compensation the exclusive remedy, to the extent that the loss does not exceed a certain minimum or "threshold" level. Under these plans, typically there is no tort remedy unless the victim's medical (or other) expenses exceed a certain dollar amount, or unless the injury sustained is one of those expressly designated as "serious," such as death, dismemberment, permanent disfigurement or impairment of some part of the body, fractures, and the like. Under the Keeton–O'Connell Plan, tort liability is abrogated unless the compensable economic loss exceeds $10,000 or pain and suffering damages exceed $5,000 in value.

(b) Some plans contain no prohibition of tort litigation. Their premise is that since plaintiff's insurer who has paid no-fault benefits must be reimbursed from the proceeds of any tort recovery obtained from a third party tortfeasor, those with small claims will usually be discouraged from pursuing them because they stand to gain too little. Perhaps more importantly, few lawyers would find it economically feasible to handle such claims. Proponents of this alternative believe that the savings thus achieved on liability insurance costs will more or less offset the increased cost of no-fault compensation, while preserving maximum individual freedom to resort to the tort system for those who feel strongly enough that they want to do so.

Much of the controversy between the proponents and opponents of no fault compensation has centered around its costs. Will no-fault increase or decrease insurance rates, and how much? The results with respect to the first generation of no-fault plans are mixed. Now that many states have experience with no-fault systems, accurate data should be available, but preliminary statistics are inconclusive.

Not counting Puerto Rico (1968), the first U.S. state to enact a no-fault compensation plan was Massachusetts, effective January 1, 1971. Today, about 15 states have true no-fault plans, and another ten or so have "add-on" plans that require that insureds be offered first-party no-fault benefits providing compensation for certain specified economic loss. Since the first wave of popularity of these plans in the 1970s, interest in no-fault has subsided; a few states have cut back or repealed their plans, and there have been no recent adoptions.

No-fault auto compensation legislation was first introduced in Congress in 1971. Originally conceived as a comprehensive national uniform plan, it did not pass in that form and so it evolved into the "National Standards For No–Fault Insurance Plans Act." This bill would have permitted the various states to enact their own versions of compulsory no-fault plans, except that state laws would be required to meet or exceed the standards set forth in some detail in the federal act as to coverages, benefits, exclusions, and limitations on tort liability. In any state whose law did not meet the federal standards (or that failed to pass any law), an even stronger federal no-fault compensation act would automatically have taken effect. Opponents of the bill argued that the states were in fact passing various forms of no-fault legislation, and that they should be permitted to continue to do so; that the subject is complex with many variables, the idea is largely untried, and thus state-by-state experimentation ought to be encouraged. The opponents prevailed, and the act failed to pass. Another federal no-fault bill was introduced in 2000 (S.B.837), but it, too, has so far failed to pass.

Some (but not all) of the arguments in favor of no-fault compensation for victims of auto accidents also apply to those injured in other ways. Thus, no-fault compensation systems have been proposed that would partly or totally replace the traditional tort remedies in areas such as products liability, medical malpractice, and premises liability, ultimately extending perhaps to all accident injuries and deaths. See, e.g., J. O'Connell, *Ending Insult to Injury: No–Fault Insurance for Products and Services* (1975); Franklin, *Replacing the Negligence Lottery: Compensation and Selective Reimbursement*, 53 Va. L.Rev. 774 (1967). Such proposals face even stiffer opposition than has no-fault auto insurance, and bring into sharp focus both jurisprudential and empirical questions about the functions and operation of the tort-litigation system. All that is certain is that vigorous and healthy debate will continue over these matters for some time to come.

E. OTHER SPECIAL LIABILITY RULES

§ 8–18. Medical and Other Professional Negligence ("Malpractice")

Negligent conduct by persons practicing a profession or, in some cases, a skilled trade (physician or other skilled health care provider, dentist, optometrist, lawyer, accountant, engineer, architect, clergy, teacher, veterinarian, etc.) is commonly termed "malpractice." The term is an unfortunate one, because it connotes a greater degree of fault than the law requires.

Professional negligence is the failure to exercise the degree of care and skill that is exercised by reasonably well-qualified professionals in that field. As such, this standard of care is similar to the standard applied in all other negligence cases, with one important exception. As to some professions (health care providers and, in some jurisdictions, others as well), the standard is not what the reasonably prudent professional ought to have done, but rather what the reasonably well-qualified professional *ordinarily* and *customarily* does in fact. In other words, the profession itself sets the standard by its own custom and practice. It is a rare case in which the court is willing to hold that the usual practice in the profession can be found to be negligent (e.g., *Helling v. Carey*, Wash. 1974).

With respect to medical doctors (and sometimes dentists and others), the standard of care has been further limited by the so-called "locality rule." A physician historically was required only to possess and apply the knowledge and use the skill and care that is ordinarily used by reasonably well-qualified physicians *in the locality in which she practices,* or, usually, in "similar localities." This frequently made it difficult or impossible for plaintiff to prove the applicable standard since other doctors in the same locality are notoriously reluctant to testify against their professional colleagues. However, with the advent of improved communication and continuing medical education, the reason for the rule has abated, and today the trend is toward its abolition.

When the profession recognizes specialists—as do medicine, dentistry, and to some extent the law—a specialist (including one who holds himself out as a specialist) is held to the higher standard of the specialized subgroup. (The locality rule is rarely applied to specialists, as their standard is typically a national one.)

In earlier times, when medical knowledge was less advanced, courts were forced to recognize divergent medical theories represented by different "schools" of medicine, and to judge doctors by the tenets of the "school" to which she belonged. Today, the accepted standards of diagnosis and treatment tend to be uniform nationally, although there are still many specific matters on which respectable medical authorities differ. This is largely a matter for expert testimony, and there is no longer need to recognize "schools" as such. Of course, where the legislature has expressly sanctioned other types of healers, such as chiropractors, podiatrists, and osteopaths, members of these groups will be judged by their own standards when acting within the areas of their competence.

Informed consent describes another special liability rule applied in professional negligence cases. As previously noted (§ 7–2, supra), tortious conduct can be authorized by consent. That consent must be based on the professional's disclosure of the material risks and alternatives to the proposed conduct so that the patient/client can make an informed decision as to the best course of action. In medical cases, at one time the prevailing standard only required the doctor to inform the patient of those risks and alternatives that doctors customarily chose to disclose. Known as the "professional standard," this is still the rule in some jurisdictions. However, it is being replaced by the "reasonable patient" standard, which gives the patient greater autonomy: the doctor must disclose those risks and alternatives of which a reasonable patient would want to be informed so as to be able to make an intelligent choice. In other words, all risks *material* to the decision of the ordinary patient in the plaintiff's position. Note that a violation of this standard does not negate the consent (so as to give rise to a battery) but rather is simply another instance of negligent conduct. The patient still must prove that the lack of proper disclosure caused him to undertake the procedure with the resulting injury.

The "Medical Malpractice Crisis" and Tort Reform. Although tort reform is a perennial, the last several decades have produced a bumper harvest. A large component of the recent reforms has been the result of dramatic increases in the cost of medical malpractice insurance premiums. Whatever the underlying reason(s) for these increases, many state legislatures were convinced that the remedy was to modify tort and procedural rules in favor of physician-defendants. Typical changes have included modifications to the medical standard of care and medical res ipsa loquitur rules; partial abrogation of the collateral source rule (see § 9–1); statutes of repose (see § 5–7); restrictions on expert testimony; arbitrary limits on the amount recoverable in a medical malpractice action, either generally or for non-economic losses; and mandatory submission of the case to a screening panel prior to taking the case to court. Some of these reform measures have been held unconstitutional, and the mix and type of changes vary from state to state, but one or more of these changes are now the law in most jurisdictions. As of this writing, proposals are being advanced to enact such reforms at the federal level.

§ 8–19. Nuisance and Environmental Law

"Nuisance" is one of those amorphous concepts in the law that cannot be concisely defined and is often misunderstood and misused. As Dean Prosser noted, at one time or another it has meant all things to all persons. The principal sources of confusion are (1) a tendency toward indiscriminate use of the term and (2) a failure to recognize and to focus upon the fact that it is in essence merely a form of action for particular kinds of *harm* with special rules as to when and how that harm may be redressed. It is the interest of plaintiff that has been invaded, and not the conduct of the defendant, which determines whether an action for nuisance will lie. Liability for interference with such a protected interest may be based upon defendant's *intent* to interfere, *negligence, strict liability* for abnormally dangerous activities, or occasionally upon violation of a *statute*. But the character of defendant's activity or conduct is irrelevant in distinguishing nuisance from other torts; it is the nature of the harm to plaintiff to which one must look. Indeed, strictly speaking, nuisance may not be a tort at all, but merely a category of certain types of harm. Unfortunately, there are a number of cases in which the term "nuisance" is used improperly and unnecessarily, as where plaintiff is actually being (or ought to be) permitted to recover under some other tort theory.

To understand nuisance at all, it is essential to bear in mind the distinction between *public nuisance* and *private nuisance*.

Private Nuisance. Properly conceived, a private nuisance is a thing or activity that substantially and unreasonably interferes with the possessor's *use and enjoyment* of his land or an interest in land.

This interference may occur in a variety of ways. For example, there may be a physical effect upon the land itself, such as by vibration, objects hurled upon it, destruction of crops, flooding, or pollution of its water or soil. Or it may consist of a disturbance of the comfort, convenience or health of the occupant, as by foul odors, smoke, dust, insects, noxious gases, excessive noise, excessive light or high temperatures, and even repeated telephone calls. Under proper circumstances it may even extend to conditions on adjoining land that impair the plaintiff's mental tranquility by the fear or offensive nature of their mere presence, such as a house of ill repute, a contagious disease hospital, stored explosives, or a vicious animal.

The important thing to remember is that the interference must be with the *use and enjoyment* of plaintiff's interest in *land*. Similar interferences that affect plaintiff only personally, and do not affect his use and enjoyment of his land, may be some other tort but they are not a private nuisance.

It will be seen that there are situations in which nuisance will be a concurrent remedy with trespass to land (§ 6–7), which, recall, protects one's right to exclusive possession against physical invasions. An interference with that right frequently will also be an interference with the use and enjoyment of the land. At one time, a trespass had to be direct; if defendant merely set forces in motion that eventually resulted in an invasion of the land, the remedy (if any) was in nuisance. And trespass could not be maintained for invasions of air-borne gases and particles not visible to the naked eye. On the other hand, nuisance, a form of the action of case, required proof of fault and actual damages; trespass did not. In its modern form, trespass requires proof of fault, but may be direct or indirect, and it has been held that microscopic particles wafted on the breeze may constitute a trespass. Thus, trespass and nuisance are now more often concurrent remedies than in earlier times.

Public Nuisance. A public nuisance is so different from a private one that it is unfortunate that the term "nuisance" is applied to both. Public and private nuisances are separate and distinct wrongs that developed independently. The area of overlap between them is not very great, and is largely accidental.

A public nuisance is an act or omission that obstructs or causes inconvenience or damage to the public in the exercise of rights common to all. It is fundamentally a catch-all collection of minor crimes, originally common law and now largely legislative in origin, to be redressed by criminal prosecution. "It includes interferences with the public health, as in the case of a hogpen, the keeping of diseased animals, or a malarial pond; with the public safety, as in the case of the storage of explosives, the shooting of fireworks in the streets, harboring a vicious dog, or the practice of medicine by one not qualified; with public morals, as in the case of houses of prostitution, illegal liquor establishments, gambling houses, indecent exhibitions, bullfights, unlicensed prize fights, or public profanity; with the public peace, as by loud and disturbing noises, or an opera performance that threatens to cause a riot; with the public comfort, as in the case of bad odors, smoke, dust and vibration; with public convenience, as by obstructing a highway or a navigable stream, or creating a condition that makes travel unsafe or highly disagreeable, or the collection of an inconvenient crowd; and in addition, such unclassified offenses as eavesdropping on a jury, or being a common scold." Prosser, § 90 at 643–45.

The interest or right that is interfered with must be one that is common to the *public* as a *class,* and not merely that of one person or even a group of citizens (except by statute in a few states where interference with the rights of a substantial number of persons is sufficient, even though no public right as such is involved). The pollution of a river is only a private nuisance insofar as it interferes with the rights of the riparian owners to make use of the water; but if it also kills the fish or impairs a public water supply it is to that extent a public nuisance.

In addition to broad, general criminal public nuisance statutes, all states have a number of specific provisions declaring certain things (e.g., bawdy houses, certain plants, houses where narcotics are sold, mosquito breeding grounds) to be public nuisances.

A private citizen has no civil remedy for the harm he has sustained as a result of a public nuisance if that harm is of the same kind as that suffered by the general public, even though he may have been harmed to a greater degree than others. A criminal prosecution is the exclusive remedy. But an individual who has sustained damage particular to him, different in kind from that of the public, may maintain a tort action for his damages. Thus, where dynamiting has thrown a large boulder onto a public highway, members of the public who use the highway (even those who use it much more frequently than most) have no action for the inconvenience caused by the obstruction. But a motorist who collides with the boulder has sustained damage of a kind different from that of the general public, and so may sue for his personal injuries.

If a public nuisance interferes with plaintiff's use and enjoyment of his land, it is a private nuisance as well. And since this injury is particular to him and different in kind from that suffered by the public, he may sue for his damages under either theory. Usually it is preferable to rely on the public nuisance theory, since in such cases certain defenses (prescriptive rights, laches, statute of limitations) are not available.

Basis of Liability: Fault. Notwithstanding some early cases to the contrary, nuisance liability is not absolute. Absent a statute, defendant's interference with plaintiff's protected interest must have been intentional, reckless, negligent, or the result of an abnormally dangerous activity (see § 3–3) such that principles of strict liability will apply. The requisite intent, if that is the theory of liability, is similar to that of other intentional torts (see § 6–1), and it is sufficient if defendant created the condition or continued his conduct after he acquired knowledge of actual harm, or a substantial certainty of future harm, to plaintiff's interest.

Thus, attempts that some have undertaken to distinguish nuisance from, for example, negligence liability reflect a fundamental misconception. Nuisance is a type of harm; negligence is one basis on which liability for that harm may be imposed.

In addition, nuisance liability may be based upon violation of a statute, and in such cases (within constitutional limits) there will be no need to find fault or some other basis beyond the requirements of the statute to support nuisance liability.

Basis of Liability: Substantial Interference. Nuisance liability requires some substantial interference with the interest involved. Where the physical condition of property is affected, it is not too difficult to distinguish the substantial from the insubstantial. This is not always so, however, in cases of personal inconvenience, annoyance, or discomfort. Generally, the standard is that of the ordinary member of that community with normal sensitivity and temperament. Similarly, plaintiff cannot, by devoting his land to an unusually sensitive use, make a nuisance out of conduct on defendant's adjoining premises that would otherwise be relatively harmless. Beyond this, whether or not the harm is substantial is a question of fact.

At one time it was thought that a nuisance did not exist unless the interference was continuing or recurring; a single interference of relatively short duration was not enough. Despite the persistence of occasional pronouncements to this effect, there is no such requirement. However, it is true that certain kinds of interferences are substantial or unreasonable only because they are continuing or recurring. And where an injunction is sought, it is obviously necessary that there be a threat of future harm.

Reasonableness of Defendant's Conduct. Not only must the interference with plaintiff's interest be substantial; it must also be unreasonable to require him to bear it, or to bear it without compensation. This balancing process, weighing the respective interests of plaintiff and defendant, is of course required in any event where the basis of liability is negligence. A similar balancing process is used in determining whether an activity is "abnormally dangerous" such that strict liability is appropriate (see § 3–3). But in the case of a nuisance, it is also a prerequisite to liability for harm that is intentionally inflicted. In effect, defendant has a privilege to cause substantial harm to an interest of the plaintiff that would otherwise be protected by the law of nuisance if, on balance, his conduct is reasonable under all the circumstances.

This reasonableness test may be applied to public nuisances, unless there is a statute that establishes the standard of conduct (i.e., makes something a nuisance per se) and therefore precludes further inquiry into the reasonableness of defendant's activity. But the primary application of the requirement is in cases of private nuisance.

The rationale behind the reasonableness requirement is that in a crowded society, some accommodation to the activities of others is necessary. Some activities are socially useful (particularly those relating to industry, commerce and trade), or at least do not deserve to be prohibited or unduly burdened, and therefore will be tolerated even though they impinge to some extent on others and on the tranquility, comfort, and quiet enjoyment of their land. At the same time, some activities may fairly be required to bear the cost of the harm they cause, where the cost is reasonable under all the circumstances.

The balancing process by which reasonableness is determined is not unlike that used to determine whether conduct is negligent. Essentially, the nature and gravity of the harm is balanced against the burden of preventing it and the utility of the conduct. More specifically, among the many factors that may be relevant are: (1) the extent and duration of the interference; (2) the character of the harm; (3) the social value of plaintiff's use of his land, or other interest invaded; (4) the burden to plaintiff of preventing the harm; (5) the social value of defendant's conduct, both in general and to the particular community; (6) the motive of the defendant; (7) the burden and feasibility of defendant preventing or mitigating the harm; and (8) the nature of the locality and the suitability of the activities or uses of the land being made by defendant and plaintiff. With respect to the latter, the dominant character of a neighborhood or area may be an important factor in determining what activities are reasonable and what a nonconforming plaintiff must reasonably endure—a sort of judicial zoning.

Courts occasionally speak of an "absolute" nuisance. Frequently this means nothing more than that a public nuisance statute has established the standard of conduct and therefore the issue of reasonableness is foreclosed. But once in a while a court will attempt to establish that a particular activity, otherwise lawful, is a nuisance per se, giving rise to liability for any harm it may cause under any and all circumstances. As in the case of most other absolutes in the law, the generalization must sooner or later admit of exceptions, in which case it is no longer absolute. Even where strict liability is asserted, a balancing process is required in order to determine whether the activity is so abnormally dangerous than liability may be imposed.

Remedies. The usual private remedy for nuisance is an action for damages. In cases of permanent nuisance (that is, of a type that probably will continue indefinitely), all damages must be obtained in one action. If the nuisance can be abated, plaintiff generally recovers all damages incurred up to the time of the trial. If defendant then fails to abate it (a continuing nuisance), the further invasion of his interest constitutes a new nuisance for which another action may be brought.

In cases of continuing and threatened nuisances, if plaintiff has no adequate remedy at law (which frequently is the case where real property is involved) equitable relief may be sought. When an injunction is requested, the court will undertake a further balancing process, taking into account the relative economic hardships that will result to the parties from the granting or denial of the injunction, as well as the interest of the public in the continuation of the defendant's enterprise. Thus, the court may find defendant's conduct so unreasonable that he must pay damages but not so unreasonable as to justify an injunction, compliance with which might require an unreasonably high expenditure of funds to abate or the ceasing of the activity altogether. *Boomer v. Atlantic Cement Co.* (N.Y. 1970). Cf. *Spur Industries v. Del E. Webb Development Co.* (Ariz. 1972) (injunction granted but *plaintiff* must pay *defendant's* cost of abatement.)

In addition, there is a limited self-help privilege to enter upon defendant's land to abate a nuisance. Usually notice to defendant and his refusal to act is first required. Only reasonable force may be used, and plaintiff may be subject to criminal or civil liability for unreasonable or unnecessary damage, personal injuries, or a breach of the peace.

Defenses. Legislation authorizing a particular activity or use of land (e.g., zoning laws, licenses) may be used to establish that it is not a nuisance. Generally, however, the courts have tended to construe narrowly the authority given to include only reasonable conduct.

While it is no defense to an action for nuisance that others are also contributing to the harm, each defendant is ordinarily liable only for the damages that he has caused. However, it is consistently held that a defendant will be liable where his conduct along with the activities of several other persons combine to create a nuisance, even though neither defendant's activity nor that of any of the others, by itself, would have been sufficient.

Contributory negligence, assumption of risk, and the doctrine of avoidable consequences are defenses to the same extent as in other tort actions.

Defendants in nuisance cases have often alleged that plaintiff assumed the risk because he "came to the nuisance" by purchasing and moving to land next to an existing and operating source of interference. The cases generally have not supported this defense, at least where plaintiff purchased the land in good faith and not for purposes of litigation. Absent a prescriptive right, which requires actual harm to the property for a certain period of time, defendant cannot require surrounding land to endure his nuisance—at least not without compensation. A purchaser is entitled to the reasonable use and enjoyment of his property the same as anyone else. Nevertheless, "coming to the nuisance" may be one factor to be considered in determining the reasonableness of defendant's conduct or activity, and also in determining whether plaintiff has suffered damage (since the purchase price of the land may reflect the existence of the nuisance).

Environmental Law. Recent years have witnessed a dramatic awakening of interest in protection of the environment against certain abuses, principally resource depletion and pollution. Pollution frequently causes physical harm, and thus those harmed have looked to tort law—especially the law of nuisance—in their search for legal remedies to combat it.

The nuisance provisions of the Restatement (Second) of Torts were drafted with a view toward expanding this remedy. In the area of private nuisance, the Restatement incorporates the concept that the plaintiff may be entitled to compensation (but not to an injunction) for substantial harm intentionally caused, even though on balance the utility of defendant's conduct outweighs the harm to plaintiff, and therefore ordinarily would be considered reasonable and hence not a nuisance. In other words, even socially very useful activities should have to pay (i.e., internalize) the cost of substantial harm they cause their neighbors, and should not have a privilege or license to deposit their wastes (make noise, etc.) upon them without charge. Section 826 provides that an intentional invasion of another's interest in the use and enjoyment of land is unreasonable if:

(a) the gravity of the harm outweighs the utility of the actor's conduct, or

(b) the harm caused by the conduct is substantial and the financial burden of compensating for this and other harms does not render infeasible the continuation of the conduct.

Section 829A was added in the Restatement (Second) to those which spell out specific applications of the balancing test used to determine whether conduct is unreasonable, expressly providing that it is if "the harm resulting from the invasion is substantial and greater than the [plaintiff] should reasonably be required to bear without compensation."

Public nuisance, which was not dealt with in the first Restatement of Torts, has been added to the second. A proposed definition of a public nuisance as a "criminal" interference with a public right was rejected on the ground that the requirement that the interference be a crime was unnecessary and too restrictive, since it still had to be unreasonable. And the standards for determining whether the interference is unreasonable are broadly stated as follows:

(a) whether the conduct involves a substantial interference with the public health, the public safety, the public peace, the public comfort or the public convenience, or

(b) whether the conduct is proscribed by a statute, ordinance or administrative regulation, or

(c) whether the conduct is of a continuing nature or has produced a permanent or long-lasting effect and, to the actor's knowledge, has a substantial detrimental effect upon the public right. § 821B(2).

With respect to the standing of a private citizen to sue for public nuisance, the Restatement (Second) preserves, so far as an action for *damages* is concerned, the common law rule that he must have suffered harm of a different kind than that of the public. Any other rule could subject a defendant to an unreasonable burden of multiple suits. But it opens the door to the development of broader standing rules in suits by private citizens to *enjoin* or *abate* a public nuisance. In such cases, § 821C would require only that plaintiff (1) have a cause of action for damages, or (2) have the requisite authority as a public official or public agency, or (3) have "standing to sue as a representative of the general public, as a member of a class in a class action, or as a citizen in a citizen's action." The latter, while not itself providing any standing rules, invites the courts to fashion them as they see fit.

There are a large number of environmental protection statutes on the books at both the state and federal level, and all jurisdictions have some sort of environmental protection agency (by whatever name). These statutes may interact with tort law in one of four principal ways:

(1) The statute may, expressly or impliedly, create a private cause of action for damages or an injunction where one would not otherwise exist.

(2) The statute may create standing for other remedies.

(3) The statute (or rules or regulations issued under it) may establish defendant's standards of conduct (e.g., permissible levels of noise or pollution) applicable in a nuisance or other tort action.

(4) The statute may preempt the field and thereby make unavailable (a) common law tort remedies, or (b) in the case of federal legislation, state statutory remedies as well. For example, this has been held to be the effect of federal automobile emission standards.

Water Rights. There are special rules applicable to the tortious interference by one with another's rights with respect to watercourses, lakes, ground and surface waters. See R. §§ 841–864.

§ 8–20. Negligent Infliction of Emotional Distress

As we have already seen (§ 6–5) the common law long refused to recognize a cause of action where the only effect of defendant's wrongful conduct was plaintiff's mental anguish, with or without some resulting physical illness. Various reasons were given—a fear of false claims, the difficulty or measuring damages, lack of precedent, a fear of the proverbial "flood of litigation," and assertions that such harm is too "remote" from the wrongful conduct and that since there can be no recovery for mere fright there can be none for its physical consequences.

The weakness of these reasons is apparent, except perhaps for the first. Spurious claims might indeed be easy to make and hard to disprove, especially where defendant never directed his conduct toward plaintiff, never made contact with him, and might not even have known of plaintiff's presence in the vicinity when he allegedly committed the act for which he is sued.

During the second half of the twentieth century, the courts came to realize that the risk of false claims is not a sufficient reason to deny a cause of action for legitimate ones, and so carved out exceptions to the general rule of nonliability. Note, however, that a cause of action has been given only in those cases where (1) the circumstances surrounding the actionable event create some inherent assurances of genuineness or (2) the equities favoring liability are strong, or (3) some combination of these two factors is present.

As previously noted (§ 6–5) an action for severe emotional distress was first allowed in cases where the harm was caused *intentionally* or *recklessly*. Where it can be shown that defendant intended to shock, frighten or severely upset the plaintiff (or that he knew that this was a highly probable result of his conduct) there is some objective assurance that plaintiff's injury is real, and his claim is reinforced by the social interest in deterring such conduct.

But suppose defendant is merely negligent, as where he drives his auto through a red light and narrowly misses the plaintiff. The circumstantial probability that plaintiff was in fact severely emotionally distressed by defendant's conduct is less; and in addition it can be argued that liability for the consequences of plaintiff's fright may be disproportionate to defendant's fault.

Thus, in cases of *negligent* conduct that inflicts severe emotional distress the law distinguishes three fact situations, which may be designated (1) impact, (2) zone of danger, and (3) bystander.

(1) Impact. Where defendant's negligence causes an impact with plaintiff's body resulting in some physical injury, plaintiff traditionally may claim damages not only for his physical injury but also for the accompanying damage to his mental equilibrium—pain, suffering, neurosis, nervousness, humiliation, apprehension, and fright. R. § 456. Such damages are said to be "parasitic" to the damages recoverable for the physical harm. By extension of this familiar and well-accepted principle, the courts have generally permitted an action for such psychic trauma and resulting physical consequences even though the physical impact was very slight and itself caused little or no bodily harm at the point of the impact. Sufficient impact has been found in a slight blow, jolt or jar; a trifling burn or electric shock; and dust in the eye or the inhalation of smoke. The requirement has even been satisfied by an impact resulting from plaintiff's own response to the fright. Thus, the courts have gone far beyond the concept of such damages as parasitic. Rather, it appears that the true function of the impact requirement is to provide a circumstantial guarantee of the validity of plaintiff's claim.

(2) Zone of Danger. At one time, the courts denied recovery for the physical consequences of emotional distress that occurred in the absence of an impact, even though plaintiff was within the zone of danger of a risk created by defendant's negligence, and plaintiff legitimately feared injury from that risk—for example, where defendant negligently drove his car and narrowly missed striking plaintiff. But most jurisdictions have abolished the impact requirement and allow such plaintiffs to recover in such cases upon satisfactory proof. Thus, the "zone of danger" rule is now the majority view.

(3) Bystander. Where plaintiff was not himself within the zone of danger, but merely witnessed a shocking event caused by defendant's conduct, most courts continue to deny recovery for plaintiff's resulting physical harm if defendant's conduct in precipitating the event was merely negligent. There is some fear of questionable claims, but perhaps more significant is the prevailing view that liability for shock to bystanders would be too great a burden when compared to the risk created by defendant's negligence.

But even here, the rule of nonliability has been rejected in exceptionally compelling cases. The leading decision is *Dillon v. Legg* (Cal. 1968), where a mother was allowed to recover for the severe emotional trauma and resulting illness caused when she witnessed defendant negligently run down and kill her child, even though she was in a position of complete safety. The court found that ordinary principles of negligence law would permit recovery, since it is entirely foreseeable by one who is negligent toward a child that its mother will be in the immediate vicinity, will witness the event, and will suffer severe shock. *Dillon* has been followed in several jurisdictions in cases involving similar facts, but it has been expressly rejected in several others (e.g., *Tobin v. Grossman*, N.Y. 1969). So far, the cases and writers have suggested that liability in such cases be limited to situations where (1) the threatened injury is a serious one, (2) plaintiff is a member of the immediate family of the person in peril, (3) the shock results in actual physical harm to plaintiff, (4) the event is of short duration, and (5) plaintiff actually witnesses the traumatic event, or at least comes upon the scene almost immediately and witnesses its aftermath. While such limitations are somewhat arbitrary, they are seen as necessary to keep liability within reasonable bounds and to restrict it to indisputably genuine claims. E.g., compare *Leong v. Takasaki* (Hawaii 1974) with *Kelley v. Kokua Sales & Supply, Ltd.* (Hawaii 1975).

Even before *Dillon,* some cases would permit a plaintiff who was himself within the zone of danger to recover not only for the fright caused by fear for his *own* safety but also for the emotional distress caused by witnessing the peril to a close relative who was simultaneously threatened or harmed by the same negligent conduct of defendant.

See generally R. §§ 306, 436, 436A.

Interestingly (and somewhat anomalously), a number of courts that would deny liability in the *Dillon* situation will permit plaintiff to recover for the mental anguish caused by witnessing damage to or destruction of his valuable personal property caused by defendant's negligence as parasitic damages in a suit to recover for such property damage. And there is a line of cases allowing recover for emotional distress to the next of kin caused by the negligent mishandling of a corpse. R. § 868.

(4) Direct Victim Cases. A line of cases is emerging allowing recovery where there is no contact or threat of physical harm, but the plaintiff is a "direct victim" of negligent conduct whose only consequence is emotional distress. Illustrative are cases where a psychotherapist engages in an improper sexual relationship with a patient, resulting in severe emotional distress to the patient's spouse, who was participating in the therapy in some way. These cases tend to require rather clear foreseeability and some sort of preexisting relationship between the tortfeasor and the plaintiff, but beyond that the scope and limits of this duty are still being worked out.

Proximate Cause. In some jurisdictions, plaintiff may recover for emotional distress negligently inflicted only if it results in some physical illness or comparable objective bodily consequences, and then only if such consequences were reasonably foreseeable. R. §§ 436A, 313. And unless defendant had actual knowledge of some special hypersensitivity of the plaintiff, he will be liable only to the extent that plaintiff's physical response to the emotional trauma was within the normal range of ordinarily sensitive persons. These limitations, which are narrower than the usual proximate cause rules (see §§ 4–4, 6–5, supra), are in keeping with the previously-discussed policy to require objective assurance of the genuineness of claims and to prevent defendants' liability from becoming disproportionate to the risk.

§ 8–21. Prenatal Harm

At one time, plaintiff could not recover for physical harm sustained prior to his birth. The justifications given were (1) a fetus is not a separate person, (2) medical proof of causation would be too speculative and this would lead to false claims, and (3) damages would be too speculative.

These reasons are, of course, extremely weak. It is undisputed that a fetus is capable of sustaining a permanent injury. The law has long accorded property and other rights to the unborn. It is difficult to understand why the medical proof should be any less trustworthy here than in other kinds of cases.

And we regularly allow a measure of speculation in calculating damages far into the future.

Thus, this duty limitation finally succumbed to unrelieved criticism. Between 1946 and 1972 the rule was totally reversed, and today a child if and when born alive may maintain an action for personal injuries suffered while in the womb as a result of defendant's wrongful conduct.

Despite some contrary dictum, it is well established that recovery may be had for injuries that occur during any stage of the pregnancy; the fetus need not have been viable or "quick" at the time. Of course, the earlier in the pregnancy the injury is thought to have occurred, the more difficult may be the proof that the injury is causally related to defendant's wrongful conduct, but this does not alter the rule.

Suppose the injuries are fatal. Where the child is born alive and subsequently dies from injuries sustained in the womb, the courts (having first allowed the action for prenatal injuries) have had little difficulty allowing the wrongful death action. But where the child is stillborn, the courts at first were hesitant to allow recovery, frequently construing the term "person" in the applicable wrongful death act to exclude the unborn. But since *Verkennes v. Corniea* (Minn. 1949) the trend has been to allow the action if the child was viable at the time of the injury, and this is now the majority rule.

These tort law developments present an interesting contrast to recent developments in the law concerning abortions, particularly *Roe v. Wade* (U.S. 1973) which held that an unborn nonviable child is not a "person" within the meaning of the Fourteenth Amendment.

"Wrongful Birth" and "Wrongful Life." The courts have unanimously refused to recognize a cause of action in favor of a child for damages caused by having been born to an unwed mother, on the ground that such damages are more then offset by the benefits of having been born at all. But most courts now permit an action in favor of the parents for negligence in performing sterilization procedures that results in the birth of a healthy child. Damages in such cases have been limited to those associated with the pregnancy and birth, and do not include the cost of the child's support.

The more troublesome issues involve the situation where the child is born with congenital or other defects, and it is alleged that the physician was negligent in failing to diagnose the child's condition in time to permit an abortion. Do the parents, or the child, have a claim? As to the parents' claim (known as a "wrongful birth" action), most jurisdictions now permit such actions, but disagree as to the measure of damages, some awarding the extra living and caretaking expenses and medical costs attributable to the impairment, others denying those expenses but allowing recovery for the parents' mental and emotional suffering. A minority of jurisdictions deny any recovery (some by judicial decision, some by statute) on the ground that it is impossible to compute damages based on the value of non-life as compared to an impaired life.

So far all but a few courts have disallowed the child's claim for having been born in an impaired condition (known as a "wrongful life" action).

§ 8–22. Alcoholic Beverages

The general common law rule was that one who sold or otherwise furnished intoxicating beverages was not liable to third persons subsequently injured by the intoxicated person. The damage was considered too remote; it was the consumption and not the sale that was the immediate cause of the harm.

There were exceptions, usually cases involving sales to known habitual drunkards or to persons known to be intoxicated or nearly so, founded upon a reckless disregard of the rights of others. But the exceptions were limited, and many courts refused to allow liability even in the face of extenuating circumstances.

Largely at the behest of the temperance movement, statutes (called "dram shop acts") were enacted in many states that imposed some form of civil liability on those engaged in the business of selling such beverages in favor of third persons injured thereby. The justification was that those trafficking in "demon rum" ought to bear the cost of its inevitable consequential harm as a part of the cost of doing business. At one time, almost half the states had such laws; today, approximately one-third do.

The majority of such statutes impose civil liability only where the sale was itself unlawful, such as to a minor, a person already intoxicated, or an habitual drunkard or other person whom the seller had previously been notified to deny. In some cases, actual knowledge of the illegality of the sale is required. But in some states, there is liability for even lawful sales that contribute to one's intoxication. Typically, recovery is allowed to plaintiffs injured or killed by the intoxicated person, and sometimes to members of the intoxicated person's family who incur expense or lose his support as a consequence of *his* injury or death as a result of his intoxication. Absent some knowledge requirement, liability is strict. No negligence need be shown, and contributory negligence is no defense. Of course, the intoxicated person cannot himself sue for his own injuries, nor can any person maintain an action who participated with him in the drinking (a defense called "complicity"). In some states there is a statutory limit on the damages; in others, punitive damages are recoverable in appropriate cases.

A majority of states have overthrown the common law rule and have created a common law dram shop action. In most of these jurisdictions, liability is predicated on statutes that regulate the liquor business and prohibit certain sales by liquor licensees (to minors, intoxicated persons, etc.). Thus, where the sale is unlawful, it is negligence per se. And the old proximate cause limitation has been swept aside and third persons injured by the intoxicated person may sue. Here also, most (but not all) of these jurisdictions limit liability to those engaged in the regulated business of selling intoxicating beverages. See, e.g., *Jackson v. Cadillac Cowboy, Inc.* (Ark. 1999).

The courts have traditionally denied recovery against persons other than commercial vendors who furnish alcoholic beverages to their guests, relatives, employees, etc. The burden of policing the alcohol consumption in social situations has been seen as too great. However, with the increased public concern about the costs imposed by intoxicated persons, especially drunk drivers, there is now a minority view recognizing tort liability based on ordinary principles of negligence, particularly where the defendant does more than merely furnish the alcoholic beverages, such as by actively assisting the intoxicated person in the use of his vehicle. In some states, however, such liability is expressly precluded by statute.

§ 8–23. Interference With Federal Constitutional Rights

A number of federal statutes have as their purpose the implementation of one or more of the rights secured to individuals by the United States Constitution, chiefly by certain amendments (I, IV, V, VI, XIV, XV).

The most important of these statutes is 42 U.S.C.A. § 1983, which implements the Fourteenth Amendment by creating a federal cause of action in tort for acts under color of state authority that deprive one of any federal constitutional or statutory right. ("State" includes political subdivisions such as cities and counties.) It provides:

Every person, who under color of any statute, ordinance, regulation, custom, or usage, of any State or Territory, subjects, or causes to be subjected, any citizen of the United States or other person within the jurisdiction thereof the deprivation of any rights, privileges, or immunities secured by the Constitution and laws, shall be liable to the party injured in an action at law, suit in equity, or other proper proceeding for redress.

Enacted in 1871, § 1983 long lay nearly dormant, having been rather narrowly construed. But in 1961, the U.S. Supreme Court in *Monroe v. Pape* breathed new life into it, holding that, contrary to popular belief, § 1983 was *not* limited to unconstitutional acts that state law purported to authorize, but rather extended to *all* deprivations of federally created rights whether lawful or unlawful under state law. "Under color of" state law thus means that the defendant, at the time he committed the act, need merely have been acting in his capacity as a state officer or employee or else have had some substantial connection with the state such that he could be said to be its instrumentality. It also ruled that the wrongful act did not have to be done with specific intent to deprive plaintiff of a federal constitutional right; § 1983 "should be read against the background of tort liability that makes a man responsible for the natural consequences of his actions."

Section 1983 is designed to prevent abuses of power by state and local officers, employees, and others acting with the authority of the state behind them. It is primarily intended to provide a remedy where state law in inadequate or, though adequate in theory, is ineffective in practice. However, it is not limited to these situations. The remedy is supplementary to remedies available under state law, and ordinarily unsuccessful resort to such remedies is not a prerequisite.

Federal jurisdiction in § 1983 cases is conferred by 28 U.S.C.A. § 1343, irrespective of diversity of citizenship or the amount in controversy. Trial by jury is available. States courts have concurrent jurisdiction of § 1983 claims.

The most significant feature of § 1983 is its enormous breadth. *All* constitutional rights guaranteed by the Fourteenth Amendment and all rights created by federal statutes are within its scope. Included are (1) First Amendment rights—freedom of speech, religion, the press, assembly, and association; (2) illegal arrest, and the use of unnecessary force during an arrest; (3) unlawful searches and seizures; (4) assault, bodily injury, and wrongful death (e.g., police brutality); (5) the right to consult an attorney; (6) reasonable access to the courts; (7) coerced confessions and other denials of the right against self-incrimination; (8) bail; (9) malicious prosecution; (10) false imprisonment; (11) the right to a fair trial (e.g., knowing use of perjured testimony, right to an impartial and unbiased tribunal); (12) various prisoners' rights (e.g., right to medical care, First Amendment rights, and protection against cruel and unusual punishment, or summary punishment), including rights of juveniles and those committed to institutions for the mentally ill; (13) invasion of privacy (e.g., police harassment, the privacy of one's body); and (14) other due process and equal protection rights, whether personal or property (*Lynch v. Household Finance Corp.*, U.S. 1972), such as freedom from discrimination based on race or sex; rights to due process in public and other employment, public housing, license issuance and revocation, grant or denial of other valuable privileges (e.g., bar admission), pension rights, social security benefits, rights to public utilities, students' rights; protection against summary garnishment, seizure or destruction of property; and voting rights—to list only some.

Since *Monroe,* there has been a dramatic increase in the number of § 1983 cases in the federal courts, to the point that they are now a significant fraction of the docket. With the broadening of the areas in which state and local government touch the lives of all persons, it is safe to predict a continuing increase in the volume of such cases.

Plaintiffs may include anyone whose rights have been violated, white, black, or otherwise, and even aliens and corporations where appropriate.

Ordinarily, the defendant will be a state or local officer or employee, since liability exists only for rights denied by state action. At least as to actions for damages, municipalities are not vicariously liable unless the deprivation is caused by "action pursuant to official policy" *Monell v. Department of Social Services* (U.S. 1978); *City of Canton v. Harris* (U.S. 1989) (inadequacy of police training must amount to "deliberate indifference"). States and state subdivisions are not subject to suit under § 1983. *Will v. Michigan Dept. of State Police* (U.S. 1989). (In addition, the eleventh amendment is a bar to suits against the states in federal courts, although *Will* is not based on the eleventh amendment.)

Except for these entities, however, the coverage of the act has been increasingly liberalized. Even private persons may be held to have acted "under color of" state law where (1) they act in concert with state or municipal officers or employees, or (2) they purport to act pursuant to state law, or (3) they act under the authority of some state statute that purports to give them the power to act, such as a state statute authorizing summary garnishment, or (4) there is a substantial state nexus with defendant's activities, as where defendant is subject to extensive state regulation (e.g., an insurance company or public utility) or receives significant state aid, either directly as in the case of grants or tax exemptions (i.e., private universities) or indirectly as where defendant is permitted to use public property or facilities (e.g., a Y.M.C.A. regularly allowed to do so). There is a large body of law as to what is state action; the courts will now look to all state involvement, support, encouragement, sanction, aid, and regulation, and the test is whether the totality of these factors is sufficiently substantial to give a "color" of state law to defendant's activities.

The nature, extent and interaction of (1) the fault required to support liability, (2) defenses, and (3) immunities in § 1983 cases are in the process of development and are not yet fully worked out. The corresponding rules of analogous torts will certainly play an important part in this process, as Justice Douglas suggested in *Monroe,* but cannot be controlling since there may be overriding policies applicable to § 1983 that are absent in the usual tort case.

As to fault, it is at least clear that no specific intent to violate another's rights is required. Here, tort law may be of its greatest value. The emerging rule seems to be that if there is an analogous common law tort, the fault required in a § 1983 action will ordinarily be the same. However, there cannot be liability for a negligent interference with a due process right protected by the Fourteenth Amendment. *Daniels v. Williams* (U.S. 1986); *Davidson v. Cannon* (U.S. 1986).

Defenses and immunities are a different matter. It is apparent that if all of the common law immunities of government and governmental employees (see Chapter 11) were available in § 1983 cases, the act would be emasculated. It is also noteworthy that the statute itself makes no reference to any immunities, and some have argued persuasively that it was intended that there be none. Nevertheless, at least in actions for *damages,* the courts have given absolute or qualified immunities to certain defendants as a matter of policy, apparently on the theory that such immunities are necessarily implicit. Thus, judges (*Pierson v. Ray*, U.S. 1967), legislators (*Tenney v. Brandhove*, U.S. 1951), public prosecutors (*Imbler v. Pachtman*, U.S. 1976), and public or court-appointed criminal defense counsel (*Minns v. Paul*, 4th Cir. 1976) are *absolutely* immune from damages suits under § 1983 for acts within the scope of their duties (an area yet to be delineated). Others have a qualified immunity, which is to say immunity for acts committed (1) in good faith, (2) with probable cause, or (3) in the exercise of their discretion, or some combination of these three. Examples include the state governor (*Scheuer v. Rhodes*, U.S. 1974) and probably other high executive officials, and school officials exercising disciplinary authority (*Wood v. Strickland*, U.S. 1975). In certain cases, the courts speak of a "qualified immunity," but what they really mean is that defendant's good faith or probable cause negates the existence of the intent required for liability.

The full effect of 42 U.S.C.A. § 1988 on § 1983 actions is yet to be determined. Section 1988 provides, in effect, that in suits under § 1983 (and certain other civil rights statutes) if issues arise as to which there is no applicable rule of federal law, or there are gaps or deficiencies in the federal law, then the law of the state in which the federal court is located may be applied. Under this provision, state law has been used to determine survival of the action, the statute of limitations, and the nature and extent of the remedy for wrongful death. On the other hand, federal common law is generally held to determine the measure of damages in the interest of uniformity, and thus for example punitive damages may be awarded even through the law of the state in which the federal court is sitting does not allow them. Some have argued, with some force, that the federal courts should fill gaps by fashioning federal common law consistent with the purpose of § 1983, rather than to borrow under § 1988 the various state laws that may themselves be inadequate or inconsistent. How far this will be done remains to be seen. But it is at least clear that state law rules that are barriers to liability (such as very short special statutes of limitations applicable to suits against state employees and common law tort immunities) will not be applied if they significantly impair the § 1983 remedy.

There are other federal statutes upon which an action for damages for discrimination may be based. These remedies are broader than § 1983; no state action is required. These include § 1981 (personal rights), § 1982 (property rights), §§ 1985 and 1986 (conspiracies), § 2000a (public accommodations), § 2000d (federally funded programs), § 2000e (employment discrimination) and §§ 3601–3631 (housing discrimination). A remedy for age discrimination is provided in 29 U.S.C.A. §§ 621–634.

Since § 1983 is limited to acts under color of state law, it does not reach deprivations of constitutional rights by *federal* officials and employees. However, it is now recognized that interference with any federal constitutional right, at least by federal personnel, gives rise to a cause of action under the Constitution itself without the necessity of implementing legislation. Therefore, a person whose constitutional rights have been violated by a federal officer or employee may sue him in federal court under the provisions of 28 U.S.C.A. § 1331 (which gives jurisdiction to the federal courts of civil actions arising under federal law) if the amount in controversy exceeds the required $50,000. *Bivens v. Six Unknown Named Agents of Federal Bureau of Narcotics* (U.S. 1971). Congress has removed exclusions for certain intentional torts by investigative and law enforcement personnel from the Federal Tort Claims Act. This principle provides a remedy for violations of constitutional rights by officers and employees of the District of Columbia, who are beyond the reach of § 1983. *District of Columbia v. Carter* (U.S. 1973). The full scope of *Bivens* is yet to be determined, but it seems clear that it is not limited to fourth amendment violations. See, e.g., *United States ex rel. Moore v. Koelzer* (3d Cir. 1972) (fifth amendment); *Paton v. La Prade* (3d Cir. 1975) (first amendment); *Butler v. United States* (D. Hawaii 1973) (same); *Wounded Knee Legal Defense/Offense Comm. v. Federal Bu-*

reau of Inv. (8th Cir. 1974) (sixth amendment). See R. § 874A.

Finally, it should be noted that racial discrimination by private citizens has been held actionable under the common law tort of infliction of emotional distress. See § 6–5, supra. Cf. R. § 866.

CHAPTER 9

DAMAGES FOR PHYSICAL HARM

§ 9–1. Compensatory Damages

When defendant's tort injures plaintiff's person or property, his basic remedy is compensatory money damages. In almost all cases, this will also be his only remedy.

The common law rules of damages for physical harm reflect three fundamental ideas:

(1) Justice requires that plaintiff be restored to his pre-injury condition, so far as it is possible to do so with money. Thus, he should be reimbursed not only for his economic ("out-of-pocket") losses, but also for his noneconomic damage (loss of physical and mental well-being).

(2) Most noneconomic losses are capable of being translated into dollars.

(3) When plaintiff sues in tort for an injury which he has sustained, he must recover all of his damages arising from that injury, past and future, in a lump sum and in a single lawsuit. R. § 910.

General vs. Special Damages. For purposes of pleading and proof, there is a distinction between general damages and special damages. *General* damages are those awarded for harms and losses which are a natural and usual consequence of the tort and injury asserted. Traditionally, these harms and losses could be proved even though plaintiff did not specifically allege them in his complaint. For example, a battery which causes bodily harm normally results in physical pain, and so "pain and suffering" was provable under a complaint for a battery which alleged only that plaintiff suffered "great bodily harm" or "a broken leg." *Special* damages are those awarded for all other compensable harms and losses. Such harms or losses must be specifically pleaded so that defendant will be on notice that damages for them will be claimed. Medical expenses, lost wages, and damages for any unusual effects of the injury (e.g., traumatic neurosis) are illustrations of special damages in a personal injury case. R. § 904.

Which items of damages are general and which are special depends, of course, on (1) the tort and (2) the general or specific injuries alleged. No hard and fast rules can be laid down, nor are they necessary for our purposes. Note, however, that in personal injury cases, plaintiff's economic or out-of-pocket losses may be referred to as "special damages" or simply "specials," and his noneconomic losses (such as pain and suffering) may be called his "general damages," irrespective of the allegations in the pleadings. Although technically inaccurate, this usage sometimes appears in judicial decisions and other legal writing.

Nominal Damages. If plaintiff establishes defendant's liability for some tort but is unable to prove any actual damages, nominal damages may be awarded. R. § 907. As the name implies, they are damages in name only, usually one cent or six cents or one dollar. Such awards are largely confined to the intentional torts (e.g., trespass to land) where actual damages need not be alleged or proved. Occasionally they may be given in other cases where plaintiff proves that he sustained some actual damage but is unable to establish the amount.

Damages for Personal Injury. As a general proposition, when plaintiff proves a compensable injury to his person, he may recover for all adverse physical and mental consequences of that injury. R. § 924. While the specific elements of damage for which recovery may be had vary somewhat among the torts, and will differ a little from one jurisdiction to the next even for a particular tort, the following types of harms are commonly compensable.

(1) *Economic Loss.* Past and future pecuniary losses and out-of-pocket expenses proximately caused by the injury are recoverable, including (a) reasonable medical expenses (doctor, hospital, nursing, tests, medicines, devices, physical therapy, and travel to obtain these services); (b) lost wages, earnings or profits; (c) the cost of substitute labor hired to do work which plaintiff can not perform because of his injury; and (d) the cost of custodial care, if

any, required because the injury has left plaintiff more or less incapable of caring for himself.

Future losses and expenses need not be established to a certainty, either as to their incidence or amount. The jury need only find it more probable than not that they will be incurred and have some reasonable basis beyond sheer speculation for their computation. Thus, where the injury impairs plaintiff's earning capacity, she may recover for future lost earnings even though not employed at the time of her injury if the jury can find that more probably than not she would be employed in the future and can determine the probable type of employment and rate of earnings. It may take into account probable future wage increases. In the case of a child, it may even find that she probably would have gone to college and obtained skilled employment, if such a finding is supported by some evidence.

Impaired earning capacity is frequently a subject of expert testimony by an economist or actuary.

(2) *Physical Pain.* Past and future physical pain—commonly referred to as "pain and suffering"—is compensable. Within broad limits, its valuation is left largely to the jury's discretion.

An oft-debated question is whether plaintiff should be permitted to use the so-called "per diem" argument to the jury in which he suggests that his past and future pain be valued in units of time (e.g., $20 per day, $2 per hour) or whether he should be limited to suggesting a lump sum for such damages. The authorities are split, with a substantial minority refusing to allow the "per diem" argument on the ground that it enhances the effects of sympathy and lends a spurious sense of accuracy to what is fundamentally sheer speculation.

(3) *Mental Distress*. In addition to physical pain, most courts will permit plaintiff to claim damages for some or all of the following mental harms: (a) fright and shock; (b) anxiety about the future, both physical (e.g., premature death, physical disability, illness, the effect on plaintiff's unborn child) and economic (whether for himself or others), unless plaintiff's fears are clearly unfounded and unreasonable; (c) loss of peace of mind, happiness, or mental health, ranging from depression through neuroses and psychoses; (d) humiliation, loss of dignity, or embarrassment caused by the physical injury, disability or disfigurement; (e) mental distress resulting from loss of the ability to enjoy a normal life; (f) inconvenience caused by the injury.

(4) *Physical Impairment*. In lieu of compensation for the mental distress caused by a physical impairment of plaintiff's body, some jurisdictions purport to base compensation on the physical impairment itself. In other words, where the injury impairs (temporarily or permanently, partially or totally) his eyesight, hearing, use of an extremity, consciousness, ability to conceive or bear children, or any other bodily function, or where plaintiff is disfigured, the jury is told to value and compensate that loss as such and not merely its mental consequences. (Such compensation is, of course, in addi-

tion to that awarded for any economic loss and pain resulting from that injury.) Of course, as a practical matter it probably makes little difference whether the jury is instructed to base compensation on the physical impairment or its mental effects, since in either case it is in reality the latter which is being valued.

Pre–existing Conditions. As previously discussed (§ 4–4), defendant's liability for damages is not mitigated by the fact that some pre-existing physical infirmity of the plaintiff was responsible for all or part of the consequences of plaintiff's injury by defendant. If plaintiff is especially predisposed or vulnerable to some illness or injury, defendant whose tort precipitates it is liable for the harm it causes even though under the same circumstances a normal person would not have suffered that illness or injury. The same is true where the injury re-activates a previous condition which had been brought under control, or aggravates an existing condition.

A corollary rule is that defendant is liable for the aggravation during treatment of plaintiff's injuries, even where such aggravation is due to the negligence of another, so long as plaintiff exercised reasonable care in selecting those in whose care he placed himself.

Present Value. If plaintiff is awarded damages for losses that he will incur in the future, he will be over-compensated unless these damages are figured at their present value, due to the fact that (1) they are received by him in a lump sum at the conclusion of the trial, and (2) money will earn interest. R. § 913A. For example, assume that plaintiff is awarded $1,000 to compensate him for lost income which, but for his injury, he would have earned ten years in the future. Presumably he can now take that $1,000 and invest it at, say, six per cent interest. Thus, ten years hence he will have not $1,000 but $1,791. Therefore, in order to provide him with $1,000 ten years from today, that $1,000 must be discounted to its present value—a sum which, together with the interest (compounded) which it will earn, will equal $1,000 in ten years. At a discount rate of six per cent, this would be about $558.

Typically, the jury is told to discount its award for future economic loss to present value, but is not told how to do so or what rate to use. Frequently this is a subject of expert testimony by a statistician, economist or actuary.

In most jurisdictions, damages for future *non-economic* harm (pain and suffering, mental distress, disability, disfigurement) are *not* reduced to present value.

Inflation. In calculating damages for future economic losses, may the jury take into account the probable continuing decline of the purchasing power of the dollar due to inflation? May plaintiff introduce expert testimony of the probability of such continued inflation? At one time the general rule was that the court would not sanction the jury's consideration of inflation on the ground that its future effects were too speculative. But today we have finally realized that interest rates include an inflation factor, and therefore it would be inequitable to reduce future damages to present cash value (using the interest rate) while denying the benefits of that same inflation to the plaintiff. Thus, almost all jurisdictions will allow inflation to be the subject of evidence and argument. In some states inflation is held to offset the discount rate and they cancel each other out, so that in these jurisdictions plaintiff's future economic loss is simply not reduced to its present value.

Taxation. The Internal Revenue Code exempts compensatory damages for personal injuries from income taxation, even though they may include damages for past and future lost earnings. 26 U.S.C.A. § 104. In some states, the nontaxability of such damages may not be the subject of evidence, argument or instructions to the jury on the grounds that (1) plaintiff would thereby be deprived of the tax benefit given him by Congress, and (2) the future effects of taxation cannot be calculated to an acceptable degree of certainty. R. § 914A. Those states also often reject evidence as to the effect of taxes on plaintiff's future earnings as too speculative. However, in other jurisdictions and under the F.E.L.A. (*Norfolk & Western Ry. Co. v. Liepelt*, U.S. 1980), the opposite rule prevails and such evidence and instructions are required.

Collateral Source Rule. As a general rule, plaintiff may recover the reasonable value of the expenses, services and lost time from work attributable to his injury (e.g., doctors' fees, hospital and other medical expenses, his wages while absent from his employment), even though he did not in fact pay for them (as where they were furnished as a gift or as a matter of professional courtesy) or he was reimbursed for such expenses from a collateral source (that is, a source other than defendant or which defendant did not fund). R. § 920A. Examples of these collateral sources include private health and accident insurance, workers' compensation, social security, disability insurance, wage continuation plans, sick leave, veterans' benefits, and public aid. (Distinguish payments received from or on behalf of a joint tortfeasor in settlement of his potential tort liability to plaintiff for the same injury; defendant *is* credited with these payments. See § 9–4, infra.) The justification for the rule is that it would be more unjust to give defendant the benefit of these payments than to permit an innocent plaintiff to recover them twice, especially since in most cases plaintiff himself arranged for the collateral benefits and paid for them. (There is, of course, no double recovery where plaintiff must repay the collateral source out of the judgment he obtains from defendant, as in the case of benefits received from the workers' compensation, public aid, and the military services.)

In some (but not all) jurisdictions, plaintiff (or the person furnishing them) may even recover the value of nursing services gratuitously furnished plaintiff by friends and relatives, on the ground that defendant is not entitled to the benefit of these services.

The collateral source rule is not without its critics, and courts occasionally allow exceptions to it, but in general it appears too well established and accepted to be changed except by statute. Some automobile accident compensation acts (§ 8–17) modify it, as do certain medical negligence statutes, but otherwise there is as yet no discernible movement to restrict or abolish it by statutes of general application.

Mitigation. Under the doctrine of avoidable consequences, plaintiff is required to make reasonable efforts to mitigate the consequences of his injury and to take steps to prevent further harm, and defendant is not liable to the extent that he fails to do so. For example, absent some legitimate reason for not doing so, plaintiff is required to make a reasonable effort to seek medical treatment for his injuries.

In some jurisdictions, this is extended to include safety precautions required or available *prior* to the injury, such as the wearing of seat belts or safety helmets, and defendant is not liable for those damages attributable to plaintiff's failure to make use of them. However, the majority rule is to the contrary.

Mere negligence in failing to mitigate damages is no defense to an intentional or reckless tort.

Of course, plaintiff may recover as an item of damages any expenses reasonably incurred in attempting to mitigate his harm, whether or not his efforts were successful, and also damages for further harm sustained as a result of reasonable efforts to mitigate his harm.

Conversely, where defendant's tort caused harm but also conferred some benefit on plaintiff, that benefit may be considered in mitigation of plaintiff's damages if it is equitable to do so.

Attorneys' Fees and Litigation Costs. The universal U.S. rule (with exceptions not pertinent here) is that the prevailing party in litigation may not recover as damages his attorneys' fees or other litigation costs in the absence of a statute expressly authorizing them. Statutes typically provide for the recovery of minor litigation expenses, such as filing and service fees, but little else.

This fact is often used to bolster arguments in favor of certain damages rules, such as the collateral source rule, the rule against a deduction for tax benefits, and damages for pain and suffering. It is said that any windfall which plaintiff receives as a result of these rules is more than offset by the fact that plaintiff must pay his own attorneys' fees and most other expenses of litigation out of the award he receives.

Harm to Personal Property. For harm to personal property that does *not* amount to conversion, plaintiff at his election may recover either:

(1) The difference between the value of the property before the tort and its value afterwards; or

(2) The reasonable costs of repair and restoration to use of the chattel, or attempts to do so, plus any diminution in its value remaining thereafter.

Ordinarily, plaintiff may recover the reasonable costs of repairs or restoration even though they exceed the value of the chattel before the harm, unless a reasonable person under the circumstances then known to him would simply have junked it and obtained a replacement.

In addition, if recovery is based on the cost of repair, he may recover any costs or damages reasonably incurred during the time he was deprived of its use (such as the cost of renting a substitute) proximately resulting from the loss of use.

The measure of damages for the conversion of personal property is its value at the time and place of conversion, plus interest from that time. Plaintiff may also recover any damages proximately resulting from loss of its use, including (in lieu of interest during that time) the cost of renting a substitute, until such time as a replacement was or could have been obtained.

Some courts will permit plaintiff to recover damages for the mental distress proximately caused by the trespass or conversion.

Damages for conversion of a chattel are mitigated if plaintiff accepts a tender of its return, or in certain cases by the tender alone. R. § 922.

Harm to Real Property. Damages for past invasions of land include (1) the difference in the value of the thing damages (or if it cannot be separately valued, the value of plaintiff's interest in the land) before and after the invasion, or, at plaintiff's election, the reasonable costs of restoration, (2) compensation for loss of use, and (3) damages for (a) bodily harm, (b) harm to chattels, and (c) mental distress (such as discomfort, inconvenience and annoyance) resulting from the invasion.

In certain cases, plaintiff may be required, or may elect, to recover for future invasions in the same lawsuit. The measure of damages for future harm is either the permanent decrease in the value of the land or the cost of preventing future harm.

§ 9–2.   Consequential Damages

Where defendant causes injury to the person of *A*, that injury will often cause damage to *B*. Such indirect or consequential damage to third persons will sometimes give rise to a separate cause of action. Such actions have generally been limited to spouses, parents, and the employer of the injured person, absent an intent to cause an injury to the third person.

Spouse. At common law, a husband was entitled to the domestic services of his wife, and to the earnings from her employment outside the home. Accordingly, when defendant's tort physically injured or incapacitated the wife so that she was unable (temporarily or permanently) to perform them, the husband was given a cause of action for loss of her services. In time the measure of damages was broadened to include his loss of "consortium," which consists of her society, companionship, affection, and sexual relations.

The wife, however, had no corresponding right to the services of her husband. She was entitled only to his support, and only he could recover for an injury that impaired his earnings or earning capacity. Hence, she had no action for loss of his services or by extension his consortium.

Beginning in 1844, Married Women's Acts or Emancipation Acts were passed in all American jurisdictions giving married women a legal identity separate from their husbands. For a long time this had little effect on either the husband's action or the denial of the wife's action, except that (1) the wife alone could not recover for her lost earnings and (2) a few courts abolished the husband's action, interpreting the act to mean that the husband was no longer entitled to an action for loss of his wife's services and throwing out with it his action for loss of consortium.

Most courts, however, continued to allow the husband's action for loss of consortium and also for loss of domestic services actually performed. As the recognition of equal rights for women increased, so did criticism of the denial of a similar cause of action for the wife. A few courts yielded in the case of certain intentional torts. Finally, *Hitaffer v. Argonne Co.* (D.C. Cir. 1950) overthrew the ban and recognized the wife's action for harm to the marital relation caused by a negligent injury to her husband, and almost all jurisdictions have since followed suit, some with the aid of recent interpretations of the various constitutional provisions on equal protection and equal rights.

Ordinarily either spouse may recover medical expenses which he paid or incurred as a result of a tortious injury to the other, to the extent that the injured spouse does not recover them in his own action.

Parents. At common law (and yet today, believe it or not) a father is legally entitled to the services and earnings of his unemancipated minor child. Thus, he (or the child's mother, if she has sole custody) may recover for loss of those services against one who negligently injures the child. A few courts permit, in addition, the award of damages for loss of the child's society, companionship and affection, but at present the majority of jurisdictions do not.

In addition, the parent may recover medical and other expenses that he paid or incurred as a result of the child's injury, and future expenses that will be incurred during the child's minority.

Children. Despite some sentiment in support of it, the courts so far have denied a cause of action to a child for loss of his parent's care, support, training, guidance, companionship, love and affection resulting from a negligent injury to the parent.

Nursing Services. The authorities are divided as to whether a member of the injured person's family may recover the value of nursing services gratuitously furnished to him.

Nature of Action. The action of a spouse or parent for consequential damages is separate and distinct from that of the injured spouse or child, and in most jurisdictions either action may be brought independently of the other. As a practical matter, all such claims are usually brought in the same lawsuit, and a few courts, fearing double recovery and the burden of multiple suits, require it.

Most courts regard the action for consequential damages as derivative, and therefore defendant usually may invoke any defense (e.g., contributory negligence) that would have been available in a suit brought by the injured person. Thus, one suing for consequential damages must first prove that the injured person could have succeeded in a lawsuit of his own, and must then establish *his* right to recover and negate any defenses asserted against him. See Restatement (Third) of Torts: Apportionment of Liability § 6.

Whether the actions are brought separately or together, there does exist a danger of double recovery for the same elements of damage. Contrary to the views of some courts, this is not a sufficient reason to deny the action for consequential damages altogether, but care must be taken to see that the damages recovered by persons other than the one injured do not duplicate those awarded to the injured person, and vice versa.

Employers. At common law, a master had a property interest in the services of his servant sufficient to support a cause of action against one whose tort deprived him of those services. But times have changed, and with them the nature of the employer-employee relationship. While there is still authority (some of it relatively recent) supporting the existence of the cause of action, most current decisions have refused to recognize it, in cases where the injury to the servant was negligently inflicted. *Steele v. J & S Metals, Inc.* (Conn. Super. 1974); *Phoenix Prof. Hockey Club, Inc. v. Hirmer* (Ariz. 1972). The action is preserved by statute in one or two states.

§ 9–3. Punitive Damages

If defendant's wrongful conduct is sufficiently serious, tort law permits the trier of fact to impose a civil fine to punish him and to deter him and others from similar conduct in the future. R. § 908. Punitive damages—also called exemplary or vindictive damages or "smart money"—are not really damages at all (even though they are usually paid to plaintiff) since presumably plaintiff has been made whole by the compensatory damages awarded in the same action. They are justified as: (1) an incentive or reward for bringing defendant to justice, especially where plaintiff's actual damages are so small that suit would otherwise be prohibitively expensive; (2) punishment for criminal or quasi-criminal offenses which often escape or are beyond the reach of the criminal law; (3) compensation for damages not normally compensable, such as wounded feelings and attorneys' fees and other expenses of litigation; and (4) the only effective means to force conscienceless defendants to cease practices known to be dangerous or tortious and which they would otherwise continue because it is more profitable to pay (or insure) compensatory damages for the harm they cause and continue them.

Punitive damages are of common law origin, but may be expressly allowed, prohibited, or regulated by statute. Generally they are not recoverable as a matter of right, but only in the discretion of the jury when justice and the public good will be served.

The common law of four states (Louisiana, Massachusetts, Nebraska and Washington) does not permit them. They may be recovered, however, even in those states if allowed by statute (e.g., under the Massachusetts wrongful death act). A few states permit them primarily on the theory that they serve compensatory functions; in Connecticut they are limited to the expenses of litigation. They may *not* be awarded in F.E.L.A. and Jones Act cases, nor sometimes in certain types of cases in particular jurisdictions (e.g., survival or wrongful death actions in some states).

To justify an award of punitive damages, defendant must have acted from a wrongful motive, or at least with gross or knowing indifference to the rights or safety of another. His conduct must have an element of outrage, similar to that which is a crime. An intentional tort usually will suffice. Most jurisdictions also allow them in cases of reckless or "willful and wanton" misconduct. Of these, some courts permit them whenever such conduct is found; others require, in addition, a finding of a kind of "malice," which in this case means a conscious and deliberate disregard of a high probability of harm. Negligence, even gross negligence, is not enough, although some courts have defined the latter as synonymous with willful and wanton misconduct and, as so defined, sufficient to support punitive damages. A fortiori, strict liability in any form will not do.

In most states, the fact that defendant's conduct also happens to be a crime does not prevent the assessment of punitive damages in a civil tort action. The double jeopardy argument has totally failed, and so has the contention that such damages can violate constitutional due process guarantees because they impose quasi-criminal punishment without the accompanying safeguards and standards of proof required by criminal law and procedure. See *Pacific Mut. Life Ins. Co. v. Haslip* (U.S. 1991). But courts will occasionally look to the criminal fines for similar misconduct as guidelines when reviewing the excessiveness of punitive damages.

Plaintiff must ordinarily prove some actual damages as a prerequisite to an award of punitive damages. But proof is usually all that is required, and a verdict for compensatory damages is not an absolute necessity. An award of nominal damages will often support a verdict for substantial punitive damages, as where the tort is particularly offensive or outrageous but no substantial damage resulted from it. On the other hand, the courts will often (especially in personal injury or property damage cases) use the amount of the compensatory damages as a guideline in judging the excessiveness of the punitive damages, and sometimes require that there be a reasonable relation between their amounts, or at least between the character of the harm and the amount of the punitive damages.

Since the function of punitive damages is ordinarily punishment and deterrence, evidence of defendant's financial circumstances is usually admissible as bearing on the amount of such damages which will be necessary to accomplish this purpose.

The whole concept of punitive damages has always had its critics, and courts frequently state that such damages are not a favorite of the law and will be scrutinized with care. Until recently, however, such awards were relatively rare and were ordinarily affirmed. But lately plaintiffs have been seeking such damages, and juries have been awarding them, with increasing frequency and sometimes in very large amounts. Thus, there is some indication that the courts are becoming increasingly watchful and may begin to place new limits on them. And the United States Supreme Court has made it clear that there are due process limits on the award of punitive damages. *BMW of North America, Inc. v. Gore* (U.S. 1996) (due process limits amount of punitive damage award); *Honda Motor Co. v. Oberg* (U.S. 1994) (due process requires judicial review of punitive damage award); *State Farm Mut. Auto. Ins. Co. v. Campbell* (U.S. 2003) (punitive damages of $145 million violates due process).

Tort reform statutes sometimes treat punitive damages, such as by placing a cap or higher level of scrutiny on such damages, or requiring proof of fault "beyond a reasonable doubt" or by "clear and convincing evidence."

One lively controversy concerns vicarious liability situations. Many courts have held that punitive damages may be assessed against an employer for any tort committed by his employee (within the course of the employment) for which punitive damages against the employee would be justified. But a substantial number of jurisdictions, supported by the Restatement of Torts (§ 909) and Agency (§ 217C), do not allow punitive damages to be awarded against an employer based upon the acts of his employee, except where (1) the employer authorized the doing and the manner of the act, or (2) the employee was unfit and the employer was reckless in employing him, or (3) the employee was working in a "managerial capacity," or (4) the employer or one of his managerial agents ratified or approved the act. These rules have particular significance in the case of corporations, which act exclusively through agents and employees.

Another problem arises where tortious conduct gives rise to multiple claims, as where many items of the same product sold to the public have the same defect which causes injury to a number of persons. If there is no class action and all the claims are brought separately, it may be appropriate to limit or deny punitive damages in each case (and especially the later ones) in order to prevent astronomical liability. See *Roginsky v. Richardson–Merrell, Inc.* (2d Cir. 1967); *Haslip*; Mo. Stat. Ann. § 510.263.

Are punitive damages insurable? Assuming that the language of defendant's liability insurance policy may fairly be read to cover them, is such coverage contrary to public policy and therefore void? On the one hand, it would be easy enough for the insurer to expressly exclude them, and its failure to do so may well have misled the insured. On the other hand, punitive damages are to punish and deter, and permitting the wrongdoer to shift his punishment to his insurance company substantially impairs or defeats that purpose. There seems to be general agreement that where the liability for punitive damages is vicarious, as in the case of a corporate defendant, punitive damages are a business risk which may be insured, at least where the tort is not that of management and where the conduct was merely reckless and not an intentional wrong. There is a split of authority as to whether one may insure his own personal liability for punitive damages. The majority view seems to be that he may not, but a substantial minority of courts hold that he can if the tort was not willful.

§ 9–4. Allocation Among Tortfeasors

Joint Tortfeasors. It is common for a plaintiff who has suffered physical harm to claim against two or more tortfeasors, usually simultaneously. This was not always so. Recall that earlier rules of tort law were oriented toward placing responsibility on a single wrongdoer. And under older rules of procedure, joinder of more than one defendant in a single tort action was possible only where all such defendants acted in concert in committing the tort, either directly (where each did a tortious act pursuant to a common plan) or where one was vicariously responsible for the tortious act of another under principles of conspiracy or joint enterprise such that a mutual agency existed.

Tort law now recognizes that the negligence (or other wrongful conduct) of more than one person, each acting independently and without a common design, may be concurrent causes of plaintiff's injury for which all may be subject to liability. For example, a passenger in an automobile may be injured by the combined negligence of its driver and the driver of another vehicle. There may be a violation of a common duty; the manufacturer, wholesaler and retailer of a defective product may all be liable to a user injured by it. Or one person may be directly liable and another vicariously liable for the same act, as in the case of a tort committed by an employee in the course of his employment.

Modern rules of civil procedure generally permit joinder in a single action of all defendants whose liability to plaintiff arises out of a single event or transaction, or even out of closely related events. But irrespective of whether such persons are sued separately or together, or are not even sued at all, multiple tort liability creates issues as to how the plaintiff's damages are to be allocated among the different persons liable for them.

Divisible Damages. It sometimes happens that different persons may be liable for separate, identifiable parts of plaintiff's harm. For example, two hunters in separate hunting parties each negligently fire at the same time; one wounds plaintiff in the arm, the other in the leg. Absent concert of action, each is liable only for the harm traceable to him. This is essentially a problem of proof of causation, previously discussed. See § 2–1, supra.

Indivisible Harm. Where two or more persons are responsible for the same harm, the traditional rule was that all whose tortious conduct is found to be a proximate cause of that harm are jointly and severally liable for all of the plaintiff's damages, along with anyone who is vicariously liable for that conduct. Under pure joint and several liability, each tortfeasor is liable for the entire harm, and plaintiff ordinarily may sue any one of them, or some or all, jointly or separately, obtain judgments for the full amount of his damages against as many as he can, and then collect his judgment from one or any combination of them, as he chooses. R. § 882. Of course, he is entitled to only one *satisfaction* for his damages, but an unsatisfied judgment against one does not bar a subsequent action against another. Thus, for example, if there are three defendants, all found liable to the plaintiff, and plaintiff's damages are $100,000, he will be given judgment against each defendant in the amount of $100,000. He can then collect that judgment from one or more defendants in any amount he likes, so long as his total collections do not exceed $100,000.

All persons who are liable to one plaintiff for the same harm are customarily referred to as joint tortfeasors, even where each acted independently and there was no joint enterprise or concert of action involved, and irrespective of whether they are sued in the same action (or indeed at all). In such cases "concurrent tortfeasors" might be a more accurate term, since only their liability is potentially joint.

With the advent of comparative fault, "pure" joint and several liability is now the minority rule. Some jurisdictions now make even joint tortfeasors only "severally" liable to the plaintiff. For example, if Defendant A's proportional share of plaintiff's $100,000 damages is found to be 30%, in those jurisdictions he will be given judgment against A for only $30,000. The majority of jurisdictions now have some form of hybrid between joint and several and several liability. Sometimes several liability is restricted to certain categories of defendants, with all others being jointly and severally liable. In other states, joint and several liability is limited to certain types of torts, or to defendants whose percentage of the total fault exceeds a certain threshhold. There are many variations. See Restatement (Third) of Torts: Apportionment of Liability §§ 10–21.

Release and Covenant Not to Sue. Plaintiff may, of course, enter into an agreement with a tortfeasor by which he promises to relinquish his claim against him in exchange for a consideration. The transaction is called a settlement. By far the greater number of all tort claims are settled without trial.

One form of instrument by which this may be accomplished is a release, in which plaintiff completely surrenders his claim. His cause of action against the released tortfeasor is extinguished. What of his claims against other potential defendants for the same harm? While plaintiff may have rights against several persons arising out of a single injury he has but one cause of action, and thus the traditional common law rule was that a release of one released that cause of action and therefore released all others potentially liable for the same harm.

This led to the development of a device known as a covenant not to sue, under which plaintiff (usually by express language in the instrument) does *not* release his claim against that person, nor his cause of action, but instead merely agrees to forego any further attempts to enforce his claim against that alleged tortfeasor, by suit or otherwise. (A slight variation is a "covenant not to enforce" in which plaintiff promises not to try to collect any judgment he may obtain, or has obtained, from that particular tortfeasor.) Usually such covenants expressly reserve plaintiff's rights against other tortfeasors. But even in the absence of such a reservation, a covenant not to sue or not to execute is held not to release or extinguish plaintiff's claims against others who may also be liable for the same harm. The consideration received in exchange for such a covenant is always less than the full amount of the damages which plaintiff claims; otherwise his cause of action is fully satisfied and the instrument is in reality a release, and will be so construed. The amount received under such a covenant is credited against any judgment plaintiff subsequently obtains against other tortfeasors, but of course has no effect on later settlements with others.

Whether a particular instrument is a release or a covenant is a question of construction not always free from doubt. It is the parties' intent as derived from the substance of the document which controls, and not the document's form of designation. Having rejected the tyranny of labels, the courts are increasingly realizing that there is no logical reason why an instrument which is in form a release of one tortfeasor should ipso facto discharge others if the parties expressly agreed that it shall *not* do so and if it is *not* intended as a full satisfaction. Accordingly, in a most jurisdictions (either by court decision or statute), under these conditions a release of one tortfeasor does not release others liable for the same harm.

The Restatement (Second) of Torts went one step further, holding that a release does not discharge others liable for the same harm unless the agreement expressly so provides. It characterized the requirement that there be an express reservation of rights in the instrument as a "booby-trap for the unwary." R. § 885. Section 885 is now superseded by the Restatement (Third) of Torts: Apportionment of Liability § 24, which reaffirms this rule. Most jurisdictions now follow this view.

One exception to the rule that a release of one tortfeasor does not release others is that in many jurisdictions, a release of Tortfeasor A automatically releases B who was liable to plaintiff solely under some rule making B *vicariously* liable for the conduct of A.

Loan Receipt Agreement. Another settlement device which has had the sanction of at least some courts is the so-called "loan receipt" agreement, whereby one tortfeasor "loans" the plaintiff a sum of money, without interest, to be repaid *only* if and to the extent that plaintiff is successful in his claims against other joint tortfeasors, and *only* from the proceeds of any amount which plaintiff eventually obtains from the others. Plaintiff ordinarily promises to use his best efforts to pursue such other claims as he may have. These are often called "Mary Carter" agreements, as they were first approved in a 1967 Florida case, *Booth v. Mary Carter Paint Co.*

Such an agreement is very advantageous to the first tortfeasor to settle, since it gives him the prospect that the entire loss will be shifted to others, and this in turn may tend to induce settlements by other tortfeasors who might otherwise have to bear the full amount of the damages if the case goes to judgment. (These effects may be altered by the rules of contribution and indemnity, to be discussed.) Since this form of settlement gives the settling tortfeasor a vested interest in the plaintiff's recovery in the lawsuit against the remaining non-settling tortfeasors, the settlement must be disclosed to the court and also to the jury if the settling party testifies.

Most of the jurisdictions that once approved *Mary Carter* agreements (including Florida) have since concluded that they are too one-sided, and now reject them as a matter of policy.

Contribution. When a plaintiff obtains a judgment against two or more joint tortfeasors, if and to the extent that joint and several liability is applicable, the plaintiff may collect that judgment from any one or less than all in any disproportion he pleases. Plaintiff's convenience and assurance of satisfaction are the main considerations; he is allowed to get his money the best way he can. If, as a result, one such defendant does in fact pay more than his proportionate share of the judgment, it might seem logical and fair that he should obtain reimbursement for the excess from the other tortfeasor(s) who, due to the luck of the collection process, paid more. The English and early U.S. common law so held, except in cases of intentional torts or acts in concert where the wrongdoers' equities were too weak to justify the court's aid.

But U.S. tort law went through a long period, lasting until late in the twentieth century, when the majority of the U.S. jurisdictions overextended this exception and denied all common law contribution among joint tortfeasors irrespective of the basis of liability, including cases of negligence and strict liability.

The "no-contribution" rule has been largely overthrown, by judicial decision or statute, and some form of contribution is now available, usually statute, in most states. (Many are patterned after the Uniform Contribution Among Tortfeasors Act, a desirable model.) Several jurisdictions allow contribution by judicial decision. The same policies that support comparative negligence also support contribution among joint tortfeasors. See Restatement (Third) of Torts: Apportionment of Liability § 23, replacing R. § 886A.

Most states allowing contribution allocate the damages among the defendants in proportion to their relative fault, much as in the case of the allocation between plaintiff and defendant under the pure form of comparative negligence. In the remainder, the damages are divided equally. Certain defendants (e.g., employer and employee) are grouped together and charged a single share.

Note that if and to the extent that a defendant is only severally liable to the plaintiff, contribution is not needed and is not available.

Contribution is still generally (but not universally) denied to willful tortfeasors.

Suppose plaintiff has sued and obtained a judgment against fewer than all joint tortfeasors. Should contribution be allowed against one against whom the plaintiff has no judgment? Some of the statutes say no, but the better rule allows it (subject, of course, to satisfactory proof of liability). However, some jurisdictions require the contribution claim to be tried in the same lawsuit, so a tortfeasor not sued by the plaintiff must be joined as a third-party defendant by the defendants seeking contribution or the right to contribution will be lost.

It is generally held (in the absence of a statute requiring otherwise) that a tortfeasor who settles prior to trial, and therefore against whom there is no judgment, may nevertheless obtain contribution from other joint tortfeasors whose liability he discharged by his settlement. He must, of course, prove the others' liability to the plaintiff and the reasonableness of his settlement.

In an action for contribution, the party seeking it must ordinarily establish that the tortfeasor from whom contribution is sought was subject to liability to the injured plaintiff, if no judgment has been obtained determining that liability. Thus, it is usually held that even defenses which only the contribution defendant could have asserted against the injured person, such as intra-family or governmental immunity, privilege, or the immunity provided an employer under the workmen's compensation act, will bar contribution. There is, however, some authority to the contrary. Of course, the fact that the statute of limitations has run on the injured person's claim against the contribution defendant is no defense in the action for contribution.

Indemnity. Contribution must be distinguished from indemnity, with which it is often confused.

Contribution is an equitable sharing of the loss; indemnification is a shifting of the entire loss from one tortfeasor to another, by operation of either (1) a prior agreement of the parties or (2) law, based on equitable considerations. While in theory the main justification for denying contribution—that the courts will not assist a wrongdoer—is equally applicable to an action for indemnity, the fact is that every jurisdiction permits indemnity at least to some extent.

Subject to restrictions imposed by statute and occasionally by public policy, parties entering into a relationship or engaging in an activity may contract in advance that one will indemnity the other for any tort liability (short of intentional wrongdoing) arising therefrom. Such agreements are relatively common, for example, in the construction industry among owners and contractors and subcontractors.

Indemnity by operation of law is based upon the concept of unjust enrichment. Restatement (Third) of Torts: Apportionment of Liability § 22, replacing R. § 886B. Although largely superseded by the adoption of contribution, when still permitted it is allowed in a variety of situations for which no concise tests or standards can be articulated. Generally speaking, it lies when there is a significant or qualitative difference between the blameworthiness of two defendants, both of whom are nevertheless legally liable to the plaintiff for his injury, such that the primary responsibility for the harm rests upon the defendant against whom indemnity is sought. It is frequently said that where the misconduct of the indemnitee (the one seeking indemnity) was merely "passive," or his fault only "secondary," indemnity will be granted against one (the indemnitor) whose wrongful conduct can be described as "active" or a "primary" cause. Such formulations are useful in some situations, but by no means do they encompass all, and they are not sufficiently precise to use in deciding cases.

Indemnity is often allowed in favor of one (such as an employer, partner, or automobile owner) whose sole basis of liability is vicarious responsibility for the tort of another. The same is true where the indemnitee acted pursuant to directions received from the indemnitor which he reasonably believed to be lawful; or where he was induced to act by a misrepresentation of the indemnitor upon which he reasonably relied. Indemnity may be allowed where the indemnitor is responsible for a defective or dangerous condition which caused injury to the plaintiff, and which the indemnitee innocently failed to discover (e.g., the wholesaler or retailer of a defective product).

Indemnity (or the same thing by a different name) is usually allowed in favor of one who is held liable for additional harm caused plaintiff by the subsequent negligence of another. For example, the original tortfeasor who is held liable for all of plaintiff's damages, including those attributable to the aggravation of his injuries by the negligence of the treating physician, may be allowed indemnity from the physician for that portion of the damages for which the physician was responsible. Other courts have reached the same result under a theory of subrogation.

With the advent of contribution, indemnity liability has been greatly restricted. Contribution has almost entirely replaced the "active-passive" form of implied indemnity. Some jurisdictions have also restricted or eliminated other forms of implied indemnity, substituting a contribution remedy. Only express indemnity remains largely unaffected by the shift to contribution.

PART III

TORT AND CONTRACT

CHAPTER 10

TORT AND CONTRACT

§ 10–1. Parties to the Contract

As we have seen, the duty upon the breach of which a tort action may be founded can arise from either of two sources: (1) a general obligation that each of us has to carry on our activities with proper regard for the interests of others; and (2) specific obligations that arise out of some relationship between two or more persons. One such relationship is a contract, which creates by agreement of the parties certain enforceable obligations that the law in most cases would not otherwise impose.

When one party to a contract fails to render the agreed performance, the other party may not only lose the benefit of his bargain, but may also suffer other kinds of injury, including physical and pecuniary harm, as a direct result. Assuming the breach to have been intentional, reckless or negligent, may the party wronged elect to sue in tort, or is he confined to his action for breach of contract? For a variety of reasons, plaintiff will usually prefer to sue in tort if he can. For example, typically the tort measure of damages will be more favorable to him.

General Rule: Misfeasance vs. Nonfeasance. For reasons mainly historical, but also because of a fear of unwarranted extensions of liability, the general rule is that where defendant's duty arises because of a contractual relationship between the parties, he is not liable in tort for harm caused by his breach of that contract where the breach consists of his failure to commence performance at all. But once having begun to perform, he may be liable in tort for his intentional, reckless, or negligent misperformance, whether consisting of acts or omissions to act. For example, one who contracts with plaintiff to cut down a tree on his property will not be liable *in tort* if he simply never arrives on the premises and the tree falls on plaintiff's house before another contractor can be engaged. But once he appears and starts to cut down the tree, he will be liable if he does so negligently, or if he negligently abandons the work halfway through, with the same result. His liability is the same as that of one who gratuitously undertakes to perform some task and does so negligently. Both are liable where their misperformance creates a foreseeable, unreasonable risk of harm to the recognized interests of the plaintiff.

The difficulty lies in determining exactly where nonfeasance ends and misfeasance begins. Many forms of conduct can logically be characterized as either. Omissions to act during the course of an ongoing activity are readily seen as misfeasance. But, perhaps for unspoken policy reasons, firing an employee and expelling a theater patron have been held to be nonfeasance. In general, however, the question is whether defendant's performance (as distinct from his promise or his preparation) has gone so far that it has begun to affect the interests of the plaintiff beyond the expected benefits of the contract itself and may be regarded as a positive act assuming the obligation beyond the mere promise to perform.

Exceptions; Liability for Nonfeasance. When the common law first began to allow an action for breach of an undertaking, it was against those engaged in the common or public callings—common carriers, innkeepers, public warehousemen, and other public servants and utilities. It was a form of tort liability, and it was soon extended to nonperformance and even to defendant's refusal to enter into a contract at all. Gradually this evolved into the action of assumpsit, a contract action in its later stages, which became the principal remedy for breach of any contract. But the original principle has been carried forward in tort law, and such defendants remain liable in tort for nonperformance.

In addition, there are certain other relations (which may or may not be based upon a contract) in which the law imposes a duty of affirmative care and for the failure of which there may be tort liability. For example, a bailee must act affirmatively to care for the goods; an employer must take steps to provide a safe place for his employee to work; a possessor of land must make the premises reasonably safe for invitees.

Such duties arise independently of the terms of the contract, and thus the tort action is limited to that which the law requires. If the contract provides for a different or greater duty, then to that extent its nonperformance must be enforced in a contract action. For example, when defendant agrees to board plaintiff's pet dog, the law will impose a duty to feed it independent of the contract, and for the failure to do so there may be a tort action; but for the failure to perform a promise to give it a rabies shot, the sole remedy is in contract.

Another exception to the general rule is that a promise made without any intent to perform it may be fraud for which a tort action in deceit will lie.

Election: Tort or Contract Action. Where the facts permit, it would seem logical to allow plaintiff to elect to bring his action in either tort or contract as he sees fit. In general, the courts have so held, at least where the issue is one of procedure (jurisdiction, venue, joinder of parties, etc.) or where plaintiff is claiming only pecuniary loss or property damage. But where the action is one for personal injury, many courts have ignored the pleadings and characterized the suit as one in tort for purposes such as determining whether the action survives or which statute of limitations is applicable.

Unjust Enrichment: Restitution. Where defendant's tort results in the unjust enrichment of defendant at plaintiff's expense, the law generally allows plaintiff to "waive" his ordinary tort remedy and sue instead for restitution of the benefit, under a completely theoretical and fictitious "contract" by which defendant impliedly promises to repay his wrongful gain to plaintiff who lost or was deprived of it. Originally a common law tort action, a form of assumpsit, it is now called "quasi-contract" and has some of the advantages of a contract action. It derives from equity and is subject to equitable principles and limitations.

§ 10–2. Liability to Third Persons Not Parties to the Contract

The duties arising under a contract between *A* and *B* will sometimes affect the interests of *C*, a nonparty, such that *A*'s or *B*'s nonperformance or misperformance of the contract may cause harm to *C*. For example, an auto mechanics's negligence in repairing an automobile causes it to crash and injure *C*, a passenger in another vehicle. May *C* sue the mechanic in tort?

Under the common law as it existed in this country until well into the twentieth century, the general rule was that as to duties created by contract, one who was not a party to the contract had no cause of action in tort for harm he suffered as a result of the parties' misperformance or nonperformance. In effect, as a nonparty he had no standing to complain of the breach, even in a tort action; he was not in "privity of contract" with the defendant.

This rule is another of those duty limitations that served to keep tort liability within manageable bounds until the maturation of our economy and the development of the institution of liability insurance. It appears to have originated, or at least to have had its first clear statement, in the notorious 1842 English case, *Winterbottom v. Wright*. The Court of Exchequer there held that the breach of a contract to keep a mailcoach in repair after it was sold gave no cause of action to a passenger in the coach who was injured when it collapsed. The holding was that there could be no action on the contract itself, but certain dicta, particularly that of Lord Abinger who foresaw "the most absurd and outrageous consequences, to which I can see no limit" "[u]nless we confine the operation of such contracts as this to the parties who entered into them," were taken to mean that there could be no action even in tort. This principle was generally followed and extended to the misperformance of any contract.

As in the case of most duty limitations, the courts soon found themselves busily engaged in creating exceptions to it. The exceptions proliferated, and today the privity barrier is largely down and relatively few vestiges of the *Winterbottom* rule survive. Ordinary principles of negligence and proximate cause for the most part now delineate the liability of a contracting party to one with whom he is not in privity. Yet even today, we occasionally see the old privity barrier in the form of a duty limitation, such as in *Kirk v. Michael Reese Hosp.* (Ill. 1987).

The classic example of the erosion of the privity rule is the history of the law of products liability, discussed elsewhere.

Nonfeasance. Just as there is no tort liability between the parties for harm caused by the nonperformance of a contract, absent some recognized exception, so there is generally no tort liability to a nonparty injured thereby. Thus, one who is hired to repair an auto but never even begins performance is not liable to a third person injured by the defect.

But here also there are exceptions, and liability to third persons for failure to commence performance may be imposed in situations where the courts have determined that a contract between *A* and *B* creates a sufficient duty toward *C* to justify it. Illustrations of such situations include: (1) the failure of a telegraph company to transmit a telegram; (2) the nonperformance by an agent of his contractual duty (a) to supervise property or persons over which he has been given control (e.g., a herd of cattle) or (b) to take certain precautions for the safety of third persons (e.g., a railroad crossing guard); (3) nonperformance of a contract to maintain, inspect or repair an instrumentality that foreseeably creates a substantial risk of harm to third persons (e.g., an elevator, a boiler, scaffolding); and (4) in some jurisdictions, nonperformance by a landlord of his contract to repair the premises. In a number of these cases, defendant's conduct might just as easily have been classified as misfeasance, bearing further witness to the illusory nature of the distinction.

One oft-cited example of nonliability in tort for nonperformance of a contract is found in cases exonerating water companies from liability for fire damage caused by their failure to perform their contractual duty to maintain adequate water pressure in their lines—e.g., *H. R. Moch Co. v. Rensselaer Water Co.* (N.Y. 1928) (Cardozo, J.). A similar result is usually reached in cases of failure to furnish other utilities and municipal services. Again, such cases could just as readily be deemed misfeasance, and the real reasons for these holdings are based upon fears of unduly burdensome liability.

Misfeasance. Once defendant has commenced performance of his contract, the general rule today is that he will be liable to nonparties for his tortious misperformance, subject of course to the usual rules of proximate cause and any other applicable limitations. The privity rule is now virtually dead in cases involving the sale of goods, and nearly so in cases involving the performance of services. Thus, our auto mechanic who negligently performs repairs on an automobile will be liable to third persons injured as a result, when and to the extent that their injuries are a foreseeable result of his negligence. An attorney who negligently drafts or directs the execution of a will may be held liable to disappointed intended beneficiaries.

It must be emphasized, however obvious it may seem, that even though privity is no longer necessary, liability to third persons does not automatically follow from the misperformance of a contract. For the most part, privity was an arbitrary duty limitation that could not be justified in terms of the underlying principles from which liability or nonliability ought to flow. But in certain cases, the privity limitation rather unartfully expressed a valid concern that liability not be so disproportionately burdensome that otherwise desirable activities be made prohibitively risky or expensive. Removal of that limitation merely laid bare the underlying dilemma and forced the courts to deal with that directly. For example, when privity of contract was required, that in itself would prevent an accountant who negligently prepared a financial statement from being liable to third persons who sustained pecuniary loss in reliance upon it. Now that privity is no longer necessary, the courts have had to face the real problem, which is the risk of very large potential liability to an indeterminate class of persons who may reasonably rely on the statement. The solution has been to limit liability for pecuniary loss for a negligent misrepresentation to those persons for whose benefit and guidance the accountant (or other actor) knows the information to be intended. This is, in effect, a special proximate cause rule. See § 15–3, infra. In the area of products liability, an analogous problem is the scope of the manufacturer's liability to "bystanders" (i.e., persons other than the user or consumer injured by the product), and the solution has been either to deny liability to bystanders or to limit liability to those bystanders whose exposure to the product the manufacturer can reasonably anticipate.

PART IV

IMMUNITIES

CHAPTER 11

IMMUNITIES

§ 11–1. Government and Its Employees

An *immunity* is a defense to tort liability that is conferred upon an entire group or class of persons or entities under circumstances where considerations of public policy are thought to require special protection for the person, activity or entity in question at the expense of those injured by its tortious act. Historically, tort litigation against units of government, public officers, and charities, and between spouses, parents and children, has been limited or prohibited on this basis.

It is frequently said that immunities differ from privileges (see § 7–1) in that the latter are narrower in scope and operate when the presence of certain facts make defendant's conduct nontortious. Thus, a privilege negates the existence of the tort, whereas an immunity recognizes that a tort has been committed but provides a defense to liability because of defendant's favored status. While perhaps technically accurate, this distinction is largely

393

semantic and is frequently not observed, and courts and writers sometimes use the two terms interchangeably. Moreover, in recent years there has been a strong trend to abolish or limit immunities, and to the extent that they remain in force at all, often it is not because of defendant's favored status but because the utility of the particular conduct in question is such that the burden of liability would be disproportionate to the risk created. Hence, what is left of the traditional immunities tends to resemble duty limitations or privileges.

Governmental or Sovereign Immunity. The most important tort immunity is that of units of government, which is frequently referred to as sovereign immunity.

The sovereign immunity concept has dual aspects, and this duality has caused controversy and confusion. One aspect is procedural, the other substantive. In its original form, under English common law, the rule was fundamentally procedural. A lawsuit could not be brought against the Crown (the sovereign) in the Crown's own courts without its consent. (This disability would, of course, apply not merely to tort actions but to all others as well.) But the doctrine eventually came to be regarded as also embodying a rule of *substantive* immunity from *tort* liability, as reflected in the oft-quoted phrase "The King can do no wrong," which was usually interpreted as meaning that the sovereign was incapable of committing a tort.

One might have expected that the United States, founded as it was upon a premise of the supremacy of the people over those who govern them and a rejection of the notion of the divine right of kings, would also have rejected the notion of sovereign immunity. But the opposite is true; the doctrine was unquestioningly accepted into the fabric of the U.S. common law. Ironically, in England the Crown had long provided other means of redress for injuries caused by royal and governmental agents.

In this country, there are three distinct levels of government—federal, state and local. Initially, each of these was uniformly held to be entirely immune from tort liability. That immunity has by now been significantly restricted (although by no means entirely eliminated) at all levels, but each has had a different history and there are important differences among them with respect to the nature and scope of their liability.

United States. From the beginning, it was taken for granted that the United States could not be sued without its consent, *Cohens v. Virginia* (U.S. 1821), and this is still the rule. R. § 895A. Congress in 1855 created the U.S. Court of Claims to adjudicate contract claims, and the Tucker Act of 1887 gave jurisdiction to the Court of Claims and the federal courts of certain non-tort claims, including those arising under the fifth amendment (prohibiting the taking of private property without compensation). But, with minor exceptions, there was no remedy against the United States for torts committed by the government against its citizens (except by private bill in Congress) until Congress adopted the Federal Tort Claims Act in 1946. 28 U.S.C.A. §§ 1346, 1402, 1504, 2110, 2401, 2402, 2411, 2412, 2671–2680.

Under this statute, the federal district courts have (exclusive) jurisdiction over suits against the United States "for money damages ... for injury or loss of property, or personal injury or death caused by the negligent or wrongful act or omission of any employee of the Government while acting within the scope of his office or employment, under circumstances where the United States, if a private person, would be liable to the claimant in accordance with the law of the place where the act or omission occurred." 28 U.S.C.A. § 1346(b). Trial is without a jury.

The Act contains a number of exceptions, mostly preserving immunity for specific governmental activities (e.g., tax assessment and collection, failure to deliver mail, military combat in time of war, actions arising in foreign countries). In addition, there are two important general exceptions. First, the United States is not liable for "any claim arising out of assault, battery, false imprisonment, false arrest, malicious prosecution, abuse of process, libel, slander, misrepresentation, deceit, or interference with contract rights"; except that the Act *does* apply to "acts or omissions of investigative or law enforcement officers of the United States Government" with respect to claims "arising, on or after the enactment of this proviso, out of assault, battery, false imprisonment, false arrest, abuse of process, or malicious prosecution." 28 U.S.C.A. § 2680(h). (The proviso was added by amendment in 1974 to assure the availability of adequate remedies for abuses of power by federal law enforcement personnel.) While it is sometimes said that (except for the proviso) the Act is limited to negligent acts or omissions, there are intentional torts that are not excluded and for which actions may be brought, such as trespass and invasion of privacy.

Second, the federal government is not liable for acts done with due care in the execution of a statute or regulation, even though it is invalid, or for "an act or omission ... based upon the exercise or performance or the failure to exercise or perform a *discretionary* function or duty on the part of a federal agency or an employee of the Government, whether or not the discretion involved be abused." 28 U.S.C.A. § 2680(a) (emphasis added). Much litigation has centered on whether the act in question involved the exercise of discretion or was merely ministerial, because almost any act by any governmental employee is arguably the product of the decision of some one who had the power to decide to act or not. The concept refers to decisions made at the planning or policy level, and for the most part does not include conduct at the lower or "operational" levels of government even though the exercise of some judgment may be involved.

In addition, the United States is not subject to strict tort liability, since the Act waives its immunity only for a "negligent or wrongful act or omission." *Laird v. Nelms* (U.S. 1972).

Agencies of the federal government share its immunity. Sometimes a statute will expressly or impliedly authorize suits against a particular agency; but if the claim is cognizable under the Federal Tort Claims Act, that is the exclusive remedy.

States. The doctrine of sovereign immunity has been uniformly applied to the state level of government. R. § 895B. (An early decision that this did not apply to suits against the states in federal court, *Chisholm v. Georgia* (U.S. 1793), was nullified by the eleventh amendment.) Most states adopted the common law rule of sovereign immunity in both its substantive and procedural aspects. Some state constitutions codify the procedural aspect of the doctrine, but expressly or impliedly allow waiver; a few expressly prohibit the giving of consent to suit.

Various justifications, all of them rather weak, have been advanced for adhering to the doctrine: there should be no liability for negligence in the performance of a duty imposed by law; a tort cannot be committed by an entire people; whatever the state does must ipso facto be lawful; a government employee who commits a tort must thereby be acting outside the scope of his authority and employment; tort compensation is not a proper use of public funds; tort liability would cause inconvenience and embarrassment to the government; and, occasionally, just "public policy." The most likely reason for its persistence is a fear that governmental tort liability would precipitate a large scale milking of the public treasury and fiscally disastrous consequences—a fear that is increasingly seen as unwarranted and outweighed by the injustice of immunity. Thus, all states have now consented (usually by statute or constitutional provision) to allow tort claims in some form and to a greater or lesser extent. Some are limited to particular types of claims (e.g., motor vehicle accidents); in many states there is a special court, agency or procedure for claims against the state. Some merely authorize the purchase of liability insurance and permit claims to the extent of the insurance.

Even where the state's sovereign immunity is discarded, of necessity certain special common law defenses unique to governmental activities remain. For example, a state is not liable in tort for the actions or inaction of its courts or legislature, nor ordinarily for the judicial or legislative acts of state administrative officers and agencies. Nor is it liable in tort for the basic planning and policy decisions of state officials involving the exercise of official discretion. See R. § 895B (3)(b) and Comment *d*.

Local Governments. Units of local government below the level of the state are in a separate category. The distinction between state and local governments derives from the fact that municipalities are regarded as having a dual character. In one sense, they are a branch of government, deriving their governmental powers from their parent state. But in another sense, they are corporate entities, much like private corporations, organized to provide various services to the residents of their areas, such as water, electricity, waste disposal, and sometimes hospitals, schools, libraries, transportation, and others. Units of local government are often referred to as municipal corporations.

The first local governmental entities were cities, towns and villages. Today, we have these and many more—counties, townships, special purpose districts of various kinds, and other separate governmental entities such as transit and utility companies. In some jurisdictions certain of these are state agencies, and thus are governed by the state immunity rules. If not, they are regarded as local governmental entities and the rules governing municipalities apply.

Russell v. Men of Devon (K.B. 1788) is usually cited as the first articulation of local governmental immunity. At that time, the idea of a local governmental *entity* had not yet developed and the action was, in effect, against the entire male population of the county. Thus, one basis for denying liability was the fact that there were no corporate funds out of which to pay a judgment.

Nevertheless, the *Russell* case was followed in this country, and local governmental immunity was at one time the universally accepted rule in the United States. It was rationalized on grounds similar to those previously noted that were offered in support of state immunity. But it was subject to the same criticisms; predictably, exceptions to it soon developed. The most important of these was based on the "governmental-proprietary" distinction arising from the dual character of municipal corporations. When the entity was acting in its governmental, political, or public capacity, it was immune. But when acting in its corporate, private, or proprietary capacity, it was subject to tort liability to much the same extent as any private corporation.

As might be expected, the courts had considerable difficulty distinguishing between governmental and proprietary functions, and there was substantial disagreement and inconsistency among the cases on this issue. Moreover, as sentiment favoring liability has increased, there was a trend to find acts to be "proprietary" whenever possible. The result was hopeless confusion.

Other exceptions developed. Local governments are always liable in nuisance. An important intermediate step on the road to abrogation was taken in many jurisdictions that held that where the local government had purchased liability insurance (as most had, since they were liable for some activities), immunity was thereby waived to the extent of the insurance coverage—a classic "Catch 22." In addition, local governments were sometimes held liable for particular activities, such as the maintenance of public ways, or for activities voluntarily undertaken, or for misfeasance. In addition, statutes began to impose liability for certain activities, such as operating motor vehicles.

Finally, beginning with *Hargrove v. Town of Co-
coa Beach* (Fla. 1957), the courts began to overthrow local governmental immunity entirely.
Largely unrestricted by constitutional or statutory
provisions, local governmental immunity until recently has remained much more a common law
doctrine than state immunity, and thus the courts
are freer to abolish it. Accordingly, *Hargrove* attracted a large following.

As in the case of the state's immunity, the abolition of the immunity of local governments has been
held not to affect certain pre-existing defenses peculiar to the activities of government. There is no tort
liability for judicial and legislative functions, nor for
the exercise of an administrative function involving
the making of a basic policy decision. R. § 895C(2)
and Comment *g*.

Comprehensive Statutes. Most states have now
enacted comprehensive statutes governing the tort
liability of state and local governmental units and
their employees. At first these statutes were passed
in response to decisions abolishing immunity, and
many of the acts are patterned after legislation
enacted in California in 1963; some follow the Federal Tort Claims Act. Several states have since
obviated the need for judicial abrogation by similar
legislation. The statutes typically recognize general
governmental liability, but reinstate limited immunities or defenses for particular kinds of activities.

Governmental Officers and Employees. The
personal tort liability of governmental officers and

employees for their job-related conduct is *not* identical to that of their governmental employer. As a general rule, in the absence of a statute, their common law liability is somewhat broader. But they are also the beneficiaries of certain special immunities.

As a general proposition, a governmental officer or employee is personally liable for his torts. R. § 895D. However, when exercising a judicial or legislative function, he shares the traditional immunity of his employer.

The highest executive officers of the federal and state governments are also absolutely immune from tort liability, except perhaps when they have so far exceeded the scope of their official discretion as to be acting clearly beyond the bounds of their authority, as when acting purely out of personal spite or malice.

Lower level executive and administrative employees possess a qualified immunity. When performing a discretionary function, they are immune from liability so long as they act honestly and in good faith. But with respect to ministerial acts, they are subject to the ordinary rules of tort liability. As to the distinction between discretionary and ministerial acts, see R. § 895D, Comments *f* and *h*.

The scope of the common law tort liability of public officers and employees is, of course, subject to statutory modification, and there are many such statutes. State governmental tort immunity acts usually apply to government employees, often making their liability coextensive with that of the government. Federal and state employees are generally liable for constitutional violations (see § 8–22, supra), but even here some (but not all) of the traditional immunities have been judicially preserved. And occasionally a statute will immunize the employee even though the government is liable for his act (e.g., negligence in the operation of a motor vehicle by a federal employee, 28 U.S.C.A. § 2679(b)).

Statutes frequently alter the usual rule that an employer may obtain indemnity from an employee for whose tort he is held liable, either by prohibiting indemnity, or, occasionally, by reversing it and requiring the government to indemnify the employee.

Public employees may be held personally liable for punitive damages, but such damages ordinarily may not be assessed against a governmental entity in the absence of statutory authorization.

§ 11–2. Charities

At one time, all but one or two U.S. jurisdictions held that charitable, educational, religious, or benevolent organizations and enterprises were immune from tort liability.

The rule was derived from an 1846 English case, which justified it on the ground that the funds of the charity should not be diverted from the donor's intended charitable purpose to so remote a use as the payment of tort claims. The parent case was overruled in England in 1866, a fact that seems to have gone unnoticed here. Moreover, that justification runs counter to well-established principles of trust law; trust assets may generally be used to satisfy tort liabilities incurred in administering the trust.

Another supposed justification is that the principle of respondeat superior does not apply to charities because they derive no profit from the employee's service. The defect in this argument is that the principal justifications for respondeat superior (see § 8–10, supra) have nothing to do with whether the employer profits from his employee's work.

With respect to the beneficiaries of the charity's services, some jurisdictions (by judicial decision or statute) restrict or deny liability on the dubious theory that they, in effect, impliedly assume the risk of the charity's negligence by accepting its benevolence. Clearly, this is quite unrealistic. One should be able to expect even a charitable enterprise to conduct itself with reasonable care, and we have seen that principles of tort law require one who undertakes to act, even gratuitously, to exercise ordinary care.

Some have suggested that charities in rendering a public service should be treated the same as a governmental unit. Aside from the fact that the justifications for governmental immunity have been discredited and the immunity itself largely abrogated (§ 11–1), the functions of charities and government qua government are seldom similar and therefore the analogy is false.

The most likely reason for the immunity is that it was thought to further a public policy that strongly favors and supports charitable enterprises, whose beneficent work might be hampered if their assets must be used to pay tort claims. But first legal writers and then the courts accepted the now-prevailing view that tort liability is a legitimate expense of any enterprise, however benevolent and worthy, and the public policy favoring charity is outweighed by the injustice of tort immunity, especially now that liability insurance has reduced the burden to manageable levels.

President and Directors of Georgetown College v. Hughes (D.C. 1942) (Rutledge, J.) effectively demolished the underpinnings of charitable immunity, and started an avalanche of decisions overthrowing it. Most states now reject it entirely, and this is the Restatement position (R. § 895E). The rest have all abolished it in part. A few have abrogated the immunity of charitable hospitals but retained it as to religious institutions and other charities. Some limit the immunity to recipients of the benefits of the charity. Some have abolished it to the extent that defendant is covered by liability insurance or to the extent that the judgment can be satisfied out of nontrust assets. And almost all will impose liability in certain situations, as when the tort is that of a managing agent, or when committed during fundraising activities, when not directly connected with the charity itself, or when it is a nuisance.

Most U.S. jurisdictions have statutes that purport to reinstate some charitable immunities, at least in part, either generally or as to certain charities. There would appear to be some question as to the constitutionality of at least some of these statutes if they are narrowly drawn to immunize certain groups or activities and not others similarly situated.

§ 11–3. Spouses, Parents and Children

In many jurisdictions, if the person injured and the tortfeasor are (or were) either (1) husband and wife or (2) parent and child, the tortfeasor may have partial immunity from suit or liability.

Husband and Wife. At common law, neither spouse could sue the other during the marriage, but only because it was procedurally impossible. A woman lost most of her separate legal identity during marriage. Her husband acquired many of her rights, and became liable for her torts. She could not sue or be sued without joinder of him as plaintiff or defendant. Thus, there could be no tort litigation inter se because the husband would have had to be on both sides of the same lawsuit.

In the United States, beginning about 1844, statutes (called Married Women's Acts or Emancipation Acts) were passed in every jurisdiction that gave a married woman a separate legal identity and separate ownership of her own property. These statutes were construed (where possible) to permit the wife to maintain an action against her husband for torts against her property interests and for torts involving only pecuniary loss (e.g., deceit). By necessary implication, the husband was given the same rights against his wife. But most jurisdictions refused to go further, and held that such legislation did not remove the bar to actions between spouses for personal torts not involving property. A few of these acts expressly prohibited interspousal litigation.

Preservation of the common law interspousal tort immunity after the passage of the Married Women's Acts required the courts to find new justifications for it, such as: (1) preservation of the peace and harmony of the home; (2) prevention of a flood of spurious litigation; (3) the availability of other remedies to the injured spouse, such as divorce or criminal prosecution; (4) protection of liability insurers from collusive suits; (5) avoidance of the danger that the tortfeasor spouse would share the benefit of the proceeds of the claim obtained from the insurer; and (6) legislative preemption (the statutes themselves being held to make the matter one of legislative concern). The immunity was thus transformed from a procedural to a substantive one.

All of these justifications have been refuted to the satisfaction of most legal writers and courts. Domestic disharmony is perhaps a *cause* of litigation, but rarely an effect; either there is no tranquility left to preserve by the time the litigation stage is reached, or else the real object of the suit is liability insurance. In the latter case, there is no reason to suppose that the trier of fact is any less able to detect spurious or collusive claims here than elsewhere. Remedies under the divorce or criminal laws are manifestly inadequate, and do not compensate for the injury. The possibility of a benefit to the wrongdoing spouse does not justify denying the injured spouse a remedy, especially since the latter is presumably capable of protecting his or her rights in the compensation fund. And, absent a controlling statute, the immunity remains of common law origin and subject to judicial control.

Thus, the trend has been to abolish this immunity; the majority of states have done away with it entirely. The Restatement (Second) rejects it (§ 895F). And many of the remaining states (a few of which have statutes expressly preserving it) recognize exceptions, as where the marriage has been terminated (by death or divorce) or where the tort occurred prior to the marriage. Most jurisdictions allow actions for intentional torts. And almost all courts now hold that plaintiff may sue one who is vicariously liable for his spouse's tort, even though his spouse is personally immune.

Parent and Child. The common law recognized no such legal unity of a parent and his child. Property and contract actions between them have always been permitted, and so have actions for torts involving property interests or pecuniary loss. And while authority is scant, there is no reason to think that the same would not have been true in other common law countries as to personal torts. But in the United States, the first reported decision on this issue was *Hewlett v. George* (Miss. 1891), which held (citing no authority) that a minor child could not sue her parent for false imprisonment. Following this case, it soon became the general rule that a parent and his unemancipated minor child were each immune from suit by the other for a personal tort, whether intentional or negligent in character.

Justifications were given for this immunity analogous to those offered in support of interspousal tort immunity. It was said that to allow parent-child tort actions would: (1) undermine parental discipline; (2) permit collusive lawsuits; (3) upset the even allocation of family resources; (4) foster useless litigation, since the parent or child might eventually inherit the recovery from the other's estate; and (5) violate a general social policy that the parent is the head of the household and as such should have an immunity like that of a sovereign.

These justifications, like those for the husband-wife immunity, have now been largely discredited on similar grounds. The principal difference in the rationale of the parent-child immunity relates to the possible effect of parental liability upon the parent's authority to discipline the child, and this authority would seem to be adequately protected by the privilege to discipline, previously discussed (§ 7–7). Whatever merit remains in the bases of this immunity is now generally regarded as outweighed by the injustice of denying compensation to one who has been tortiously injured, especially when one or more of the foregoing justifications are absent.

Thus, a strong minority of states have now abolished this immunity generally; this is the Restatement position (R. § 895G). Note, however, that this does not mean that the liability of a parent will be the same as if the plaintiff was a stranger. Aside from the privilege of discipline, it is sometimes said that there is no liability where the alleged negligent act involves an exercise of parental discretion in the provision of food, clothing, housing, and other necessities and care, or that a parent is not liable for the ordinary risks inherent in intrafamily activities and relations. In some cases the courts may simply be saying that defendant's conduct was not negligent under the circumstances, one of which was the family relation; but other courts may be preserving a portion of the former immunity.

Among the remaining states, a number of exceptions to the immunity have evolved. Most now hold that there is no immunity for bodily harm intentionally or recklessly inflicted. In some jurisdictions there is no immunity where the risk is unrelated to the status of the parties as parent and child, as in the case of harm inflicted in the course of a business activity of the defendant. Some will allow an action where the parent-child relation has been terminated by the death of either party, or for the wrongful death of the other parent. And it is generally agreed that the immunity of the parent or child is a personal one that does not protect a third party who is vicariously liable for the tort of either, such as his employer.

It is uniformly held that the immunity extends only to unemancipated minor children, and that it does not apply to persons who only stand in loco parentis.

Siblings and Other Kin. Brothers, sisters, and other kin are not, by reason of their relationship, immune from tort liability to one another. R. § 895H.

PART V
SURVIVAL AND WRONGFUL DEATH

CHAPTER 12

SURVIVAL AND WRONGFUL DEATH

§ 12–1. Survival of Tort Actions

At common law, all causes of action for personal torts abated with the death of either the tortfeasor or the person injured, regardless of the cause of death. "Actio personalis moritur cum persona." Except as modified by statute, that remains the general rule today.

This is one of the best examples of a rule wholly without rational support, which persisted solely because of stare decisis. It probably originated from the fact that in its inception, tort law was an inseparable part of the law of wrongs, whose main functions were retribution and punishment. See § 1–3, supra. Thus, if the tortfeasor died, he could no longer be punished and so the entire action abated, including the criminal punishment and the civil remedy, if any. If the tortfeasor was responsible for a death, the killing was frequently a felony, in which case the crown executed the tortfeasor and

413

confiscated his property, and so there was nothing left with which to compensate the victim's survivors. The civil remedy was said to be "merged into the felony." If injured person died from some other cause, he no longer required compensation and the crown could still punish the tortfeasor's wrong, and so the victim's civil remedy died with him.

By statutes enacted in the fourteenth century, actions for the loss, damage or conversion of personal property were allowed to survive the death of the plaintiff (but not that of defendant). But actions for torts against real property or against the person (e.g., assault, battery, false imprisonment, negligent personal injury, defamation, malicious prosecution, and usually misrepresentation) were still within the common law rule of abatement when the various United States received the law of England.

Contract actions, however, have always survived. This has led to attempts, usually unsuccessful, to characterize plaintiff's suit as one for breach of contract even though the gist of the action is negligence or some other tort theory—for example, where plaintiff is injured in an accident while a passenger on a common carrier and sues for breach of the contract of carriage.

All jurisdictions have more or less modified the common law rule, almost always by statute.

States. State survival statutes usually provide that in certain specified types of cases, plaintiff's cause of action does not abate because of his death or because of the death of the tortfeasor, but survives in favor of plaintiff or his personal representative. However, the statutes vary widely as to the types of actions that survive and the conditions under which they may be brought.

The statutes are of two types. In some, either all tort actions or all tort actions with certain listed exceptions survive. In others, only those actions named survive. This creates problems of construction, since frequently the statute lists categories such as "injury to persons or property" instead of the names of particular torts.

About one-third of the states provide for the survival of (1) all tort actions or (2) all tort actions except defamation. The remainder are a potpourri of inclusions and exclusions. In general, actions for harm to tangible property (real or personal) survive the death of either party. Personal injury actions also survive in almost all jurisdictions, but in many cases with limitations on the damages recoverable. In a few states, personal injury actions do not survive the injured person's death except as part of an action for that death. Actions for injury to one's character or reputation often do not survive. Non-survival of actions for deceit, invasion of privacy, malicious prosecution, injuries to personal relations (e.g., seduction, alienation of affections), and false imprisonment is not uncommon. Actions for consequential damages sometimes do not survive the plaintiff's death.

At one time it was the general rule that wrongful death actions did not survive the death of the tortfeasor, but today in most states they do.

The result of this diversity is a maze of inconsistencies and incongruous results. For example, there are jurisdictions in which a cause of action for legal malpractice for the negligent failure to file a personal injury lawsuit prior to the expiration of the statute of limitations does not survive the death of either the plaintiff or the negligent lawyer, even though the personal injury action itself would not abate on the death of either plaintiff or defendant. And in other states, where both plaintiff and his auto are damaged in an automobile accident, the action for damage to his car survives but not his action for his personal injuries (if he dies from other causes).

Thus, there is a tendency to broaden the survival statutes, both by amendment and by judicial interpretation. And at least one state has held that an exception to its general survival statute for defamation actions is unconstitutional. *Moyer v. Phillips* (Pa. 1975). It is safe to predict that eventually all or almost all tort actions will survive.

The measure of damages in a survival action is generally the same as it would have been if no one had died. Of course, plaintiff's death terminates the accrual of certain kinds of future damages that he otherwise could have recovered (future pain and suffering, mental distress, medical expenses, loss of earnings, disability, etc.) based on his life expectancy before he died, and recovery may be had only for those damages that actually accrued prior to his death. R. § 926. And the survival statutes in a few jurisdictions expressly limit in other ways the damages recoverable where plaintiff is the one who died.

Where defendant tortiously injures plaintiff who subsequently dies from those injuries, plaintiff's survivors or estate may have either a survival action or a wrongful death action or both. Special problems arise from this situation that will be discussed in the two sections that follow.

In most jurisdictions, defendant's death terminates plaintiff's right to seek punitive damages, and in some states so does the death of the plaintiff.

Federal. F.E.L.A. and Jones Act actions survive. The appropriate state survival statute applies in actions under the Federal Tort Claims Act, and in admiralty claims by nonseamen. But there is no general maritime survival action, and the Death on the High Seas Act, which limits recovery to pecuniary losses suffered by surviving relatives, is the exclusive recovery for deaths that occur on the high seas. *Dooley v. Korean Air Lines Co.* (U.S. 1998).

§ 12–2. Wrongful Death

Where defendant's tort proximately causes fatal injuries to another, decedent's family usually sustains a measurable loss. During some periods of the development of the common law, this loss was at least partly compensated, usually in the same action in which the crown punished defendant for the killing. There is some evidence of compensation for wrongful death in the earliest U.S. tort law.

However, an English trial judge (Lord Ellenborough) is reported to have remarked in 1808 that "in a civil court, the death of a human being could not be complained of as an injury." *Baker v. Bolton.* Thenceforth this was taken to be the common law rule both in England and the United States (Hawaii alone to the contrary).

No satisfactory reason for this rule has ever been suggested. Lord Ellenborough offered none. Perhaps he was thinking of the rule of nonsurvival (§ 12–1) which, however, would apply only to the injured person's own damages and not to those sustained by his next of kin. It has been suggested that the rule originated in the common law doctrine by which the civil remedy merged into a felony, but this would not explain its application in a nonfelony cause such as *Baker.* Some courts, apparently struggling to rationalize the rule, spoke of the impossibility of calculating the pecuniary value of a human life or expressed a repugnance to undertake so crass a task. Perhaps the real reason for the initial judicial acceptance of the rule was an unexpressed fear of huge and largely unreviewable verdicts by juries sympathetic to widows and orphans and intent on punishment.

Criticism of the rule mounted rapidly, culminating in its abrogation in England in 1846 by a statute known as the Fatal Accidents Act, or more commonly Lord Campbell's Act. It provided that "whensoever the death of a person shall be caused by wrongful act, neglect, or default, and the act, neglect, or default is such as would (if death had not ensued) have entitled the party injured to maintain an action and recover damages in respect thereof, then and in every such case the person who would have been liable if death hand not ensued shall be liable to an action for damages" by decedent's personal representative on behalf of his spouse, parent or child. Beginning with New York in 1847, every U.S. jurisdiction has followed suit.

Wrongful death statutes are of two types. The majority are modeled upon Lord Campbell's Act, which is a true "wrongful death" act and creates an entirely new cause of action for the damages resulting to certain next of kin from the death. The remaining states have only "survival acts," which merely preserve the cause of action that was vested in the decedent at the moment of his death and enlarge it to include the damages resulting from the death itself.

The survival-type remedy for wrongful death was primarily intended to foreclose the problem of double recovery and multiplicity of litigation that could arise in the situation where the decedent survived his injuries for a period of time and then died from them. In such cases, his representative could have an action for his personal injuries and the losses arising from them and also an action for his death and the losses arising from it under a wrongful death act. There could be overlap in the measure of damages in the two actions; hence no separate wrongful death cause of action was created. Unfortunately, a few states construed their statutes of this type to mean that there could be no recovery at all for wrongful death where the death was instantaneous, since in such a case the decedent himself never had a cause of action capable of surviving. Such a construction is obviously wrong, and most states with survival-type statutes have held to the contrary.

Nevertheless, in those jurisdictions having a personal injury survival statute and a separate remedy for wrongful death, two distinct causes of action ordinarily will arise where the accident victim lived for a while after the accident before succumbing to it. In most of these jurisdictions, either action may be brought independently of the other or they may be brought in the same lawsuit, at plaintiff's option. If brought separately, double recovery is prevented by disallowing claims for the same elements of damage in both actions or by limiting the survival action damages. However, in some states the actions must be consolidated; in others the causes of action are automatically merged; in a few plaintiff must elect between the survival action and the wrongful death action; and occasionally the survival action is held to abate, either entirely or as to certain elements of damage (e.g., pain and suffering).

Under most statutes, any tort theory that would have supported a personal injury action will support an action for wrongful death—an intentional tort, reckless or negligent behavior, strict liability (product or otherwise). A few courts once held that there could be no wrongful death action for breach of warranty, but these decisions if not yet overruled are of doubtful current validity.

The usual rules of proximate cause apply in wrongful death cases, notwithstanding some older decision narrowly construing the term "caused" that appears in most statutes.

In addition to the death acts of general application, most statutory tort actions (e.g., F.E.L.A., dram shop acts) contain their own provisions for recovery in the event of death. If not, then an appropriate general death act will be held to apply.

The Death on the High Seas Act (46 U.S.C. §§ 761–768) provides a remedy for deaths occurring more than one league (three nautical miles) from U.S. state or territorial shores on or over international waters, but the act limits recovery to "pecuniary losses" suffered by surviving relatives

The fundamental justice of allowing recovery for wrongful death, and the universal existence of the remedy, have led many to urge a reconsideration of the rule of *Baker v. Bolton* and its progeny and a recognition that there exists a common law action for wrongful death independent of any statute. These urgings went unheeded until the landmark decision of the United States Supreme Court in *Moragne v. States Marine Lines, Inc.* (U.S. 1970), which held that there is a wrongful death action under general principles of admiralty law. Following *Moragne,* Massachusetts in *Gaudette v. Webb* (Mass.

1972) recognized the existence of a common law wrongful death action separate and apart from the Massachusetts wrongful death statute, thereby allowing the wrongful death act's statute of limitations to be tolled under a different statute.

Moragne and *Gaudette* must not be read too broadly. Even if they are generally followed, the result will be that the general common law and statutory rules of tort law will apply in wrongful death cases, but *only* if and to the extent that they do not conflict with the provisions of an applicable wrongful death statute. The wrongful death act will still control as to those matters on which it speaks. However, these decisions do create the possibility that wrongful death act provisions that significantly limit the rights and remedies of plaintiffs thereunder, as compared to plaintiffs in other similar personal injury actions, could be held unconstitutional as a denial of the equal protection of the laws. If the wrongful death action is no longer solely of legislative origin, then the legislature is no longer free to limit or restrict that remedy in any manner it chooses.

§ 12–3. Wrongful Death: Beneficiaries and Damages

The wrongful death statutes specify or designate those who may recover under them. The primary beneficiaries are ordinarily the deceased's spouse and children. Parents are sometimes designated beneficiaries, primary or secondary. Under many statutes these are the sole beneficiaries, and if the deceased left none surviving then no wrongful death action may be brought. Some statutes extend benefits to other relatives, but often only if they were in fact dependent upon the deceased and sometimes only if there is no beneficiary in a higher class. Under a few statutes the recovery is paid to the deceased's heirs at law whoever they may be, or is simply distributed to the beneficiaries of his estate like any inherited sum. It may be reached by creditors of the estate.

In most jurisdictions the action must be brought by the decedent's personal representative, and if there is none (because the probate estate is too small) one will be appointed for this purpose. In some states the action may be brought directly by certain beneficiaries, and in a few others it must be.

The damages that may be awarded in a wrongful death action and the methods of calculating them constitute a large and complex subject, chiefly because of the wide variety of wrongful death statutes and even wider variety of judicial interpretations of them. R. § 925.

In general, for purposes of the damages issue the various acts may be roughly grouped in two categories: (1) "loss to the survivors" statutes (e.g., Lord Campbell's Act and those patterned after it); and (2) "loss to the estate" or "value of the life" statutes. "Loss to the survivors" statutes are by far the most common, and the discussion that follows applies primarily to them. Differences under the "loss to the estate" statutes will be briefly noted.

Traditionally, wrongful death damages have been limited to the *"pecuniary loss"* resulting from the death, either by express language in the act itself or by judicially discovered implication. "Pecuniary loss" usually refers to the loss of the support, services and contributions that the survivors would have received from the decedent but for his death.

Loss of Support and Contributions. Where decedent leaves a spouse and/or minor children, the most common measure of loss of support and contributions is the decedent's anticipated future earnings (including fringe benefits) less that portion that he would have expended for his personal needs. In computing his probable future earnings, his prospects for advancement and wage increases may be considered.

In the case of beneficiaries other than his spouse and minor children, their damages are usually based on the actual amount of the support or contributions that they could reasonably anticipate having received. Proof of their financial circumstances may be relevant on this issue. Actual dependency is sometimes required.

Loss of Services. Pecuniary loss is also held to include the loss of the services that decedent would have performed for the survivors but for his death, as such services are capable of monetary valuation. They consist primarily of the household, domestic and familiar chores that members of a family usually perform for each other. In the case of a deceased parent, it includes the parental care, guidance, training and education that the children would have received, both during their minority and (in some states) thereafter.

Loss of Probable Inheritance. At one time most jurisdictions would not allow as an element of damages the probable inheritance that the survivors would have received from the decedent if he had lived out his normal life expectancy and left an estate. Such damages were regarded as too speculative. Today, a growing number of jurisdictions permit recovery of this item upon satisfactory proof that an estate would have been accumulated and its amount, provided the same funds are not already included in the measure of damages for loss of support.

Valuation and Proof of Pecuniary Loss. The bases for computing the survivor's loss of support, contributions and services are the decedent's life expectancy and work life expectancy (how long he could be expected to earn his income), the life expectancies of the beneficiaries, and for some purposes the remaining period of the minority of his children. Standard mortality tables are admissible, but the jury may also consider other evidence that the decedent's or beneficiary's life span would likely be longer or shorter than the average. From these the jury can compute the number of years during which each beneficiary will incur each item of damage.

In valuing the beneficiary's probable future loss, the jury may also consider the actual support, contributions and services rendered in the past, and the decedent's "habits"—that is, his relevant character traits (e.g., his industry, thrift, sobriety, familial concern, and the like).

The same damages rules apply in wrongful death cases as in other personal injury cases (discussed in § 9-1, supra). Future pecuniary loss must be reduced to its present cash value. The collateral source rule and the rules concerning the effects of taxation and inflation are the same.

In view of the complexity of the damages issues, expert testimony by an economist or actuary is common in wrongful death cases.

Nonpecuniary Loss: Consortium. The traditional rule was that, except where expressly authorized by the statute, nonpecuniary losses were not compensable. This included the loss by the spouse, children, parents, or others of the decedent's society, companionship, love and affection and, in the case of the spouse, conjugal relations. However, most jurisdictions now permit the jury to award damages for these losses. (Some classify them as pecuniary losses.) In some states there is a monetary ceiling on the amount that may be given for such damages.

Nonpecuniary Loss: Mental Distress. Most jurisdictions still refuse to allow damages for the grief and mental anguish suffered by the survivors as a result of decedent's death. But several states do permit them, including three or four by statute.

Medical Expenses. If not recovered in the survival action, the medical expenses incurred between the deceased's injury and death usually may be recovered by the person who paid them, or by the estate, either in the wrongful death action or (in some states) in a separate action.

Funeral, Burial and Administration Expenses. Some states do not permit recovery of the decedent's funeral and burial expenses on the ground that the tortfeasor did not cause them but merely accelerated the date of their payment. However, a majority of jurisdictions allow them to be claimed. A few permit recovery of the fees and expenses of the administration of decedent's estate.

Loss to the Estate. As previously noted, in a minority of jurisdictions (chiefly those having a survival-type death statute) wrongful death damages are measured by the loss to the decedent's estate and not by the loss to the survivors. In these states, the primary measure of damages is either (1) his future earnings minus his personal expenses, or (2) less commonly, his probable future accumulations or net savings, or (3) occasionally, his future gross earnings. Under these statutes, damages for loss of services are frequently not recoverable, except that they are usually allowed where the act provides for payment of the wrongful death damages directly to certain statutory beneficiaries. Damages for nonpecuniary loss are almost never allowed under this type statute. On the other hand, damages for medical, funeral and burial expenses are almost always recoverable.

Punitive Damages. As to punitive damages, there is a split of authority. Some statutes expressly authorize them. In other states, the courts have allowed their recovery. But in a number of jurisdictions, punitive damages may not be recovered, usually on the ground that the wrongful death statute is construed to permit reimbursement only for pecuniary loss and hence is limited to compensatory damages.

Punitive damages are the *only* damages recoverable under the Alabama wrongful death act.

Deaths of Children and Older Parents. Special problems arise under the "loss to the survivors" type of statute where the death is that of a minor child. In most cases, it is difficult to prove pecuniary loss, since any loss of income or services that the child would have furnished to his parents is more than offset by the savings to the parents of the costs of the child's support. Nevertheless, the courts have usually permitted verdicts in the parents' favor to stand, so long as not too large, notwithstanding their lack of any real evidentiary basis. Sometimes this is accomplished by the assumption that the child would give the parents contributions and services throughout their lifetime, and might even support them in their old age. In some jurisdictions, the courts recognize a "presumption" of some substantial pecuniary loss in the event of the death of direct lineal kin that will support a verdict. Some refuse to permit deduction of the costs of rearing the child, or recognize a "loss of investment" theory. *Wycko v. Gnodtke* (Mich. 1960). And in a few states the statute makes special provision for damages in the case of the death of a child. The problem is lessened in those states that permit recovery for nonpecuniary loss, and today large awards are often sustained for loss of the child's or parent's society.

A similar problem exists where only adult children survive the death of an older parent. In such cases, a measure of speculation or a presumption will usually support at least a modest award for pecuniary loss, and in some state damages for nonpecuniary losses will permit a substantial verdict.

Under statutes that base damages on the loss to the estate (or "value of the life"), the age and status of the survivors is of lesser or no importance.

Limits. At one time, almost half of the states' wrongful death acts contained express dollar limits on the total amount of the damages that could be awarded for a person's death. All such general limits have now been abolished. However, several states have limits on particular elements of damage (e.g., nonpecuniary loss) or for certain deaths (e.g., minors) or as to certain beneficiaries (e.g., collateral heirs).

The Warsaw Convention (as modified) limits air carriers' liability for deaths on certain international flights to $75,000, unless the result of "willful misconduct."

Distribution. Under most wrongful death acts, the court or jury allocates the damages among the various beneficiaries in accordance with their loss. Under some statutes, the proceeds to as provided in the statute or in accordance with the state's intestacy laws. Some acts establish classes of beneficiaries that take consecutively; others provide one exclusive list. And there is a variety of rules as to when the beneficiary must survive to take and whether or not the estate of a deceased beneficiary is entitled to a share.

§ 12–4. Wrongful Death: Defenses

As a general rule, any defenses that defendant could have invoked in an action by decedent for his injuries (had he lived) may be asserted in a survival or wrongful death action by or on behalf of his survivors. R. § 494. This is true not only as to the survival-type death action (where such a rule has some logic, since the beneficiaries' action is wholly derivative) but also in the true wrongful death action (e.g., Lord Campbell's Act) despite the fact that under the latter type of statute the action is not derivative but is an entirely new and separate action. For example, decedent's contributory negligence is a defense or damage-reducing factor in an action for damages for his death. (In general, where comparative negligence is the law it will apply in wrongful death cases.) See Restatement (Third) of Torts: Apportionment of Liability § 6.

Similarly, where decedent lived for a while before dying from his injuries, and during that time obtained a judgment or settlement of his cause of action for those injuries, such judgment or settlement is usually a bar to a wrongful death action, even as to those damages arising solely from the death itself. Again, while there is some justification for this result under a survival-type statute, it makes little sense as to actions under a true wrongful death act where the cause of action does not even accrue until the death. Accordingly there is a minority view that decedent's judgment or settlement does not bar a wrongful death action under the latter type of statute, at least to the extent of the compensable damages arising out of the death.

Where decedent, prior to his death, sued for his injuries and lost on the merits, the wrongful death action will ordinarily be barred under principles of res judicata.

Suppose a *beneficiary's* negligence contributed to the death. Under those statutes based on a "loss to the estate" theory, the negligence of a beneficiary is no defense and does not bar or reduce his share in the recovery. However, under most acts, which proceed on the theory of compensating the loss to the survivors, the rule is different. The contributory negligence of the sole beneficiary (or of all beneficiaries) is a defense or damage-reducing factor. Where one or more (but less than all) beneficiaries were negligent, in most jurisdictions their negligence is a defense only as to them and usually the damages are reduced pro tanto. See Restatement (Third) of Torts: Apportionment of Liability § 6, replacing R. § 493.

In a few states, the contributory negligence of one parent used to be imputed to the other in an action for the wrongful death of their child. This rule is certainly moribund, if not completely dead, and the contrary majority rule is much to be preferred even in community property states. Restatement (Third) of Torts: Apportionment of Liability § 6, replacing R. § 494A.

Logically, the intrafamily immunities (§ 13–3) should not apply in wrongful death cases. The reasons for the immunity no longer apply with sufficient force to bar recovery where the victim of the tort is dead. There is a split of authority on this issue, but the trend is to abolish the immunity in death cases.

By extension of the collateral source rule, it is generally held that the remarriage of decedent's spouse, or the adoption of his children by the new husband or wife of his spouse, does not mitigate the damages. There is, however, a minority rule to the contrary.

Generally, decedent's familial misconduct (separation, abandonment, desertion, nonsupport, adultery) with respect to his children or spouse (absent divorce) is not a bar to an action for his wrongful death, but may be shown to the extent that it affects the probability and amount of future pecuniary loss by the survivors. However, a parent's abandonment or nonsupport of his child ordinarily will bar an action by the parent for the child's death.

As is by now apparent, wrongful death and survival are complex subjects with great variety and inconsistency among the statutes and decisions. Prosser states (§ 127):

The impression gained from a survey of the law of wrongful death and survival is that both the statutes and the decisions sometimes fall short of what is needed to provide compensation and avoid costly windfalls. Much improvement might be made by a comprehensive statute, but recent statutes have not always been logical or neutral, and no doubt the law will continue to need thoughtful and vigorous judicial action to fill the gaps that inevitably exist in all statutes, including, or especially, the wrongful death acts.

*

PART VI
INJURIES TO OTHER INTERESTS
CHAPTER 13
DEFAMATION

§ 13–1. Defamation

The law of defamation encompasses two torts, libel and slander. In general, libel is a written defamatory communication; slander is an oral one. In the next section we will discuss the differences between the two, but here we examine the common elements and principles.

Defamation is an invasion of one's interest in his good reputation and good name. Like the other torts in this Part VI, the injury is to a "relational" interest, in this case plaintiff's relationship with others in the community as it is affected by others' opinions about him. Thus, a defamation must be communicated to third persons; if communicated only to the plaintiff it might constitute intentional infliction of emotional distress, but it is not an actionable defamation.

The elements of a defamation action are (R. § 558): (1) a false and defamatory communication

435

concerning another; (2) an unprivileged publication to a third party, the publication being intentional or at least negligent on the part of defendant; (3) in some cases, depending on the status of the defendant, a showing of some degree of fault on the part of defendant in knowing or failing to ascertain the falsity of the statement; and (4) in some cases, proof of special damages. Some defamatory statements are actionable "per se," i.e., without proving special damages.

What Is Defamatory? A communication is defamatory if it tends to harm plaintiff's reputation in the community, either by (1) lowering others' estimation of him, or (2) deterring others from associating or dealing with him. R. § 559. Examples include communications that expose plaintiff to hatred, contempt, or ridicule; that reflect unfavorably on his morality or integrity; which impair his financial reputation; or which impute that plaintiff has a disease or other physical or mental attribute or deficiency such that others will be deterred from associating with him. The examples are endless.

One important question is the standard by which the defamatory character of the communication is to be determined. Normally it is sufficient if plaintiff is defamed in the eyes of any substantial and respectable group, even though a small minority of the community. However, it is not defamatory if the minority's views on that subject are so antisocial or extreme that it would not be proper for the courts to recognize them. For example, calling the plaintiff a "civil rights activist" is not defamatory, even though a substantial minority of the community in which plaintiff resides would so regard it.

Truth. A defamatory statement is not actionable unless it is false. R. § 581A. Traditionally, truth has been regarded as an affirmative defense on which defendant has the burden of proof. In cases involving issues of public interest, however, the first amendment now requires that plaintiff bear the burden of proving the statement's falsity. Additionally, the law now requires plaintiff to establish defendant's *fault* with respect to the falsity of the statement in at least some defamation cases.

Who May Be Defamed. Any living person—as well as corporations, partnerships, and unincorporated associations—may be defamed. R. §§ 561, 562. But unless a statute otherwise provides, no action lies for the defamation of a deceased person. R. § 560. Whether the action survives plaintiff's death depends on the local survival statute.

Meaning of Communication. A communication is defamatory only if the recipient understands it in a defamatory sense, and understands that it was so intended. R. § 563. If the recipient reasonably so understands it, it does not matter that he is mistaken. In determining how the recipient understood it, the context of the statement is considered.

In determining the meaning of a communication, extrinsic facts and circumstances known to the recipient are taken into account. For example, the statement "John Smith resides in Pleasantville" may be found to be defamatory if one or more recipients know that Pleasantville is a state mental hospital.

At common law, if a statement was not defamatory on its face, plaintiff was required to plead the extrinsic circumstances that gave it a defamatory meaning; this was called the "inducement." He then had to set forth the communication verbatim, and then explain the defamatory meaning he claimed to have been understood; this explanation was called the "innuendo." These terms and requirements are still in effect in some jurisdictions.

Application to Plaintiff. The communication must have been understood by the recipient (correctly, or mistakenly but reasonably) as intended to refer to plaintiff. R. § 564. The applicability of the defamatory matter to plaintiff may depend upon on extrinsic facts or circumstances known to the recipient. If so, common law pleading rules require such facts or circumstances and the manner in which they connect the defamatory matter to plaintiff to be set forth. This portion of the complaint is called the "colloquium." For example, suppose defendant publishes a novel about the widow of an assassinated U.S. president who marries a Greek shipping magnate. In a libel action, plaintiff may show that people who read the story reasonably understood it to be "of and concerning" her, even though the character in the story had a dissimilar name and the work purported to be fiction.

As a general rule, no action lies for the publication of defamatory words concerning a large group or class of persons, since the words cannot reasonably be understood as applying to any one individual—for example, "all the doctors in this town are quacks," there being several dozen doctors. But a member of a small group may recover if a statement may reasonably be understood as applying to him—for example, "that jury was bribed" or "most of the players on that football team are on drugs." And so may a member of any size group if the circumstances indicate that the statement was intended to apply to him. R. § 564A.

Types of Defamatory Communications. Typically, a defamatory communication consists of a statement of fact. R. § 565. It may be direct or indirect, as where words or pictures imply a defamatory meaning about plaintiff without so stating directly.

At common law, a defamatory statement of opinion (if not privileged) was actionable the same as one of fact. This rule appears to have been modified by recent constitutional law interpretations.

If the defamatory opinion is based entirely on facts (a) known to those making and receiving the statement, or (b) stated as a predicate to the opinion, *Gertz v. Robert Welch, Inc.* (U.S. 1974) seemed to indicate that the first amendment permits one to express one's opinion, however misguided or debatable, without defamation liability. "Under the first amendment, there is no such thing as a false idea."

This is analogous to the common law privilege of fair comment. However, this dictum in *Gertz* must be read narrowly. If and to the extent that the opinion implies the assertion of defamatory facts as the basis for the opinion, it may be actionable. *Milkovich v. Lorain Journal Co.* (U.S. 1990).

Similarly, humorous writings, verses, cartoons, or caricatures that may be understood as making a statement about plaintiff are similarly protected, at least the extent that they represent merely negative opinions not implying false facts. *Hustler Magazine, Inc. v. Falwell* (U.S. 1988). Profanity and similar statements, directed at plaintiff in anger and obviously intended as mere vituperation or abuse, ordinarily cannot be taken literally and therefore are not defamatory.

To attribute a fabricated quotation to the plaintiff may be defamatory. *Masson v. New Yorker Magazine, Inc.* (U.S. 1991).

§ 13–2. Libel and Slander

Libel is the publication of defamatory matter by (1) written or printed words or (2) embodiment in physical form (e.g., photos, cartoons, sculpture, film, video tape, sound recordings), or (3) any other form of communication that has potentially harmful characteristics comparable to those of written or printed words. R. § 568.

Slander is the publication of defamatory matter by spoken words, transitory gestures, or other form of communication not amounting to a libel.

The factors to be considered in distinguishing libel and slander are the area of dissemination, the deliberate and premeditated character of the publication, and the persistence or permanency of the publication. Radio and television publications are regarded in most jurisdictions as libel, unless otherwise provided by statute.

In most jurisdictions, any libel is actionable per se, that is, without proof that plaintiff sustained any special harm or damage from the publication. Even if plaintiff cannot or does not prove actual damages, the trier of fact can infer harm sufficient to support an award of compensatory or nominal damages. R. § 569. In a minority of U.S. jurisdictions, a libel which is not defamatory on its face and which requires reference to extrinsic facts to establish its defamatory meaning is not actionable without proof of special harm. This is sometimes called libel per quod.

Publication of a slander is not actionable without proof of special damages unless it defames plaintiff in one of the four following ways (R. §§ 570, 575): (1) it imputes to plaintiff conduct that constitutes a crime punishable by imprisonment or involving moral turpitude (R. § 571); (2) it imputes that plaintiff has a venereal or other loathsome and communicable disease (R. § 572); (3) it imputes to plaintiff conduct, characteristics, or a condition that would adversely affect his fitness for the proper conduct of his business, trade, profession, or office (R. § 573); or (4) it imputes unchastity or serious sexual misconduct (R. § 574). If actionable without proof of special damages, it is called "slander per se"; if not, it is "slander per quod."

In this context, special harm or damages refers to the loss of something having economic or pecuniary value, which results from the harm to plaintiff's reputation. It does not include plaintiff's emotional distress and resulting bodily harm (which may, however, be compensated if the defamation is otherwise actionable).

§ 13–3. Publication

The term "publication" is a term of art; it does not mean that the defamatory matter must be "published" in any formal sense. Publication is merely the communication of defamatory matter by defendant to someone other than the plaintiff.

Defendant is not liable for an unintended or accidental publication. The publication must have been intentional or the result of the defendant's negligence. In most jurisdictions, publication to defendant's agent is sufficient (but may be privileged). If dictated with the intent that it be reduced to writing (a letter, telegram) it is libel. Defendant is liable for a publication by his agent where he directed or procured it.

Multiple Publications (R. § 577A). Each of several communications to a third person by the same defendant is a separate publication. A single communication heard at the same time by two or more third persons is a single publication. One edition of a book or newspaper, or one radio or TV broadcast, one exhibition of a motion picture, or a similar aggregate publication is deemed a single publication.

For each single publication, only one action can be maintained in which plaintiff must claim all damages resulting from that publication. This raises issues of venue, statute of limitations, and choice of law when the publication is received in more than one state.

Liability of Republisher. One who repeats or otherwise republishes a defamation is subject to liability to the same extent as if he had originally published it. R. § 578. Thus, for example, where a libel is published in a newspaper, magazine, or book, the author, editor, printer, publisher, and owner are all subject to liability as a publisher. One who broadcasts defamatory matter by radio or television is subject to the same liability as an original publisher. R. § 581(2).

One who only delivers or transmits defamatory matter published by a third person (news dealers and delivery boys, bookstores, libraries, telephone and telegraph companies, mail or message deliverers) is subject to liability only if he knows or has reason to know of its defamatory character. However, this exception does not apply to broadcasters. R. § 581.

Defendant is liable for the republication of his defamatory statement by another if (a) the third person was privileged to repeat it or (b) defendant authorized or intended the repetition, or (c) the repetition was reasonably foreseeable. See R. §§ 576, 622A. Defendant is ordinarily not liable for a repetition by plaintiff.

§ 13–4. Fault

At common law, defamation liability was strict. Defendant did not have to be aware of the falsity or defamatory character of the statement, or even be negligent in ascertaining these things; nor need he have intended or foreseen any harm, or that the statement could be understood as referring to plaintiff. The only fault required was with respect to its publication: defendant had to intentionally or negligently publish the matter.

It is now well established that the first amendment to the United States Constitution imposes fault requirements, at least in the case of defamatory matter concerning public officials, public figures, or matters of public concern when defendant is exercising the freedom of the press protected by that amendment. These decisions have led some states to impose fault requirements as common law rules, even where not strictly required by constitutional law.

Public Official, Public Figure. Under *New York Times Co. v. Sullivan* (U.S. 1964) and its progeny, one who publishes a false and defamatory communication concerning a public official or a public figure with regard to his conduct, fitness, or role in that capacity is subject to liability only if defendant (a) knows that the statement is false and that it defames plaintiff, or (b) acts in reckless disregard of these matters. R. § 580A.

A *public official* is a governmental employee who has (or appears to have) responsibility for or control over the conduct of governmental affairs, and may include even relatively low-ranking personnel, such as police officers. To receive the benefit of this special first amendment protection, the defamatory statement must concern the official's fitness for or performance in the office.

A *public figure* is one who has achieved a degree of fame or notoriety, either generally or as to a particular public issue or controversy. The voluntary nature of plaintiff's participation is a factor to be considered. The statement must affect plaintiff in his public capacity. Examples from the cases include a well-known college football coach; a retired Army general who had taken a prominent controversial position on racial segregation; candidates for public office; but not a socially prominent woman did no more than sue her very wealthy husband for divorce.

The requisite fault is "actual malice" (sometimes described as "constitutional malice"). Here, malice does not have its literal meaning. "Actual malice" means nothing more than knowledge of the statement's false and defamatory character or a reckless disregard of these matters, as when a statement is published despite a high degree of awareness of its probable falsity, or with serious doubts as to its truth. Actual ill will need not be proved. The availability of time and opportunity to check the truth of the statement may be relevant. Proof of defendant's fault must be clear and convincing.

The cases that impose the foregoing fault requirement so far have involved public statements in the press, media and books. It remains to be seen whether these fault requirements apply to other forms of communication, though most jurisdictions do not distinguish between media and non-media cases in applying these rules.

Private Persons, Private Matters. Under *Gertz v. Robert Welch, Inc.* (U.S. 1974) and its progeny, one who publishes a false and defamatory communication concerning a private person, or concerning a public official or public figure with regard to a purely private matter (i.e., not affecting his conduct, fitness or role in his public capacity) is subject to liability only if defendant (a) knows that the statement is false and that it defames plaintiff, or (b) acts in reckless disregard of these matters, or (c) acts negligently in failing to ascertain them. R. § 580B.

After *Gertz,* strict liability for defamation published in the press, media, and possibly books is unconstitutional, regardless of the status of plaintiff. However, the states are free to determine the degree of fault required for defamation actions by persons described in the preceding paragraph, so long as at least negligence is required.

So far, the majority of states passing on the question have followed the *Gertz* criteria, so that in those jurisdictions *all* those persons described above need only prove that defendant was *negligent* in ascertaining the falsity and defamatory character of the statement. However, under a minority view, if the defamation concerns a matter of *general* or *public interest,* even those persons described above are required to prove that defendant either (1) knew that the statement was false and that it defames plaintiff, or (2) acted in reckless disregard of these matters (i.e., the same as for public officials and public figures).

Those persons described above need only prove the requisite fault by a preponderance of the evidence.

Private Communications. It remains to be seen whether the *Gertz* rule applies to publications other than in the press, media or books. At least one state court has held that it does not, and has sustained a verdict based on strict liability for a private libel. In addition, U.S. Supreme Court rulings appear to indicate that the *Gertz* rule will apply only when the subject matter of the defamation involves an issue of public interest.

§ 13–5. Defenses

Consent. Plaintiff's consent to the publication of defamatory matter concerning him is a complete defense. R. § 583. However, defendant may be liable for a republication that results from plaintiff's honest inquiry or investigation to ascertain the existence, source, content, or meaning of the defamatory publication. R. § 584.

Absolute Privilege: Judicial Proceedings. During the course of performing their functions in judicial proceedings, judges and judicial officers, attorneys, parties, witnesses, and jurors are absolutely privileged to publish defamatory matter that has some relation to the proceeding. R. §§ 585–589.

Absolute Privilege: Legislative Proceedings. A member of Congress or a state or local legislative body is absolutely privileged to publish defamatory matter in the performance of his legislative functions. A witness is absolutely privileged to publish defamatory matter as part of a legislative proceeding in which he is testifying or in communications preliminary to the proceeding, if the matter has some relation to the proceeding. R. §§ 590, 590A.

Absolute Privilege: Executive and Administrative Officers. An executive or administrative officer of the United States, or a governor or other superior executive officer of a state, is absolutely privileged to publish defamatory matter in communications made in the performance of his official duties. R. § 591.

Absolute Privilege: Husband and Wife. A husband or wife is absolutely privileged to publish defamatory matter to the other. R. § 592.

Absolute Privilege: Publication Required by Law. One who is required by law to publish defamatory matter is absolutely privileged to publish it—

for example, an newspaper required to publish an official notice. R. § 592A.

Conditional or Qualified Privileges. At common law, certain defamatory communications are *conditionally* or *qualifiedly* privileged, so that defendant is not liable provided he meets all the conditions or qualifications. R. § 593. As to these privileges, the chief limitation is that defendant must (1) *believe* his statement to be true, and (2)(a) in some jurisdictions, have *reasonable grounds* for believing it to be true, or (b) in other jurisdictions, not have acted *recklessly* in failing to ascertain its truth or falsity. But the *N.Y. Times* and *Gertz* cases, when applicable, require plaintiff to prove that defendant acted either recklessly or negligently in ascertaining the truth or falsity of the statement. Thus, if and to the extent that *N.Y. Times* and *Gertz* apply, the existence of a conditional privilege is partly or totally irrelevant. Therefore, the following privileges apply only when and to the extent that they are not superseded by the *N.Y. Times* or *Gertz* rules.

Protection of the Publisher's Interest. Defendant's defamatory communication is conditionally privileged when the circumstances cause defendant to correctly or reasonably believe that (1) the information affects a sufficiently important interest of defendant, and (2) the information will be of service to the recipient in the lawful protection of that interest. R. § 594.

Interests of defendant worthy of protection include, for example: (a) any lawful business or pecuniary interest, other than his interest in competition for prospective advantage (e.g., defamation to obtain customers); (b) his bodily security; (c) his present interest in land, chattels, or intangible property; (d) his family; and (e) his own reputation. In each case, the value of defendant's interest is to be balanced against the harm to plaintiff's reputation if the defamatory matter is false.

Protection of Interest of Recipient of Third Person. Defendant's defamatory communication is conditionally privileged when the circumstances cause defendant to correctly or reasonably believe that (1) the information affects a sufficiently important interest of the *recipient* or a *third person,* and (2) the recipient is one to whom (a) defendant is under a *legal duty* to publish it or (b) its publication is otherwise within generally accepted standards of decent conduct. R. § 595.

Important factors in determining whether the publication is within generally accepted standards of decent conduct include whether (a) it is in response to a request, rather than volunteered by defendant, or (b) a family or other relationship exists between the parties. R. § 595.

Examples of this category include fiduciaries discharging their duties; reports to proper authorities that defendant believes plaintiff is about to commit a crime against another; in most states, reports by credit agencies; communications among members of a trade association; reports to an employer about the character or conduct of a present or prospective employee; and communications to a close friend about the character or conduct of a member of his family, made in response to a request for such information.

Protection of a Common Interest. Defendant's defamatory communication is conditionally privileged when the circumstances cause defendant to correctly or reasonably believe that another who shares a common interest is entitled to know it. R. § 596. Thus, business partners and associates in a business enterprise may exchange information about employees and others; co-owners of real or personal property may communicate concerning their common interest in that property; and members of religious, fraternal and charitable organizations can discuss the qualifications of officers, other or prospective members, and association activities.

Family Relationships. Defendant's defamatory communication is conditionally privileged when the circumstances cause defendant to correctly or reasonably believe that: (1) the recipient's knowledge will help protect the well-being of a member of defendant's immediate family; or (2) the recipient's knowledge will help protect the well-being of a member of the immediate family of the recipient or a third person, and the recipient has requested the information or is a person to whom its communication is otherwise within generally accepted standards of decent conduct. R. § 597. For example, defendant tells his sister that he has seen the plaintiff, her husband, in the company of prostitutes. Or the defendant, a minister, writes an unsolicited letter to F's father telling him that plaintiff, F's fiancé, is a felon. The communications are conditionally privileged.

Public Interest. Defendant's defamatory communication is conditionally privileged when the circumstances cause defendant to correctly or reasonably believe that a sufficiently important public interest requires its communication to a public officer or other person who is authorized or privileged to take action if it is true. R. § 598. Examples include reporting a crime or anticipated crime (unless absolutely privileged); reporting misconduct or incompetence by a public official or employee; and petitions for legislative action.

Inferior State Officers. Lower level state or local government employees who are not entitled to an absolute privilege have a conditional privilege for communications required or permitted in the performance of their duties. R. § 598A.

"Abuse" (Loss) of the Privilege: Knowledge, Recklessness or Negligence Concerning Falsity. Prior to *Gertz,* in some jurisdictions a conditional privilege was lost if defendant did not honestly believe the truth of his statement, or if he did not have "reasonable grounds" to believe in its truth. It remains to be seen whether this rule has any purpose after *Gertz.*

Other jurisdictions have held that a conditional privilege is lost only if defendant knows that the statement is false or acts in "reckless disregard" as to its truth or falsity. Where *Gertz* or *N.Y. Times* applies, any conditional privilege will be irrelevant. R. § 600 adopts this version of the rule.

Defendant may be privileged to publish a defamatory *rumor* or *suspicion,* even though he believes or knows that it is untrue, *provided:* (1) he states the defamatory matter as a *rumor* or *suspicion* and not as a fact; and (2) the publication is reasonable, considering the relation of the parties, the importance of the interests affected, and the harm likely to be done. R. § 602.

Purpose. There is no conditional privilege unless defendant publishes the defamatory matter for the *purpose* of protecting the interest that gives rise to the privilege, R. § 603, and reasonably believes the publication to be *necessary* for that purpose, R. § 605.

Excessive Publication. There is no conditional privilege to the extent that defendant knowingly publishes the defamatory matter to a person outside its scope, unless he reasonably believes that such publication is a proper means of communicating it to a proper person. R. § 604.

Unprivileged Matter. The privilege is lost to the extent that defendant adds unprivileged matter to the communication. If not severable, the entire privilege is lost. R. § 605A.

Fair Comment on Matters of Public Concern. At common law, there was a qualified privilege for what was called "fair comment" (i.e., publicly expressing one's opinion) on matters of public concern. This former privilege appears to have been subsumed under the constitutional right to express such opinions without defamation liability. See text at 437–38, supra; R. § 566.

Special Types of Privilege: Report of Official Proceeding or Public Meeting. Defendant is privileged to publish defamatory matter in a report of an official action or proceeding or of a meeting open to the public that deals with a matter of public concern, provided the report is accurate or a fair abridgment of the occurrence reported. R. § 611. Although the Restatement omits this limitation, the privilege probably does not extend to matter published solely for the purpose of harming the person defamed. As a matter of constitutional law, as applied to the press and news media, plaintiff must also establish defendant's fault (as defined in *N.Y. Times* and *Gertz*) in failing to make a fair and accurate report.

Special Types of Privilege: Transmission of Message by Public Utility. A public utility under a duty to transmit messages is privileged unless the utility knows or has reason to know that the message is defamatory and that the sender is not privileged to publish it. R. § 612(2). This privilege may apply even when the utility knows that the message is false.

Special Types of Privilege: Providing Means of Publication. One who provides a means of publication of defamatory matter published by another is privileged to do so if the other is privileged to publish it. R. § 612(1).

§ 13–6. Damages

Types Recoverable. Damages that may be recoverable in a defamation action include (a) nominal damages, (b) general (or "presumed") damages for harm to reputation, (c) damages for proved special harm caused by the harm to plaintiff's reputation, (d) damages for emotional distress and resulting bodily harm, and (e) punitive damages.

Nominal Damages. One who is liable for a libel or slander actionable per se is liable for at least nominal damages. R. § 620.

General Damages (R. § 621). At common law, once defendant's liability was established, the jury could award plaintiff general damages for harm to his reputation, whether plaintiff proved actual harm or not. In most jurisdictions these are known as "presumed" damages. In the absence of such proof, the jury could compensate plaintiff for the harm to his reputation that normally would be assumed to flow from a defamatory publication of the nature involved. However, *Gertz* holds that the first amendment prohibits the states from permitting recovery for presumed damages unless plaintiff proves defendant's knowledge of the defamation's falsity or his reckless disregard for its truth; otherwise, proof of actual harm is required. "Actual harm" is not limited to pecuniary loss; it includes such intangibles as harm to plaintiff's reputation and emotional distress. No specific dollar value of such harm need be shown.

Nevertheless, in *Dun & Bradstreet, Inc. v. Greenmoss Builders, Inc.* (U.S. 1985), the Supreme Court held that a state could award presumed damages when the plaintiff was a private figure and the speech did not involve any issue of public interest or concern.

Special Damages. Special damages (i.e., economic or pecuniary loss) resulting from the defamation may always be recovered. In the case of slander per quod (and libel per quod in some jurisdictions), such damages are a prerequisite to liability. R. § 622.

Emotional Distress and Bodily Harm. Once defendant's liability is established, damages for emotional distress and resulting bodily harm are recoverable. R. § 623.

Punitive Damages. The common law generally allows punitive damages in a defamation action when defendant's conduct involves "actual malice," which usually means an intent to harm plaintiff or a reckless disregard of whether or not he will be harmed. The constitution prohibits punitive damages, at least against the press and media defendants, unless plaintiff proves defendant's knowledge of the statement's falsity or his reckless disregard for its truth.

Mitigation. By statute in some jurisdictions and common law in most others, a retraction by defendant is not a complete defense, but may be considered in mitigation of plaintiff's damages. Other mitigating circumstances may also be considered. Statutes in a few states limit the amount a plaintiff can recover unless a demanded retraction, correction, or clarification has not been published.

Right of Reply. Statutes requiring a newspaper to publish plaintiff's reply to a defamatory statement previously printed in it are unconstitutional.

CHAPTER 14

PRIVACY

§ 14–1. In General

The tort action for invasion of privacy was stimulated by an 1890 Harvard Law Review article by Warren and Brandeis. At present, the tort encompasses four distinct wrongs (R. § 652A):

1. **Appropriation** of plaintiff's name or likeness;

2. **Intrusion** upon plaintiff's privacy or private affairs;

3. **Public disclosure of private facts** about plaintiff; and

4. Placing plaintiff in a **false light in the public eye**.

Other forms (or variations on these forms) may develop in the future; these categories are not limitations. And there may be overlap between these forms in a particular case.

The action for invasion of privacy is recognized in most jurisdictions (but not in all forms). In some it is affected by statute.

Privileges. The absolute, conditional and special privileges to publish defamatory matter (see § 13–

5) also apply to the publication of any matter that is an invasion of privacy. R. §§ 652F, 652G.

Damages. In an action for invasion of privacy, plaintiff can recover damages for: (1) harm to his interest in privacy; (2) mental distress, if of a kind that normally results from such an invasion; and (3) special damages.

Persons Who May Sue. Unless otherwise provided by statute, and except for appropriation, an action for invasion of privacy can be maintained only by a living individual whose privacy is invaded. R. § 652I. Whether an action survives plaintiff's death depends on the local survival statute.

§ 14–2. Appropriation

Defendant is subject to liability for appropriating the name or likeness of plaintiff for his own use or benefit. R. § 652C. For example: Without permission, defendant uses the name and photograph of plaintiff, a famous basketball player, in an advertisement for defendant's bread.

Unless otherwise required by statute, the use need not be for business or commercial purposes. Thus, defendant has invaded plaintiff's privacy when defendant signs plaintiff's name to a telegram to a senator urging him to vote against a particular bill. Many states, however, do impose a business or commercial purpose requirement.

Defendant must use plaintiff's name for the purpose of taking advantage of plaintiff's reputation, prestige or other value associated with his name or likeness. Merely adopting a name identical to that of another, or using another's name in a communication or publication, is not an invasion of privacy unless the purpose is to appropriate the benefit of its commercial value.

§ 14–3. Unreasonable Intrusion

Defendant is subject to liability for intrusion (physical or other) upon the solitude, seclusion, or private life and affairs of plaintiff, provided the intrusion would be highly offensive to a reasonable person. R. § 652B.

The forms of intrusion are varied—unpermitted entry into plaintiff's home or hospital room; an illegal search of plaintiff's person or property; tapping plaintiff's telephone; using mechanical aids to observe plaintiff's private activities in his home; opening plaintiff's personal mail; and persistent and unwanted communications or close physical presence.

The tort is complete when the intrusion occurs. No publication or publicity of the information is required.

The intrusion must be into what is, and is entitled to remain, *private*. Photographing or watching plaintiff in a public place, or inspecting or copying nonprivate records, is not actionable.

The intrusion must be highly offensive to the ordinary person, resulting from conduct to which the reasonable person would strongly object.

The courts are beginning to recognize a constitutional right of privacy, to be free from excessive or unreasonable governmental intrusion. In addition, we are witnessing a rapid proliferation of federal and state statutes protecting personal information and records from access or disclosure without the permission of the subject.

§ 14–4. Public Disclosure of Private Facts

Defendant is subject to liability for giving publicity to some private fact about plaintiff, provided the fact publicized would be highly offensive to a reasonable person and is not a matter of legitimate public concern. R. § 652D.

The information about plaintiff need not be published in the media. It is sufficient if it is disclosed so as to be likely to become public knowledge.

In this case, the facts disclosed are true. Thus, there is no liability for facts that are already known by, or available to, the public. The facts must be intimate or at least private details of plaintiff's private life, the disclosure of which would be embarrassing, humiliating or offensive. And plaintiff's right to keep these facts private is balanced against the legitimate interest of the public. Thus, there are fewer "private" facts of the famous and those in high positions.

Constitutional Limitations. The first amendment freedoms of the press and speech are a further limitation of this tort, and permit publication of private facts that are matters of legitimate public concern or interest—i.e., "news."

Persons who have voluntarily become public figures, and even those involuntarily in the public eye by being part of a newsworthy event, cannot complain of the publication of facts, otherwise private, which are of legitimate public concern or interest in connection with that person, activity, or event. This legitimate concern may even extend to the family and close friends of the public figure, and to some facts about persons who were public figures at some time in the past.

§ 14–5. False Light in the Public Eye

Defendant is subject to liability for giving publicity to a matter that places plaintiff before the public in a false light, provided (a) the false light would be highly offensive to a reasonable person, and (b) defendant had knowledge of the falsity of the matter and the false light it created, or acted in reckless disregard of these matters. R. § 652E.

Relation to Defamation. In this case, the information communicated about plaintiff is false. Thus, if it is also defamatory, an action for libel or slander may be an alternative remedy. However, it is not necessary to this action that plaintiff be defamed. It is enough that he is given unreasonable and highly objectionable publicity that attributes to him characteristics, conduct or beliefs that are false. For example, a photograph of plaintiff, an honest taxi driver, is used to illustrate a newspaper article on the practices of taxi drivers who cheat the public. Plaintiff has an action for both libel and invasion of privacy. In fact, a few courts have rejected this particular tort action as creating, in effect, an unwarranted extension of defamation liability.

Highly Offensive. The matter must be highly offensive to a reasonable person. Thus, relatively minor inaccuracies or fictions in an otherwise accurate and favorable story about plaintiff are not actionable.

Constitutional Limitations. *Time, Inc. v. Hill* (U.S. 1967) extended the *N.Y. Times* rule to this type of invasion of privacy action, requiring plaintiff to prove by clear and convincing evidence that defendant knew of the statement's falsity or acted in reckless disregard of its truth or falsity. Whether the *Gertz* case has modified this rule (to include negligence in the case of private individuals), and the extent to which this limitation applies to others than the press and media, has yet to be decided.

CHAPTER 15

MISREPRESENTATION AND NONDISCLOSURE

§ 15–1. Remedies for Misrepresentation

The concept "misrepresentation" is another of those surrounded by much unnecessary confusion, largely because of the wide variety of cases in which it plays a role.

Some sort of misrepresentation is often an element of many different torts. An untrue assertion may be an integral part of some other intentional tort, such as battery, false imprisonment, conversion, or intentional infliction of emotional distress. It is the essence of defamation and the tort of injurious falsehood. Malicious prosecution and interference with contractual relations often involve a misrepresentation. There are numerous other examples. We are not concerned with such misrepresentations in this chapter.

For the most part, the tort action of deceit or misrepresentation discussed here is limited to cases involving some business or financial transaction between the parties in which one of them has sustained a pecuniary loss. While perhaps there is no reason why the same or similar principles could not be applied in noncommercial situations, or to damages for physical harm (R. §§ 310, 311) there has been little occasion for doing so. The other nominate tort actions generally have provided adequate remedies.

Assume, then, that defendant in the course of some business or financial transaction makes a misrepresentation to plaintiff, or to another. (The term "representation" includes both verbal and nonverbal assertions. See § 15–4.) Plaintiff acts or refrains from acting in justifiable reliance upon that representation, and as a result sustains a pecuniary loss, for which he now seeks to hold defendant responsible. Can he do so?

As we shall see, whether he can or not depends upon several interacting variables, principally (1) whether defendant *knew* that his representation was false (or knew that he had no knowledge of whether it was true or false, which amounts to the same thing)—a concept called "scienter"; (2) the legal theory upon which plaintiff bases his action; and (3) the type of remedy he seeks, and if he seeks damages, the measure of those damages.

Historical Development. As we have seen, it was not until comparatively late in its evolution that the English common law began to differentiate tort and contract actions. Prior to the eighteenth century, the remedy for misrepresentation was a form of the action of case known as "deceit," and as such belonged to the tort family. But until *Pasley v. Freeman* (K.B. 1789) the action was not available unless the misrepresentation was a part of some contractual dealings between the parties. At the same time, during this period, no scienter was required if there *was* privity of contract and if the representation amounted to what we now refer to as an express warranty.

During the eighteenth century, the contractual nature of warranty came to be recognized and assumpsit (which had become the remedy for breach of contract) replaced deceit as the appropriate form of action for breach of warranty. Since liability for breach of warranty is strict (no intent to deceive is required), this left open the question whether the *tort* action of deceit could be maintained in cases other than where the misrepresentation was intentionally fraudulent.

That question was answered in the negative in the leading English case of *Derry v. Peek* (H.L. 1889), where the court concluded that defendants were at most negligent in representing in a prospectus that they had the right to use mechanical motive power, instead of horses, in the operation of their tramway. It held that the action of deceit would not lie unless defendant made a false representation (1) knowing it to be false, (2) without belief in its truth, or (3) in reckless disregard of whether it was true or not. Meanwhile, the tort (noncontractual) nature of the deceit action had been reinforced by the *Pasley* case, which held that it would lie even where there was no privity of contract between the parties.

Before discussing the modern form of the tort action of deceit or "misrepresentation," as it is now sometimes called, note must be taken of other remedies for false representations. The failure of some courts and writers to see that the applicable rules of law do and should vary according to the theory of the action or defense asserted has resulted in no little confusion and error.

Other Remedies and Defenses Based on Misrepresentation

Breach of Warranty. An untrue statement made to induce plaintiff to enter into a contract (usually, but not always, a contract for the sale of goods) may amount to a warranty if it has sufficient characteristics of (1) a promise or (2) an affirmation of a fact that is promissory in nature. (Warranties made in connection with the sale of goods are governed by the Uniform Commercial Code.) Although having it origins in tort law, an action for breach of an express warranty is now regarded as a contract action and is subject to special defenses and limitations not applicable to a tort action. But if the representation is a warranty and if breach of warranty is the theory of the action, the defendant's liability is strict in the sense that no scienter is required.

Equitable Relief. Courts of equity have long recognized misrepresentation as one basis upon which a transaction may be avoided. Equitable remedies include rescission or reformation of a contract, or imposition of a constructive trust or equitable lien to prevent unjust enrichment. Since in a suit in equity plaintiff does not seek damages but restoration of the status quo ante equitable relief may often be given even though the misrepresentation was entirely innocent.

Restitution at Law. Not to be outdone by equity, courts of law developed a restitutionary remedy much like the equitable remedy of rescission, whereby plaintiff elects to rescind the transaction, tenders back to defendant that which was received from him, and recovers the amount by which defendant was unjustly enriched (ordinarily the amount plaintiff paid). An innocent misrepresentation is likewise one basis upon which such relief may be had.

Defenses. Fraud or misrepresentation may provide an equitable defense to an action at law for breach of a contract, and some courts will even allow rescission by defendant (where the requirements of equity are otherwise met) based on an innocent misrepresentation. In addition, a misrepresentation may provide a basis for asserting an equitable estoppel, even when the untrue statement was innocently or negligently made.

The requirements and conditions of these various remedies are beyond the scope of this discussion, and they are noted merely to distinguish them from the tort action.

§ 15–2. Basis of Liability

The elements necessary to establish a prima facie case in an action for deceit or misrepresentation include the following.

(1) **Representation.** There must be a false representation, ordinarily of a fact, made by defendant.

(2) **Scienter.** The traditional common law action of deceit required that defendant know that his statement is false, or that he make it in conscious ignorance or reckless disregard of whether it is true or false—a concept here referred to as "scienter."

(3) **Intent to Induce Reliance.** Defendant must have intended that plaintiff act (or refrain from acting) in reliance upon the representation.

(4) **Justifiable Reliance.** Plaintiff must have justifiably relied upon the representation in acting or failing to act.

(5) **Damage.** Plaintiff must have sustained actual damage as a result of his reliance.

One of the most important and controversial issues in this branch of tort law has been whether plaintiff is always required to prove scienter in order to maintain a tort action for deceit, or whether defendant may be liable where he was merely negligently or even innocently ignorant of the falsity of his statement. Let us first, then, consider this question. Other issues concerning the remaining elements of the cause of action will be taken up in succeeding sections.

Deceit: Scienter. It is, of course, everywhere agreed that defendant will be liable in a tort action of deceit when all five of the elements listed above are present. In such cases, deceit is an intentional tort, analogous to those discussed in Chapter 6.

In order to establish scienter, plaintiff must prove, according to the classic formulation in *Derry v. Peek,* that "a false representation has been made (1) knowingly, or (2) without belief in its truth, or (3) recklessly, careless whether it be true or false." Compare § 526 of the Restatement, where it is stated that a misrepresentation is fraudulent if the maker

(a) knows or believes that the matter is not as he represents it to be,

(b) does not have the confidence in the accuracy of his representation that he states or implies, or

(c) knows that he does not have the basis for his representation that he states or implies.

As Judge Cardozo stated, "Fraud includes the pretense of knowledge when knowledge there is none." *Ultramares Corp. v. Touche, Niven & Co.* (N.Y. 1931).

Scienter is, of course, only one aspect of the requisite intent. Defendant must intend to make a representation, he must intend that it be directed to a particular person or class, he must intend that it convey a certain meaning, he must intend that it be believed, and he must intend that it be acted upon in a certain way. But in the ordinary case, there is no real dispute about these matters, and they are either clearly present or easily inferred. If there is an issue of intent, it will usually be whether defendant had any intent to *deceive*—that is, scienter.

Note that if this *intent* existed, defendant's *motive* is irrelevant (except perhaps on the issue of punitive damages). In other words, if he intended to deceive another, he is subject to tort liability notwithstanding the fact that he did not intend to harm him, and in fact thought that he was benefiting him.

It may, of course, be difficult in many cases to prove what defendant knew or did not know at the time he made his representation. But the usual rules of circumstantial evidence apply, and if plaintiff can show that it would have been unlikely or unreasonable for defendant to have believed his statement to be true, then the trier of fact may infer that he knew it was false, or at least that he knew that he lacked the knowledge which his statement asserted or implied that he had. However, if defendant can convince the trier of fact that he actually believed his statement to be true, however unreasonably, then his misrepresentation was at most negligent, and scienter is not established.

Negligent Misrepresentations. Even though defendant honestly believed his erroneous statement to be true (and therefore lacked scienter), he may have been negligent in (1) failing to exercise reasonable care to ascertain the true facts, or (2) failing to possess or apply the skill and competence required by his business or profession (e.g., attorney, accountant, surveyor, product manufacturer), or (3) in the manner in which he expressed his assertion. May he be held liable in tort for that negligence?

If defendant's negligent misrepresentation proximately causes *physical harm* to plaintiff, all courts are agreed that ordinary principles of negligence law apply and plaintiff may maintain a negligence action for his damages (assuming, of course, that he can establish the usual elements of a negligence case). R. § 311.

Suppose, however, that plaintiff sustains only *pecuniary* loss as the result of his reliance upon a negligent misrepresentation. A few U.S. courts have broadened the action of deceit to encompass negligence, but the great majority have followed *Derry v. Peek* in refusing to recognize the traditional *deceit* action as extending to merely negligent misrepresentations. At the same time, however, most U.S. jurisdictions have held that a common law *negligence* action may be maintained for a negligent misrepresentation that causes only pecuniary harm. This is the approach of the Restatement (R. § 552), and since 1963 of English law. Now that the common law forms of action have lost most of their significance, the nomenclature is of little importance, since the elements of the cause of action based upon a negligent misrepresentation are the same under either theory (deceit or negligence).

However, if the negligent misrepresentation causes only pecuniary loss, there are two important departures from the usual rules of negligence law. First, unlike the ordinary negligence case where defendant's duty to plaintiff arises when he undertakes to act, even gratuitously (see § 4–5), it is generally held that there is no duty to exercise reasonable care in making a representation unless defendant has a pecuniary interest in the transaction. In other words, there is no liability for negligent gratuitous or "curbstone" statements. R. § 552, Comments c and d. At the same time, the pecuniary interest need not be a direct or immediate one. Thus, if made in the course of defendant's business, the requisite pecuniary interest may be found, even though defendant himself receives no pecuniary benefit from that particular transaction.

Second, if only pecuniary loss results, the scope of defendant's liability to third persons not in privity of contract with him is somewhat narrower than it should be under the usual rules of proximate cause, as will be discussed in § 15–3, infra.

Innocent Misrepresentation. Suppose that defendant honestly believed that his representation was true and he was not negligent in failing to ascertain its falsity, but it nevertheless turns out that it was in fact untrue. Or, assume that plaintiff simply cannot *prove* that defendant's misrepresentation was fraudulently or negligently made. In either event, assume further that plaintiff acted in justifiable reliance upon the representation and sustained a loss.

As we have seen, various remedies may be available to plaintiff. He may be able to obtain equitable relief, or he may have an action at law for restitution. If the statement was a term of a contract, he may have an action for breach of contract. If the statement amounts to a warranty made in a sales transaction, plaintiff may have a contract action for breach of warranty. This remedy extends to both physical harm and pecuniary loss cased by misrepresentation. (Of course, all of these remedies are subject to the special limitations, defenses, and measures of damages applicable to such actions.) And if the misrepresentation causes physical harm, and is made in connection with the sale of goods by one engaged in the business of selling such products, there may be strict liability. See Restatement (Third) of Torts: Products Liability § 9; R. § 402B. But may a plaintiff who has sustained only *pecuniary loss* as a result of an innocent misrepresentation elect to maintain a *tort* action in deceit or misrepresentation for that loss?

There is a line of cases, representing a distinct minority of jurisdictions, which may be interpreted as authorizing a tort cause of action in deceit upon the basis of an innocent misrepresentation, or upon the basis of presumed or constructive fraud, which amounts to the same thing. Such cases typically involve a business transaction in which defendant has a personal pecuniary interest and has made an unequivocal statement concerning a material fact, purportedly of his own knowledge, which turns out to be untrue. In some of these cases, the courts apparently confused deceit with other remedies. Nevertheless, such cases have lent support to the view of a number of legal writers that as between an innocent plaintiff and an innocent defendant who caused the loss, the latter should bear it, and plaintiff ought not to be confined to contract, equitable or restitutionary remedies that may or may not be available to him. This view prevailed in the A.L.I. debates over the Restatement (Second) of Torts; § 552C provides:

(1) One who, in a sale, rental or exchange transaction with another, makes a misrepresentation of a material fact for the purpose of inducing the other to act or to refrain from acting in reliance upon it, is subject to liability to the other for pecuniary loss caused to him by his justifiable reliance upon the misrepresentation, even though it is not made fraudulently or negligently.

(2) Damages recoverable under the rule stated in this Section are limited to the difference between the value of what the other has parted with and the value of what he has received in the transaction.

Note that liability is limited to the parties to the transaction, which must be a "sale, rental or exchange" transaction (although by a Caveat the A.L.I. does not preclude extensions beyond such transactions) and the damages recoverable do not include the benefit of the bargain or consequential damages. This limitation of damages is not supported by most of the existing cases.

Strict liability in tort for innocent misrepresentation has been and continues to be the subject of a lively controversy, and has a number of distinguished opponents. While the Restatement's damage limitation removes one objection to strict tort liability, some writers argue with vigor that where the misrepresentation is innocent, principles of contract or warranty law, equity, and restitution are more appropriate remedies as they include special limitations, defenses and other rules of law more properly designed to govern commercial situations where there has been no fraud or negligence. See, e.g., Hill, *Damages For Innocent Misrepresentation*, 73 Colum.L.Rev. 679 (1973).

§ 15–3. Scope of Liability

To whom shall the defendant be liable for his misrepresentation?

This issue raises questions of policy similar to those involved in the doctrine of proximate cause (§ 4–4, supra). In general, while rules of proximate cause extend liability to the limits of foreseeable harm in cases of personal injury and property damage, the scope of liability for a misrepresentation that causes only pecuniary loss has been narrower, based upon judicial fears of a potentially devastating burden of "liability in an indeterminate amount for an indeterminate time to an indeterminate class" of persons who might foreseeably rely upon an erroneous statement of fact. *Ultramares Corp. v. Touche, Niven & Co.* (N.Y. 1931) (Cardozo, J.). Also, the scope of liability varies according to whether the deception was intentional, negligent, or innocent.

Intent to Deceive. The doctrine of transferred intent (§ 6–1) is inapplicable to the intentional tort of deceit. In fact, at one time liability for deceit was limited to those specific persons whom defendant in fact intended to influence and to transactions of the type in which defendant sought to induce reliance. *Peek v. Gurney* (H.L. 1873): Restatement (First) of Torts § 531. Thus, liability did not extend to remote purchasers or investors, or to an agent who bought for himself in reliance upon a representation intended to influence his purchase on behalf of his principal. Of course, even under this rule, if defendant intends his representation to influence several persons or a class of persons, as when he publishes it in a newspaper advertisement or furnishes it to a credit-reporting agency, his liability will extend to any member of the class to whom the statement was directed.

The trend of the cases has been to expand liability beyond these limits and extend it to persons whom defendant did not in fact consciously desire to influence, but whose reliance upon the representation he had special reason to anticipate—in other words, persons whose receipt of, and reliance upon, the communication was not merely foreseeable but *highly* foreseeable. The first steps in this direction were taken in cases involving a representation contained in a transferable document representing some property interest (e.g., a negotiable instrument, a stock certificate, a certificate of title), or affixed to an article of commerce (e.g., the label of a product), R. § 532, or contained in a report required by law to be made and filed or published for the benefit of a certain class of persons, R. § 536 (liability being limited, of course, to members of the class intended to be protected). These have now become specific applications of the general rule, embodied in the revised Restatement (Second) § 531, that defendant's liability includes the "persons or class of persons whom he intends *or has reason to expect* to act or to refrain from action in reliance upon the misrepresentation, for pecuniary loss suffered by them through their justifiable reliance in the type of transaction in which he intends *or has reason to expect* their conduct to be influenced." (Emphasis added.) In a Caveat, the Institute "expresses no opinion" and thereby leaves open the possibility that liability may be even further extended in the future to persons whose reliance upon the representation was merely reasonably foreseeable.

Negligent Misrepresentations. Where plaintiff sues to recover for a pecuniary loss caused by a negligent misrepresentation, the ordinary rules of proximate cause applicable to negligence actions for physical harm (§ 4–4) do not apply. As in the case of fraudulent misrepresentation, liability was at first limited to the person or class of persons for whose guidance the information was furnished, and to the same or a substantially identical transaction as the one in which it was supplied. Restatement (First) of Torts § 552. It was early recognized, however, that there need not be privity of contract between plaintiff and defendant, but defendant was not liable unless he had actual knowledge of the specific person or persons for whose use the representation was intended. Thus, if *A* takes a quantity of beans to defendant, a public weigher, to be weighed for the purpose of certifying the weight to *B*, a purchaser, and defendant negligently certifies an incorrect weight causing a loss to *B*, defendant will be liable to *B* if he knew that the certification was intended for *B*'s use, *Glanzer v. Shepard* (N.Y. 1922), but not if he was unaware that it was to be relied upon by *B*, notwithstanding the fact that defendant could reasonably anticipate that some third person would be shown and rely upon the certification. *Ultramares Corp. v. Touche, Niven & Co.* (N.Y. 1931) (accountants certifying corporate financial statement). The courts seemed to envision defendant's negligent misrepresentation, once having been released into the world, being relied upon by unknown numbers of third persons, or by one such third person for a purpose not contemplated (but, in retrospect, foreseeable) by the defendant, causing a catastrophic pecuniary loss out of all proportion to defendant's fault and constituting an unbearable burden on defendant's socially useful activity. But if the third person and his proposed use of the information is *known* to the defendant before the representation is made, defendant can make an informed decision as to whether to proceed with the transaction and the price he must charge in order to assume the known risk.

The courts have come to realize that in many cases, limiting liability to *known* third persons is unduly restrictive, and most jurisdictions have expanded liability beyond this point, although not so far as in the case of fraudulent misrepresentations. Typically the defendant in these cases is a professional or a skilled tradesman who is engaged in the business of furnishing information upon which others customarily rely—accountants, surveyors, abstractors, attorneys, and the like. There seem to be two types of cases. In one, typified by the accountant, the defendant's representation is of a kind that may be used and relied upon by, and cause pecuniary loss to, a number of third persons. In these cases, while a few courts still required that such third persons be specifically known, most have held that if the group is sufficiently limited in number, liability will extend to members of that group if defendant merely knew that one or more persons in that group would receive and rely upon his representation, even though defendant had no knowledge at the time he furnished the information of their identity or of the particulars of the transaction in which the information would be used. This is the rule that is apparently codified in the revised Restatement (Second) of Torts, § 552(2), where liability for a negligent misrepresentation extends to a loss suffered

(a) by the person or one of a limited group of persons for whose benefit and guidance he intends to supply the information, *or knows that the recipient intends to supply it;* and

(b) through reliance upon it in a transaction that he intends the information to influence *or knows that the recipient so intends* or in a substantially similar transaction. [Emphasis added.]

See Comment *h*.

In another group of cases, typified by surveyors and title abstractors, defendant knows that the information he furnishes will be used by a succession of persons whose specific identity is presently unknowable, but in all probability only one such person will suffer a loss as a result of the negligence: the persons making use of the information at the time the error is discovered. In these cases, there is a tendency to extend liability to all persons who foreseeably will use and rely upon the information. *Rozny v. Marnul* (Ill. 1969); *Williams v. Polgar* (Mich. 1974).

Certain kinds of statutes (e.g., securities laws) require defendant to furnish, file, or publish information for the protection of a particular class of persons. If such information is negligently erroneous, a member of that class who relies upon it to his injury in a transaction for which the protection was intended may sue. R. § 552(3).

Strict Liability. To the extent that strict tort liability for an innocent misrepresentation has been recognized, plaintiff may recover only if he was a party to the transaction in which the representation was made and was the person to whom the representation was directed. R. § 552C.

§ 15–4. Representation and Nondisclosure

Words and Conduct. As already noted, a representation that is the basis of an action usually consists of oral or written words. But conduct that is intended as an assertion of fact may amount to the same thing. Exhibiting a document without authority to do so; turning back an automobile's odometer; and packaging, arranging or camouflaging goods so as to conceal a known defect are no less misrepresentations than words to the same effect.

Form of Words or Conduct. A misrepresentation may take any form; the only requirement is that the ordinary person would be misled. It need not be an indisputably false assertion about the subject matter of the transaction, as "This is a 1977 car" when in fact it is a 1975. Thus, ambiguous statements reasonably capable of both a true and a false meaning are misrepresentations if the false meaning is reasonably understood—e.g., a statement that the land's yield is "5,000" which the plaintiff understands to mean bushels but which is in fact dollars. Even a statement literally true, but so phrased as to be calculated under the circumstances to mislead, may be actionable. And so may untrue statements that profess ignorance of the facts, or that send plaintiff in search of erroneous or nonexistent facts, or otherwise conceal the truth.

Nondisclosure. Traditionally, consistent with the doctrine of caveat emptor, antagonists in a business transaction were under no duty affirmatively to disclose even essential facts to each other. So long as there was no active misrepresentation— no statement or assertion—one party could stand silent, knowing that the other was ignorant of facts that would significantly alter the bargain, and consciously take advantage of the other's ignorance.

The rule that silence cannot amount to a misrepresentation is, however, subject to several important exceptions. R. § 551.

(1) *Fiduciary or Confidential Relation.* It has always been held that where parties stand in a fiduciary or confidential relation to one another, they are not true antagonists and there is a duty to deal in the utmost good faith and to make full and fair disclosure of all material facts. Such relations include principal and agent, guardian and ward, executor and beneficiary of an estate, bank and investing depositor, trustee and cestui que trust, attorney and client, physician and patient, majority and minority stockholder, and the like. The same is true of certain types of contracts, such as suretyship or guaranty, insurance, partnership, and joint venture. Members of the same family are often in this class.

(2) *Incomplete Statements*. Clearly, if the defendant makes any statement of fact at all, he is required to disclose enough to prevent his assertion from being an incomplete and misleading half-truth. For example, the statement, "This car was driven only by a sweet little old grandmother" would be a misrepresentation unless it were also disclosed that she drove it in stock car races.

(3) *Subsequently Acquired Information*. If defendant makes a material assertion and subsequently acquires new information that makes the original statement untrue or misleading, he is under a duty to disclose the new information if he knows or believes that plaintiff is still acting on the basis of the original statement.

(4) *Newly Discovered Reliance*. Defendant may have knowingly made a false statement but without any expectation that plaintiff would rely upon it, in which case the false statement would not serve as the basis for a deceit action. However, when defendant subsequently discovers that plaintiff, in a transaction with him, is in fact about to act in reliance upon it, he has an affirmative duty to disclose its falsity.

(5) *Basic Facts*. Beyond this, there is a growing trend to find an affirmative duty to disclose essential facts known to one party to a transaction when that party has special access to those facts that the other does not, and in other cases where there is some reason why nondisclosure would be uncon-

scionable or at least very unfair. The Restatement § 551(2)(e) classifies them as

> facts basic to the transaction, if he knows that the other is about to enter into [the transaction] under a mistake as to [such facts], and that the other, because of the relationship between them, the customs of the trade or other objective circumstances, would reasonably expect a disclosure of those facts.

Note that such facts must be "basic," and not merely material. This duty is in the process of being extended to buyers as well as sellers. Some recent cases have gone beyond the Restatement, particularly its requirement of circumstances indicating an expectation of disclosure, and it has been suggested that the "law appears to be working toward the ultimate conclusion that full disclosure of all material facts must be made whenever elementary fair conduct demands it." Prosser, § 106.

§ 15–5. Reliance

The requirement of justifiable reliance in the law of misrepresentation is but a special application of the general principle of cause in fact (§ 2–1). Clearly, defendant's false statement is not responsible for plaintiff's harm unless plaintiff acted or refrained from acting in reliance upon the misrepresentation, believing it to be true. And, as in the cause-in-fact cases, the statement must have been a material and substantial factor in influencing plaintiff's conduct. R. §§ 546, 547.

By the same token, plaintiff's reliance need not be the sole cause of his loss. Plaintiff need not, and often does not, rely entirely upon defendant's representation, and the mere fact that he made an independent investigation or possessed other facts that he took into account does not of itself defeat recovery or establish that he did not rely upon defendant's false statement, since such investigation or facts themselves may not have been conclusive. The test is: did plaintiff accord defendant's statement any substantial weight in arriving at a decision on the course of action he would take. This question is ordinarily for the jury.

Justifiable Reliance. There is a further limitation, that the plaintiff's reliance must have been justified. R. § 537. In effect, this is simply a device by which the court may take the case from the jury and hold as a matter of law that plaintiff's loss was entirely his own responsibility. If the representation is so preposterous, or so obviously contrary to known or obvious facts, that no rational person of plaintiff's intelligence, experience and education would believe and act upon it, then plaintiff will not be heard to say that he in fact did so rely. Note, however, that this is *not* the same as contributory negligence (notwithstanding those few courts who thought otherwise). In an action based upon a negligent misrepresentation, contributory negligence may be a defense, but that is not the equivalent of unjustifiable reliance. The standard is primarily a subjective one, much like assumption of risk. Thus, if plaintiff is unusually gullible, ignorant, or stupid, he may honestly and justifiably have believed a misrepresentation that a normal person would not. Conversely, a plaintiff who has special expertise, competence, knowledge, or experience must use it, and he may be unjustified in relying upon a false representation that the ordinary person without those attributes would be justified in accepting at face value.

At one time, under the influence of the prevalent doctrine of caveat emptor, persons dealing at arm's length in a business transaction were required to be highly skeptical of each other's statements and could not justifiably believe them if a reasonable independent investigation would have revealed the truth. This is no longer true; it is now held, at least as to assertions of fact, that the recipient may justifiably rely upon them without further investigation even when their falsity could have been easily and quickly discovered, unless something known to him or apparent in the situation at hand should have served as a warning to him that the statement ought not to be accepted without further inquiry. R. §§ 540, 541A.

Materiality. Reliance includes both (1) belief and (2) acting or refraining from acting in response to that belief. Therefore, *justifiable* reliance includes the element of *materiality*—that is, plaintiff is not justified in acting or refraining from acting upon a representation, however justified he may be in believing it, unless the matter represented is of sufficient importance that a reasonable person's conduct would ordinarily be influenced by it in the transaction in question. R. § 538. Thus, in the usual case a representation by an auto salesman that the car was previously owned by a federal judge (when in fact it was owned by a law professor) would not be sufficiently material that plaintiff would be justified in relying upon that representation as a substantial factor in his decision to buy the car.

While the standard is generally that of the reasonable person, if the misrepresentation is fraudulent and the maker knows that its recipient is specially—even peculiarly or idiosyncratically—disposed to regard it as important, then that representation may be found to be material as to him even though it would not be as to the average person. For example, if defendant knows that plaintiff believes in astrology and falsely represents that the astrological signs strongly favor the transaction in question, the representation may be deemed material.

§ 15–6. Opinion, Prediction, and Intention

Opinion. It is commonly stated as a general rule that no action for misrepresentation may be based upon a false opinion, as distinguished from a misrepresentation of fact. This is but a special application of the requirement that plaintiff's reliance upon defendant's assertion be justifiable. As a general proposition, everyone is entitled to his own opinion, and therefore a reasonable person who is about to enter into a business transaction must form his own opinion from the facts and is not justified in relying upon the opinion of another party to the transaction whose judgment is presumably biased by his own self-interest. However, this rule is subject to important exceptions and qualifications, which have expanded somewhat with the waning of the doctrine of caveat emptor, so that today more often than not a statement of this rule is followed by an explanation why it does not apply to the instant case.

One must, of course, first determine whether the statement in question is one of fact or opinion. In many cases, this is no simple task, since its form, while usually important, is not controlling and there is no clear line that divides one from the other. Which it is depends primarily upon the context in which the statement is made, and the sense in which its recipient understands (or ought to have understood) it. For example, the unequivocal statement "there is water under this land" may be merely an opinion if plaintiff understands that defendant has no definite or first-hand knowledge of the matter. Conversely, there may be statements made, for the sake of politeness or modesty, in the form of opinions that reasonably may be understood as assertions of fact.

In general, an opinion is a statement that is not based upon positive knowledge of the matter asserted but represents an inference or conclusion about that matter that has been drawn from other facts.

Note, therefore, that even if reliance upon the opinion was not justified, there may be an actionable representation of fact implied within it. For example, the statement "in my opinion this chair belonged to George Washington" may be held to amount to a representation that defendant has no knowledge of facts that would cast doubt upon its authenticity, or that he knows facts that would support its authenticity. R. § 539.

Statements indicated that the maker believes a fact to be true (or probably true) but is less than certain are also deemed opinions. R. § 538A.

Quantity, Quality, and Value. Statements of quantity ("this tract contains 120 acres") ordinarily may be taken as statements of fact. But statements of quality ("this is the finest widget money can buy") and value ("this land is worth $500 per acre") traditionally have been classed as opinions upon which no reliance can justifiably be placed—mere sales talk or "puffing" that notoriously is exaggerated and which the prudent buyer is expected to discount. However, the courts have come to recognize that some representations of quality and value may be sufficiently definite and specific that the jury may be permitted to find that reliance upon them was justified. This is especially true of statements of value.

Law. Statements as to the law (made by other than a lawyer) were once commonly said to be mere assertions of opinion upon which no reliance could be placed (except that representations as to the law of a foreign state were deemed statements of fact). This was sometimes said to be based on the patent fiction that everyone is presumed to know the law, but the true rationale was that each person must determine for himself as best he can what the law is, and may not rely upon what the other party to the transaction says it is. It is now recognized, however, that they are the same as other assertions and may be either opinion or fact depending upon the form and circumstances of the statement. For example, a statement that a statute has been repealed may be deemed a statement of fact. In addition, a statement of law may expressly or impliedly contain representations of fact that may be relied upon. Thus, a statement that a corporation has the legal right to do business in a state may in a proper case be taken as a representation of the fact that all necessary steps have been taken to qualify the corporation in that state, upon which reliance may justifiably be placed. R. § 545.

Justifiable Reliance: Relation of the Parties. Even though a representation be classified as a statement of an opinion, the courts have recognized a number of situations in which reliance is nevertheless justified. One of the most important of these is when there is some fiduciary or other relation of trust and confident between the parties—attorney-client, principal-agent, insurer-insured, partners, members of the same family, and many others—just as in the case of liability for nondisclosure (§ 15–4, supra).

Justifiable Reliance: Special Knowledge or Access to Facts. Another situation in which reliance upon an opinion may be found to be justified is when there is some disparity between plaintiff and defendant with respect to their knowledge, expertise, or access to the relevant facts upon which the opinion is based. In essence, an opinion is a shorthand form of expression summarizing or synthesizing a group of underlying facts. When defendant has access to those facts and plaintiff does not, reliance may be justified, as when a jeweler represents the value of a diamond or a patent attorney represents that an invention is patentable, even though the parties are antagonists in a bargaining transaction. One the same basis, reliance upon an opinion may be justified when defendant is not an expert but knows that plaintiff cannot gain access to the underlying facts, such as when the subject matter of the transaction is located at a distance, or plaintiff is ignorant or illiterate, or defendant employs concealment or trickery to prevent access to the facts. R. § 542.

Justifiable Reliance: Disinterest. Plaintiff may be justified in relying upon the opinion of one whom he reasonably believes to be disinterested in the transaction, provided that the fact that such person holds the opinion is material. R. §§ 539, 543.

Prediction. Predictions of the future are notoriously unreliable, and will not support an action for misrepresentation even if disingenuously made.

Predictions, however, carry with them the implied representation that the speaker knows no facts presently existing that are inconsistent with the predicted fact, and as in the case of all other opinions such an implied representation (if false) may be actionable if the speaker purports to have special knowledge of, or access to, such presently existing facts.

Intention. A statement that the speaker or another person presently intends to do (or not do) something in the future is generally regarded as a statement of fact that is actionable if untrue. R. §§ 530, 544. In the classic simile of Lord Bowen, "The state of a man's mind is as much a fact as the state of his digestion." Of course, a statement of opinion also reflects the present state of the speaker's mind, but the difference is that in the everyday affairs of life persons necessarily and properly rely upon what others say they intend to do or not do, whereas they do not so rely (absent one of the special circumstances discussed in this section) on the opinions of others. One very common illustration of a statement of intention is a contractual promise, and if plaintiff can prove that defendant actually intended not to perform such a promise at the time it was made, he may be able to sue in deceit and have the benefit of the several advantages of the tort action over the action for breach of contract.

§ 15–7. Damages for Misrepresentation

Being a direct descendant of the common law action of case, a tort action for misrepresentation requires proof of actual damages, even when the misrepresentation was fraudulent. Nominal damages may not be given.

In addition, principles of causation much like those previously discussed (§§ 2–1, 4–4) require that there be a casual connection between the misrepresentation and the plaintiff's harm, and that the harm be a foreseeable result of reliance upon the false statement. R. § 548A. For example, even though defendant induces plaintiff to buy certain corporate stock by means of false representations, he will not be liable for plaintiff's loss when the corporation goes bankrupt due to unforeseeable subsequent events unrelated to the falsity of the statements; but he will be liable if plaintiff can establish that the corporation probably would have weathered the misfortune if its condition had been as represented, or if the subsequent events, though unrelated to the misrepresentation, were foreseeable.

Measure of Damages: Intentional Misrepresentation. In a tort action for misrepresentation, the measure of plaintiff's primary damages may be either (1) his *out-of-pocket* loss (the difference between the value he gave and the value of what he received) or (2) his loss of the *benefit of the bargain* he thought he had made (the difference between the value he gave and the value of what he would have received if defendant's representation had been true). For example, assume that defendant induces plaintiff to buy a widget for $5,000 by making false representations that, if true, would have made the widget worth $6,000. In reality, the widget's true value is $3,000. Under the out-of-pocket rule, plaintiff's damages are $2,000; using the benefit-of-the-bargain rule, $3,000.

For purpose of discussion, let us first assume that the representation was fraudulent.

If the representation was unrelated to any contract between the parties, then obviously the measure of primary damages must be plaintiff's out-of-pocket loss since there is no bargain of which he can be given the benefit.

Where the representation was contractual, about one-fifth of U.S. courts that have considered the matter nevertheless have limited plaintiff's primary damages to his out-of-pocket loss, usually on the theory that compensatory damages in a tort action are always measured by and limited to those necessary to make plaintiff whole; if he wishes the benefit of his bargain, he must sue in contract where that is the proper measure of damages. But the overwhelming majority of jurisdictions (about two-thirds) apply the benefit-of-the-bargain rule, reasoning that the form of the action should make no different in the measure of damages where the only difference between actions in contract and deceit is that the latter has the additional element of fraud.

In addition, it is said that confining plaintiff to the out-of-pocket rule would allow a defendant to induce a sale by misrepresentations and escape tort liability where the sales price approximated the actual value of the product sold, perhaps leaving plaintiff holding the bag containing something far different from what he thought he was getting and which he cannot use or readily dispose of. (These arguments appear to unduly minimize the availability of other remedies.)

The difficulty is that there are a number of cases in which the rigid application of one or the other of these rules will work an injustice. Thus, several jurisdictions, following the lead of *Selman v. Shirley* (Or. 1938), permit plaintiff to recover as primary damages either (1) his out-of-pocket loss or, at his option, (2) the benefit of the bargain if (a) the representation amounts to a warranty or (b) he can prove the benefit-of-the-bargain damages to a sufficient degree of certainty. This (without the warranty option) is the position taken by the Restatement. R. § 549.

Whatever the measure of primary damages, all courts permit plaintiff to recover, in addition, his consequential damages (e.g., out-of-pocket expenses caused by the misrepresentation, damages for physical harm). R. § 549. Thus, where plaintiff purchases a machine for his factory in reliance upon the seller's misrepresentations, he may recover (in addition to his loss on the purchase price) shipping costs, costs of installation, expense resulting from the fact that the machine failed to do the job, and for damage to raw materials that the machine destroyed during attempts to make it work (subject, of course, to the usual rules of proximate cause).

If a fraudulent misrepresentation was calculated to cause harm, punitive damages may be sought.

Measure of Damages: Negligent Misrepresentation. There appears to be very little case law on the measure of damages for a negligent misrepresentation. The Restatement takes the position that the usual tort damages rules will apply, and plaintiff may recover his out-of-pocket loss and consequential damages, but not the benefit of the bargain. R. § 552B.

Measure of Damages: Strict Liability. Here, also, the case law allowing recovery in tort for an innocent misrepresentation appears inconclusive on the issue of damages. Although nothing in the cases requires any such limitation, the Restatement confines the damages in these cases to plaintiff's out-of-pocket loss, thus excluding both the benefit of the promised bargain *and consequential damages* and creating what amounts to a restitutionary remedy in tort law clothing. R. § 552C.

*

INDEX

References are to pages

499

†